Philokalia
The Bible of Orthodox Spirituality

by
Anthony M. Coniaris

Orthodox Spirituality for the Lay Person

Preface by Stanley S. Harakas

Light & Life Publishing Company
Minneapolis, Minnesota

Light & Life Publishing Company

Copyright © 1998
Light & Life Publishing Company

Fifth Printing. 2018
Anthony M. Coniaris
Library of Congress Card No. 98-92036

All rights reserved. No part of this book may be reproduced, stored in a retrieval system, or transmitted in any form or by any means, electronic, mechanical, photocopying, recording, or otherwise, without the written permission of Light & Life Publishing Company.

ISBN 1-880971-38-0

Preface

The *Philokalia* is a treasure of the Orthodox spiritual life. For several reasons, however, it is a buried treasure, inaccessible to the ordinary Orthodox Christian because its primary audience is the Orthodox monastic community. Consequently, there is a distance between the text of the *Philokalia* and the clergy and the laity of the Church who are not monastics.

This sometimes has meant that non-monastic Orthodox Christians assume a pseudo-monastic appearance and mindset so that they can share in this spiritual treasure. But the Lord has pointed out that this is a distortion: "He said to them, 'Not all men can receive this saying, but only those to whom it is given'" (Matt. 19:11).

While the high and noble calling of the monastic is given to some and not to others, the call to spiritual living is addressed to all Orthodox Christians. They, however, must live the spiritual life in the context of *their* calling: diocesan hierarch, parish priest, lay person, cantor, choir member, church school teacher, parish council member, philanthropic society member, husband, wife, parent, daughter, son, employer, employee, creative artist, public servant, educator, business person, laborer, engineer, nurse, physician, scientist, gardener, administrator, and so on.

If Orthodoxy is the truth of God, then it must be applicable to everyone in every morally acceptable situation of life. To deny that would be to deny the Incarnation of Christ. Jesus Himself said:

> "As Moses lifted up the serpent in the wilderness, so must the Son of man be lifted up, that *whoever* believes in him may have eternal life." For God so *loved the world* that he gave his only Son, that *whoever* believes in him should not perish but have eternal life. For God sent the Son *into the world*, not to condemn the world, but *that the world might be saved through him* (John 3:14-17).

In the last chapter of his book, Fr. Anthony tells us that the purpose of this book is: "to bring Orthodox spirituality out of the monasteries into our everyday living." Rather than weaken the importance and significance of monasticism for Orthodox Christianity, it does just the opposite. Monasticism is shown to have captured the fullness of Orthodox spiritual life. The *Philokalia*, as Fr. Anthony describes it, is the Bible of Orthodox spiritual living.

What this book does is to translate the *Philokalia*, not from its original Greek, but from its original format as it arose in the monastic tradition of Eastern Orthodox Christianity. The translation is into a format that can be appropriated by Orthodox Christians who want to live spiritually in the life-circumstances to which they have been called. This book seeks to convey the foundational truths about the spiritual life to those of us called to live the Christian life "in the world." Thus, this book is a "translation" of the *Philokalia* in the sense that it expresses and rephrases the main ideas of the Orthodox spiritual method and way, in the garb of the common life of ordinary believers who are seeking to grow spiritually.

To do this, Fr. Coniaris extensively quotes from the writers of the *Philokalia* itself. But he also quotes the Holy Scriptures, well-known and not so well-known Church Fathers, liturgical texts, as well as spiritual writers from other traditions of faith who have come to appreciate the depth of the Eastern Orthodox Christian spiritual way. Not missing as well, is that Coniaris hallmark: pithy and illuminating stories,which he draws not only from ordinary life but also from the ancient wisdom of the ascetic Fathers. In the early chapters of the book are extensive quotations from the wonderfully beautiful, though not often chanted, *Akathist to our Victorious Lord Jesus*.

Just as the *Philokalia* does, this book focuses on the inner spiritual journey. It includes chapters on themes such as the Jesus Prayer, *Nepsis* (Inner Attention), Asceticism, Theosis, the Passions, the Gift of Tears, the Spiritual Ladder, Spiritual Synergy, Hesychasm (the Practice of Silence), the Relationship of Mind and Heart, the Inner Closet and the Inner Flame, the Life of Prayer, and the Reading of Scripture. The topics are the same as in the *Philokalia*: only in the outer clothing, their "presentation" changes, so they may become accessible to "the rest of us."

Also, just as the *Philokalia* does, Fr. Anthony connects the inner struggle for spiritual growth with the worship life of the Church, especially the sacramental life (Baptism, Eucharist, Chrismation) and, in addition, with outreach to others, such as philanthropy (almsgiving) in Christian love. But the focus is on our inner, spiritual world.

It will be as no surprise if those who read this book come to a deepening of their spiritual life. Nor will it be a surprise if the reading of this book ultimately leads to an understanding and meaningful reading of the original *Philokalia*. Nor, will it be a surprise if this book helps those who read it, put into actual practice the spiritual message of the *Philokalia*. Nothing but good can come from the reading of this book.

Read this book expecting your mind to be lead to new understandings about the Orthodox Christian spiritual life. And you will understand.

Read this book with the expectation that your heart will be touched and moved. And your heart will be warmed.

Most importantly, read *Philokalia—The Bible of Orthodox Spirituality* expecting to grow spiritually. And you will.

Fr. Stanley Samuel Harakas
Archbishop Iakovos Professor of Orthodox Theology, Emeritus
Holy Cross Greek Orthodox School of Theology,
Brookline, Massachusetts

Introduction

Alexander Solzhenitsyn believes that we have lost our spiritual focus today and have undergone a process of spiritual dispersal and squandering of spiritual values. The result is a vacuum—an inner, aching spiritual and moral vacuum that attracts people to all sorts of gurus and spiritual charlatans. People are searching for spirituality. Such a search indicates that, despite the relative comfort provided by technological progress, there is a felt need to reconnect with our spiritual roots and find a deeper purpose for living. It is this kind of a Christian spirituality that the *Philokalia* provides.

It is concerned with themes of universal importance: how man may develop his inner powers and awake from illusion; how he may overcome fragmentation and achieve spiritual wholeness; how he may attain the life of contemplative stillness and union with God.

The writings of the *Philokalia* are not only for monks. Many of the Hesychast writers go out of their way to assure us that unceasing prayer, vigilance, ascesis, and the other counsels are for monks and lay people as well, since all were created in the image of God and all are striving for the same theosis, or union with God. In fact, St. Tikhon calls on every Christian to become an "untonsured monk."

The purpose of this book is to accomplish exactly that: to bring Orthodox spirituality out of the monasteries and into our everyday living. As the *Philokalia* is a rich anthology of the writings of the Fathers, so we have endeavored to bring to you, albeit on a far limited basis, a similar anthology of many of the writings of the Fathers of the *Philokalia* on the several subjects they discuss.

In addition to the Fathers of the *Philokalia*, we have taken the liberty to include other Church Fathers who have been influenced by the *Philokalia*, such as St. Theophan the Recluse, etc.

The *Philokalia* is a great legacy we have received from the holy Fathers and Mothers of our Church. But an inheritance is not ours until we claim it. Our prayer is that we come to understand and claim the great spiritual treasures the Church has bequeathed to us through the *Philokalia*. The result will be holy lives that will bring glory to God, the Father, the Son, and the Holy Spirit.

– The Author

Table of Contents

Part One
Introducing the Spiritual Life

Chapter 1 The *Philokalia*: The Bible of Orthodox Spirituality.........2
Chapter 2 The Beautiful One is Jesus..........................10
Chapter 3 The Orthodox Spiritual Life: What It Is................19
Chapter 4 The Orthodox Spiritual Life: Maturing 26
Chapter 5 The Orthodox Spiritual Life: Renewal.................31
Chapter 6 The Orthodox Spiritual Life: The Jesus Prayer 41
Chapter 7 The Orthodox Spiritual Life: The Power of Jesus' Name ...53
Chapter 8 The Orthodox Spiritual life: The Call to Perfection........71

Part Two
Orthodox Spirituality According to the Fathers of the Philokalia

Chapter 9 *Nepsis* or Inner Attention 87
Chapter 10 Asceticism......................................112
Chapter 11 Theosis...131
Chapter 12 The Passions 147
Chapter 13 The Gift of Tears.................................171
Chapter 14 The Ladder to Heaven.............................183
Chapter 15 Spiritual Synergy.................................196
Chapter 16 *Hesychasm*—The Practice of Silence.................215
Chapter 17 *Kyrie Eleison*, Lord, Have Mercy....................237
Chapter 18 Descend with the Mind into the Heart 250
Chapter 19 The Inner Closet 258
Chapter 20 The Inner Flame 262
Chapter 21 The Fathers of the *Philokalia* and the Bible...........268
Chapter 22 Prayer According to the Fathers of the *Philokalia*.......282

Part One

INTRODUCING THE SPIRITUAL LIFE

CHAPTER ONE

The Philokalia: The Bible of Orthodox Spirituality

The Philokalia is the "treasury of watchfulness, the keeper of the mind, the mystical school of prayer of the heart ... the paradise of the Fathers ... the deep teaching of Christ, the trumpet which calls back the grace ... the instrument itself of deification."

– St. Nicodemos of the Holy Mountain

CHAPTER ONE

The Philokalia: The Bible of Orthodox Spirituality

Fr. George Florovsky, one of the great theologians of the Orthodox Church, called the *Philokalia,* "that famous encyclopedia of Eastern piety and asceticism which... is increasingly becoming the manual of guidance for all those who are eager to practice Orthodoxy in our time."

What is the *Philokalia*?

"Love of the Beautiful"

Derived from two Greek words, "love" and "beauty," the word *Philokalia* means "love of the beautiful, the exalted, the good." It is an anthology of spiritual writings by some thirty Church fathers, ranging from the fourth to the fifteenth century, assembled by two modern saints of the Orthodox Church: St. Macarios Notaras (1731-1805), Archbishop of Corinth, and St. Nicodemos the Agiorite (1749-1809). The full title tells much about the contents of the books which constitute five volumes in English: *Philokalia of the Sacred Spiritually Wakeful Individuals: Compiled from Our Holy and God-bearing Fathers, by Which the Mind is Purified, Illumined, and Perfected Through the Practical and Ethical Philosophy.* The manuscripts of the *Philokalia* were found in the libraries of the Holy Mountain—"dusty and moth-eaten," writes Nicodemos in his Prologue.

Two Collections of Philokalia

In the history of Orthodox thought, the title *Philokalia* has been given to two collections of Christian writings. At about 360 A.D., the Cappadocian Fathers compiled a selection from the works of Origen under this title. This work focused on Origen's important theological questions, exegesis of Scripture, and the spiritual life. In the 18th century, St. Nicodemos of the Holy Mountain and St. Macarios Notaras put together an anthology of writings on prayer written by

Byzantine authors from the 4th to 15th century. This second *Philokalia* was much larger than the one assembled by the Cappadocian Fathers, running into five heavy volumes.

Brief History of the Philokalia

The first text of the *Philokalia* was prepared by Macarios who, on visiting Mount Athos in 1777, gave it to the monk Nicodemos to complete and edit. Nicodemos added an introduction and brief biographies of the Fathers whose writings are included in the book. Nicodemos had the text ready for the printer after two years, during which time he also edited other manuscripts Macarios had given him. One was *Evergetinos* and the other, *Concerning Continual Communion*. Financed by John Mavrocordatos, Prince of Moldavia, all three works were published in Venice in 1782. Mavrocordatos' name appears on the title page of this monumental work of 1,207 pages.

The parts played by Macarios and Nicodemos in the composition of the *Philokalia* cannot be determined with any exact precision, but we do know that their collaboration must have been very close, resulting in a spiritual classic that has been called the Bible of Orthodox spirituality.

Writings Included in the Philokalia

The *Philokalia* consists of the most representative Orthodox ascetic and mystical treatises, starting with the writings of St. Anthony the Great and continuing with those of Evagrius of Pontus, Nilus of Ancyra, Diadochus of Photice, Maximus the Confessor, John Damascene, Philotheus the Sinaite, Symeon the New Theologian, Nicephorus the Monk, Kallistos and Ignatius Xanthopoulos, Gregory the Sinaite (who probably codified the manuscripts of the treatises of all of the above), and others. Of all the Church Fathers, St. Maximus the Confessor occupies more space in the *Philokalia* than any other Father.

It is to be noted that the writings of St. Isaac the Syrian were not included in the first edition of the *Philokalia*, although considerable excerpts from St. Isaac's writings had been included in the 11th century spiritual anthology known as *Evergetinos*. This absence, however, was remedied in the Russian (1884) and Romanian (1991) editions of the *Philokalia*.

Its Influence

The *Philokalia* was destined to have a profound influence on the spiritual life not only of Greece but of the entire Orthodox world. Eleven years after its publication, a Slavonic translation, differing slightly in content, was published in Moscow under the title of *Dobrotolubiye*. The translator was the eighteenth century Russian monk Paissy Velichkovsky, who had gone to Mount Athos in 1746, stayed there for seventeen years, and then settled in Moldavia. He and his monks are credited with a spiritual revival that took place in Russia at the end of the eighteenth and the beginning of the nineteenth centuries.

Between 1876 and 1890, a five-volume Russian version of the *Philokalia* was published. Translated by the Russian monk Theophanes the Recluse with help from monks of the Monastery of Optino and the Theological Academy of Moscow, this translation of the *Philokalia* influenced the writing of the spiritual classic *The Way of a Pilgrim*, one of the finest and most popular manuals of Eastern Orthodox spirituality.

This is how the pilgrim describes the *Philokalia* in this famous Russian spiritual classic:

Ah, how much new knowledge, how much wisdom that I never yet possessed was revealed to me in this book. As I began to put it into practice I tasted a sweetness I could not even have imagined until now. Often I spent an entire day sitting in the forest, carefully reading the Philokalia and learning many wondrous things from it. My heart burned with a desire for union with God through interior prayer.

The English-speaking world owes a great debt of gratitude to G.E.H. Palmer, Philip Sherrard, and Kallistos Ware, for undertaking the translation of the complete *Philokalia* into English from the original text of St. Nicodemos in five volumes, as published by Astir Publishing House in Athens (1957-1963). The *Philokalia* signaled the beginning of a revival in monastic spirituality and patristic learning—a revival that is still going on today.

Study Books on the Philokalia

A series of study books on the themes of the *Philokalia* has been planned. The general topic is THEMES FROM THE PHILOKALIA. They are intended mainly for the average lay person. They will comprise a series of separate volumes on the various themes of the *Philokalia*. The purpose of the series is to make the treasures of the *Philokalia* easily accessible and comprehensible to the lay person. The first such volume in this series was published in 1988 by Light and Life Publishing Company. The theme of volume 1 is WATCHFULNESS AND PRAYER. It was written by Archimandrite Ioannikios and translated from the Greek by Jeannie Gentithes and Archimandrite Ignatios Apostolopoulos. The second volume, THEMES FROM THE PHILOKALIA: THE INTELLECT Vol. 2, was published in Greece. Other volumes are expected to follow.

The Purpose of the Philokalia

St. Nicodemos describes the purpose of the *Philokalia* when he tells us that through the sacrament of baptism we have all received the "seeds" of the perfecting grace of the Holy Spirit for our growth in the life of Christ. This ember of grace received in baptism must be fanned into a new flame in our hearts. The *Philokalia* outlines exactly how this ember of grace can be fanned into a flame of faith. He writes:

Because, brethren, we have fallen into sins after baptism and consequently have buried the grace of the Holy Spirit which was given to us at our Baptism, it is necessary that we make every effort to recover that original grace which is found deeply buried underneath our passions, like an ember in the ashes. This ember of grace we must fan into a new flame in our hearts. In order to do that, we must remove the passions from our hearts as ashes from a fireplace, and replace them with the firewood of obedience in the life-giving commandments of the Lord. We can blow upon the spark with heartfelt repentance of the mind and with the repetition of this prayer: "Lord Jesus Christ, Son and Word of God, have mercy on me." When this prayer remains permanently in our heart, it cleanses us from the ashes of the passions, and finding the ember of grace within, it strikes up a wondrous and strange fire. This fire, on the one hand, burns away the temptation of evil thoughts, and, on the other, it sweetens the whole inner person and enlightens the mind.

St. Nicodemos Describes the Philokalia

St. Nicodemos laments the fact that we have forgotten the task of our sanctification, deification, and salvation. But his lamentation changes into unspeakable joy with the publication of this "spiritual book," the *Philokalia,* which he calls: *treasury of watchfulness, the keeper of the mind, the mystical school of the prayer of the heart. A book which is the excellent pattern of the practical virtue and the infallible directive of contemplation, the paradise of the Fathers, the golden series of virtues. A book which is the deep teaching of Christ, the trumpet which recalls back the grace; in two words, it is the instrument itself of deification.*

St. Nicodemos' Invitation to Read the Philokalia

St. Nicodemos invites his readers to read the *Philokalia* with these words:

Come, therefore, come and eat the bread of knowledge and wisdom, and drink the wine which spiritually delights the heart and dispels all the material and immaterial things because of deification—which is caused by the liberation of ourselves—and become inebriated with the truly alert inebriation. Come all you who are participants in the Orthodox way, together, laymen and monks, all of you who seek to find the kingdom of God which is hidden in the field of your heart. And this is the sweet Christ. Thus being freed from the imprisonment of this world and the wandering of the mind, with your heart purified from the passions, with the awesome unceasing invocation of our Lord Jesus Christ together with the collaborating virtues, which this book teaches, you will be united among yourselves, and united this way, you will all be united with God, according to the prayer of our Lord to his Father, who said, "So they may be one, as we are one" (Jn 17:11).

A Treasure House of Spiritual Wisdom

A treasure house of spiritual wisdom, the *Philokalia* has become one of the most widely read books in the Orthodox as well as the non-

Orthodox world. Asked why he became a Zen monk, a former Protestant Christian said, "Because I could not find any spirituality in my church." If anyone is searching for spirituality—God's true spirituality—his thirst will be quenched beyond expectation not in Zen or Buddhism or Hinduism but in the spirituality of the Sweet Jesus as it is brought to us through the *Philokalia*. Some feel that the influence of the *Philokalia* among the Orthodox is second only to the Bible. And indeed it is, because the *Philokalia* is nothing more than a living out of the Bible.

Is The Philokalia Revelant Today?

Alexander Solzhenitsyn believes that we have lost our spiritual focus today and have undergone a process of spiritual dispersal and squandering of spiritual values. The result is a vacuum—an inner, aching spiritual and moral vacuum that attracts people to all sorts of gurus and spiritual charlatans. People are searching for a spirituality. Such a search indicates that, despite the relative comfort provided by technological progress, there is a felt need to reconnect with our spiritual roots and find a deeper purpose for living. It is this kind of Christian spirituality that the *Philokalia* provides.

It is concerned with themes of universal importance: how man may develop his inner powers and awake from illusion; how he may overcome fragmentation and achieve spiritual wholeness; how he may attain the life of contemplative stillness and union with God.

For Monks Alone?

The spiritual path outlined in the *Philokalia* is inextricably bound up with the specific sacramental and liturgical life of the Orthodox Church. To attempt to practice it apart from its sacramental and liturgical moorings is to cut it off from its living roots. It will wither and die.

Furthermore, the *Philokalia* was written not only for those living within the sacramental and liturgical framework of the Orthodox Church, but, more specifically, for those living in the Orthodox monastic tradition. Does this mean that the counsels of the *Philokalia* are only for monks? Many of the hesychast writers go out of their way to assure us that unceasing prayer and the other counsels are for monks and lay people as well, since all were created in the image of God and are striving for theosis. What is essential is that, whether within or outside a monastic environment, the advice of a qualified spiritual father or elder be sought. If such guidance is not to be found, then active participation in the sacramental and liturgical life of the Church is always essential. The counsels of the *Philokalia* are like a beautiful fruit tree whose roots are nourished by the rich liturgical and sacramental life of the Orthodox Church.

Thus, the *Philokalia* can be used by what St. Tikhon calls the "untonsured monks," the lay people, to develop and grow in the spiritual life. Adapting St. Tikhon's remarks on monasticism as a call for the laity, Alexander Bukharev wrote, "The black monastic habit does not save a person. The one who wears the white habit (the white baptismal robe), who has the spirit of obedience, humility and purity, such a one is a true monk of interiorized monasticism." That includes all baptized lay people.

Claim Your Inheritance

We Orthodox Christians have received many great legacies from our holy fathers and mothers through the Church:
1. the deposit of grace that we receive in holy baptism;
2. the sacraments;
3. the divine liturgy;
4. the Holy Bible;
5. the awesome privilege of prayer;
6. the true apostolic faith, and
7. the *Philokalia*, the Bible of Orthodox Spirituality.

But an inheritance is not ours until we claim it. And we cannot claim it if we are not even aware of it. May we accept and claim for ourselves the great spiritual treasures our Church has bequeathed to us through the *Philokalia*.

CHAPTER TWO

The Beautiful One Is Jesus

"Beauty serves ... to prepare the soul for ... encounter with God."

– Nicholas Arseniev

CHAPTER TWO
The Beautiful One Is Jesus

If *Philokalia* is "the love of the beautiful," let us remember that the "beautiful" one is none other than the Lord Jesus. As Dostoyevsky wrote,

In the world there has been only one positively beautiful person—Christ. Therefore, the appearance of this wonderful, infinitely beautiful person is in itself an infinite miracle. The entire Gospel of John is devoted to precisely this. In it, St. John declares that the whole miracle is in the incarnation alone, in the very manifestation or emergence of the beautiful.

Beauty Will Save the World

God is the source of all that is truly beautiful, resplendent with God's glory. "Such beauty," wrote Dostoyevsky, "created by God, will ultimately save the world." "Blessed is the mind which, passing by all creatures, constantly rejoices in God's beauty," wrote St. Maximus the Confessor. God is love; but He is also the source of all that is truly beautiful. Beauty is the outer expression of God's resplendent glory. Such beauty will indeed "save the world." "Who can gaze at His (God's) face and remain without divine eros for such beauty?" said St. Gregory of Nyssa.

If there is any authentic beauty in the world, it is but a reflection of the beauty of Christ.

When Genesis 1:31 tells us that "God saw everything that He had made, and, indeed, it was very good" (the Greek word for good here means "beautiful"), it is telling us that the source of all authentic beauty in the world is God.

St. Augustine on God's Beauty

St. Augustine of Hippo wrote, "The beauty of everything is in a way their voice by which they praise God. The sky...the earth cry, YOU MADE ME, NOT I. And as He made all things, and nothing is better than He is, whatever He made is less than He is. So do not let what He made please you so as to drag you away from Him who made them. If you love what He made, love much more Him who made them. If the things He made are beautiful, how much more beautiful is He who made them!" (Expositions of the Psalms).

St. Basil on God's Beauty

Is there anything more wonderful than Divine Beauty? Is there a more charming conception than that of the magnificence of God? . . . It is for this reason that the face of Moses was glorified during his conversation with God, because he participated in that Divine Beauty.

There are those who believe that when Moses asked to see God and was shown briefly only the backside of God, that "backside," they believe, must have been the awesome beauty of a magnificent sunrise or sunset.

C. S. Lewis said once, "The sweetest thing in all my life has been the longing to find the place where all the beauty came from."

Quotations from the Philokalia

A few brief quotations from the *Philokalia* are given below to enable you to taste the style and beauty of content of this classic work.

1. **On the passions:**
   None but Jesus Christ Himself, unifier of what is disunited can give your heart lasting peace from passions.
2. **On achieving union with Christ through love:**
   All men are made in God's image; but to be in His likeness is granted only to those who through great love have brought their own freedom into subjection to God. For only when we do not belong to ourselves do we become like Him who through love has reconciled us to Himself. No one achieves this unless he persuades his soul not to be distracted by the false glitter of this life.
3. **On true wisdom:**
   When the heart has acquired stillness it will perceive the heights and depths of knowledge; the ear of the still intellect will be made to hear marvelous things from God.
4. **On prayer:**
   While you are praying, the memory brings before you

fantasies either of past things, or of recent concerns, or of the face of someone who has irritated you.

The demon is very envious of us when we pray, and uses every kind of trick to thwart our purpose. Therefore he is always using our memory to stir up thoughts of various things and our flesh to arouse the passions, in order to obstruct our way of ascent to God.

5. **On resisting demons:**

   A person's heart will not be freed from demonic thoughts, words and actions until it has first purified itself inwardly, uniting watchfulness with the Jesus Prayer.

6. **On the purification of the heart:**

   He who wishes to cleanse his heart should keep it continually aflame through practising the remembrance of the Lord Jesus, making this his only study and his ceaseless task.

7. **On humility:**

   In order to prevent the human intellect from thinking that it is god, God has subjected it to ignorance and forgetfulness, so that in this way it may acquire humility.

8. **On silence:**

   When the door of the steam bath is continually left open, the heat inside rapidly escapes through it; likewise the soul, in its desire to say many things, dissipates its remembrance of God through the door of speech, even though everything it says may be good... Timely silence, then is precious, for it is nothing less than the mother of the wisest thoughts.

9. **On the Jesus Prayer:**

   With your breathing combine watchfulness and the name of Jesus, or humility and the unremitting study of death. Both may confer great blessing.

10. **On guarding the heart and mind:**

    Stand guard and protect your intellect from thoughts while you pray. Then your intellect will complete its prayer and continue in the tranquillity that is natural to it. In this way He who has compassion on the ignorant will come to you, and you will receive the blessed gift of prayer.

11. **On watchfulness**:
> *Be watchful as you travel each day the narrow but joyous and exhilarating road of the mind, keeping your attention humbly in your heart...and invoking Jesus Christ.*

"We Cannot Forget That Beauty"

For the Orthodox, beauty is a vital part of the world and of the life of the Church. "We cannot forget that beauty" is a phrase which echoes in the mind of many who enter into the world of Orthodox spirituality; the beauty lies in both the externals of the Churches and the liturgy, and also in the inner life and holiness of the saints...

                                    - John Baggley

Beauty is Truth

Beauty is Truth
Truth is beauty...
That is all you need
To know.
             -Keats

God Made Us Beautiful

"At the beginning in Paradise," says St. Theodore the Studite, (759-826) "God made us beautiful through the high dignity of being in His image and likeness." Whereas the Bible states simply that "God made us in His image and likeness," St. Theodore draws out the meaning of Scripture by affirming that "God made us beautiful." This divine beauty is reflected in and through all the various things that the Creator has formed, but it shines out pre-eminently from God's living icon, the human person.

                             -Bishop Kallistos Ware

Inner Beauty

Though we travel the world over to find the beautiful, we must carry it within us, or we find it not.

                                      -Emerson

The Beauty of Jesus

The Prophet David, pouring forth a good word, says to his King, Christ the Lord: "Thou art fairer than the children of men." The Lord Himself created His bodily vesture as He wished. Had He wanted to reveal Himself to the world as physically the fairest among all the sons of men, He could have done so. But we have no record in the Gospel of His drawing men to Himself and impressing them by His physical appearance. He Himself said: "The flesh profiteth nothing" (John 6:63). It is clear, then, that David is not speaking of the physical beauty of Christ the King but of His spiritual, divine beauty. This is, in any case, clearly seen in the succeeding words of the Psalmist: "Full of grace are thy lips." The unrivaled beauty of the Son of God is not, therefore, in the shape and form of His lips but in the stream of grace that flows from them. The Prophet Isaiah said about Christ: 'When we saw Him, He had no comeliness' (Is. 52:2-3). How, then, do Isaiah and David agree? Perfectly well. David spoke of Christ's inner beauty and Isaiah of His external, humiliated state. We did not see Him as a king or a rich man, Isaiah wants to say, but as a servant and a sufferer.

- *The Prologue*, Bishop Nicolai Velimirovic

Bishop Nonnus on Beauty

There is a beautiful story told by the Desert Fathers that describes how the soul should strive to keep itself attractive for the Bridegroom.

As a group of bishops was meeting in Antioch, a procession of actresses passed by. Among them was the first and most beautiful of actresses bedecked with extravagantly beautiful robes and jewels. As she rode by, bare of head and shoulders with not so much as a veil upon her, the bishops groaned and turned away their heads as from a great sin.

But one of the bishops, Nonnus, did not turn his eyes away from her. Rather, he gazed upon her intently and said to the other bishops, "Did not the sight of her beauty delight you?"

The bishops answered him nothing. Nonnus persisted and said, "I was greatly delighted with her beauty and I believe that God will one day set her in judgment upon us and our episcopate. How many hours has this woman spent in her chamber, bathing and adorning herself that there may be no stain in all her body's beauty. All of this in order to please men! And yet we who have the greatest of all lovers, the splendid Bridegroom upon Whom the Cherubim dare not look, we adorn not our souls and care not so much as to wash the filth from our miserable souls.

-From the Desert Fathers

Beauty as a Principle of Life

Dostoyevsky wrote, "Beauty will save the world...Today I realized that what Dostoyevsky meant is that beauty must be our principle in life—that beauty is not a perception, an influence, to be found outside us; it is a principle which must characterize the way we do everything. Everything we do must be done in beauty, with grace... Everything we do, even digging a ditch or scrubbing the floor, must be done in beauty.

-Nancy Forest-Flier

Who But God?

Consider the tribes of birds, and varieties of form and color, both of those which are voiceless and of songbirds. What is the reason of their melody, and from whom came it? Who gave to the grasshoppers the lutes in their breasts, and the songs and chirruping on the branches, when they are moved by the sun to make their midday music, and sing among the groves, and escort the wayfarer with their voices? Who wove the song for the swan when he spreads his wings to the breezes, and makes melody of their rustling?

-St. Gregory the Theologian

To Behold the Beauty of the Lord

One thing I have asked of the Lord, that will I seek after; that I may dwell in the house of the Lord all the days of my life, to behold the beauty of the Lord and to inquire in his temple (Psalm 27:4).

Why Beauty in Churches?

An Orthodox Church is beautiful. Whether we enter a large, ancient cathedral or a small mission parish, we will "behold the beauty of the Lord." Why is the Church beautiful? Because it leads us into the presence of God Who is truly Beautiful.

Are we not "churches"? Are we not "temples of the Holy Spirit"? Must we not keep ourselves spiritually beautiful? As the church building is beautiful, so must our thoughts and actions. Our inner life must be beautified as we all work to become saints.

The Emissaries of St. Vladimir

Like the emissaries of St. Vladimir, one who has entered an Orthodox Church "cannot forget that beauty." Beauty is in the vestments, the icons, the singing, and in the eyes and hearts of the worshippers. May this beauty draw us closer to the living God and may we shine with this same beauty, becoming a light in a darkened world. "O Lord...sanctify those who love the beauty of Thy house."

Anonymous

Qualities that Render the Soul Beautiful

The book is...termed "love of the beautiful" (Philokalia) because it is directed to the virtues, which the writers in it view as qualities that render the soul beautiful and thereby God-like.

- Constantine Cavarnos

"You Alone are an Icon of Eternal Beauty"

For this is the safest way to protect the good thing you enjoy: by realizing how much your Creator has honored you above all other creatures. He did not make the heavens in His image, nor the moon, nor the sun, nor the beauty of the stars, nor anything else which surpasses all understanding. You alone are an icon of Eternal beauty, and if you look at Him, you will become what He is, imitating Him Who shines within you, whose glory is reflected in your purity. Nothing in all creation can equal your grandeur. All the heavens can fit in the palm of God's hand...and though He is so great...you can wholly embrace Him. He dwells within you...He pervades your entire being...

-St. Gregory of Nyssa

The only positively beautiful Person Who ever lived was the Lord Jesus. To be created in His image is to be created in the image of beauty. To be holy as He is holy is to be beautiful. To live in Christ is to abide in beauty.

To know Him we need to love Him as much as Fyodor Dostoyevsky did when he wrote:

Sometimes God sends me moments in which I am utterly at peace. In those moments I have constructed for myself a creed in which everything is clear and holy for me. Here it is: to believe that there is nothing more beautiful, more profound, more sympathetic, more reasonable, more courageous and more perfect than Christ, and not only is there nothing, but I tell myself with jealous love, that there never could be.

Please Note

The following six chapters will deal with the general theme: INTRODUCING THE SPIRITUAL LIFE. The chapter titles will be as follows:

The Orthodox Spiritual Life: What it Is
The Orthodox Spiritual Life: Maturing
The Orthodox Spiritual Life: Renewal
The Orthodox Spiritual Life: The Jesus Prayer
The Orthodox Spiritual Life: The Power of Jesus' Name
The Orthodox Spiritual Life: The Call to Perfection

The last part of the book, Part Two, will deal specifically with the spirituality of the *Philokalia*.

CHAPTER THREE

The Orthodox Spiritual Life: What It IS

Orthodox Spirituality is taught and exemplified through the lives of the Fathers, Mothers, and Saints of all ages. There we find living and concrete examples of what spirituality is.

CHAPTER THREE

What Is Orthodox Spirituality

To be authentically spiritual is not something abstract. It is something very concrete and practical. "Spiritual" means simply to be filled with the Spirit—the Holy Spirit, the third Person of the Godhead. Even the body becomes spiritual when it is filled with the grace of the Holy Spirit. It becomes a temple, a church, as St. Paul states. St. Theophan wrote, "Spiritual life comes entirely from His most Holy Spirit. We have our own spirit but it is void of power. It begins to gain strength only when the grace of God flows into it."

Spirituality needs to be re-discovered today because if we are not filled with the Holy Spirit, there are many unholy, evil spirits out there waiting to rush in and fill the vacuum. It is not only nature but also the soul that abhors a vacuum. You will either be filled with the Holy Spirit and be free, or you will be filled with evil spirits and be a slave to them.

From behind the Iron Curtain a few years ago, a Romanian pastor wrote,

Materialism has created an immense spiritual vacuum. As long as the scientific world was shielded with a conviction of absolute knowledge, the emptiness was not felt. But in moments of tragedy when science could no longer give a confident answer, the emptiness was felt. Man's soul can never be satisfied with purely material and cultural goods. Man thirsts for a spiritual world and cannot be satisfied with less than a living contact with that spiritual world.

People are searching for spirituality today. A huge number of books on spirituality are being published. At the entrance to a bookstore in a shopping mall there was a huge display entitled GIFTS OF THE HEART AND SOUL. Most of these books were from the New Age movement, which is a collection of all the heresies that ever existed from the beginning of time. If you were looking for the Bible and the section on World Religions, you had to go to a rather tiny section in the rear of the store.

Sales of New Age books on spirituality, however, have surged from 5.6 million to over 10 million. Angels and chats with God—which New Age books emphasize—bring more direct inspiration and are to be believed more than the word of God. People are looking for spirituality, but they are looking for it in the wrong places. What they are getting is demonology disguised as Christian spirituality. One of the greatest of all spiritual classics—The *Philokalia*—remains relatively unknown while people seek to satisfy their thirst by drinking from the broken cisterns of New Age that hold no water.

What is the true "spirituality" that people are seeking?

Where Do We Find Spirituality?

Orthodox spirituality is not abstract or mysterious. It is to be found in the living word of God as it is preserved in the Sacred and Apostolic Tradition of our Church. And it comes to its fullest expression and incarnation in the teaching, but above all, the life and being of our Lord Jesus Christ. Its various aspects are described in the *Philokalia*.

Spirituality is encountered in the permanent and ever renewed experience of a praying life which is that of the whole church: the liturgy, sacraments, especially through the sacrament that enables us to dwell in Christ and He in us: the Holy Eucharist.

Finally, Orthodox spirituality is taught and exemplified in and through the lives of the Fathers, Mothers, and Saints of all ages. There we find living and concrete examples of what spirituality is.

All of Life Can Become Spiritual

Orthodox spirituality does not distinguish between the spiritual and the non-spiritual, i.e., the secular. If life is filled with the Holy Spirit, then all of life becomes spiritual. If you would read through the Prayer Book of the Church, the *Euchologion*, you would see that the liturgy and prayer life of the Church embrace all the activities of daily life with its blessings and prayers for everything, from crops to flowers to wells to just plain water. Once filled with the Holy Spirit, everything becomes spiritual. St. Symeon the New Theologian wrote in his *Hymn of the Divine Love*: "We become members of Christ, and Christ becomes a member of us...unworthy as I am, my hand and my foot are Christ. I move my hand and my hand is Christ; for God's divinity is indivisibly united with me. I move my foot, and lo! it glows as God himself..." Once sanctified by the Holy Spirit all of life—the cosmos itself—becomes spiritual or Spirit-filled.

The Real Spiritual Life

A person who is spiritual takes God into every area of life. He asks questions such as, "What sort of person does God want me to marry? What career does God want me to follow? Where does He want me to go to college? What does God want me to do in this particular situation?" These are spiritual questions.

Some Aspects of Spirituality

True spirituality manifests itself in what we desire most in life.

1. First, do we desire to be holy rather than happy?

2. A person may be considered spiritual when he seeks the honor of God advanced through his life even if it means temporary dishonor or loss for himself.

3. The spiritual person desires to take up his cross and follow Jesus.

4. A Christian is spiritual when he tries to look at everything from God's point of view and not from the viewpoint of public opinion.

5. Another desire of the spiritual person is the willingness to suffer or die for righteousness rather than to live in unrighteousness.

6. The spiritual person desires to see others advance spiritually even at his expense. Like Jesus his purpose in life is to serve, not to be served.

7. The spiritual person habitually makes judgments based on eternal rather than temporal values.

8. The truly spiritual person is a living, praying, worshipping member of the Body of Christ, the Church, who partakes of the sacraments regularly and prays daily for the infilling of the Holy Spirit.

St. John Chrysostom Describes Orthodox Spirituality

St. John Chrysostom described Orthodox spirituality when he wrote:

The sun gives forth light; it cannot help doing so. Animals breathe in and out; they cannot help doing so. Fish swim in rivers and the sea; they cannot help doing so. What, then, are the things which a Christian cannot help doing? First of all, a Christian cannot help praying. To be a Christian is to regard God as a loving Father; and it is natural to talk and listen to one's parents. Second, a Christian cannot help praising God and giving praise to him. To be a Christian is to affirm God as creator of the universe; and when a Chrisitan looks at the beauty and glory of what God has made, praise and thanksgiving pour from the lips. Third, a Christian cannot help being generous. To be a Christian is to acknowledge that everything belongs to God, and that human beings are merely stewards of what they possess; so they naturally want to share their possessions with those in need. Fourth, a Christian cannot help reading the Scriptures and also studying the insights of other Christians. To be a Christian is to rejoice in the power of the Holy Spirit; and the Spirit speaks to us through the Scriptures and through the insights of our spiritual brothers and sisters.

Take Off Your Shoes

In the well-known Biblical passage, Moses sees the burning bush, from which the presence of God calls out to him, "Take off your shoes, for the place on which you are standing is holy ground" (Exodus 3:5). All of spiritual life is an effort to take off our shoes in the presence of God. When you stand at the kitchen stove, that is an altar. When you are teaching at school, that is an altar. When a mother or father gets up at 3 A.M. to respond to a crying infant, that is an altar. When you are doing your homework, that is an altar. When you are bathing your infant, that is an altar. When you are cooking a meal for your family, that is an altar. We do not lock Jesus in Church when we leave for home; we take him with us. We leave church to celebrate "the liturgy after the liturgy." All of life can be spiritual, filled with the Spirit of God, permeated with God's presence and glory.

Every action of the Christian should be a spiritual act, inspired and guided by the Holy Spirit. Spirituality is in effect, opening all of life to God. It can be described biblically as "being holy as God is holy", "seeking first the kingdom of God and His righteousness," "putting on Christ," "being filled with all the fullness of God."

St. Seraphim of Sarov taught that the "true Christian life" is to be "clothed with the Holy Spirit." To live is "to be in the fullness of the Spirit."

Streams of Living Water

Jesus said in John 7:37-38:

If anyone is thirsty, let him come to me and drink. Whoever believes in me, as the Scripture has said, streams of living water will flow from within him. By this He meant the Spirit, whom those who believed in Him were to receive.

Jesus is telling us in these verses, "Drink the living water of my Holy Spirit. And here's my promise: You will be flooded with such an outpouring of life that not only will you be filled, you will overflow. The fountain of my Spirit will spring up inside you, flooding you with so much life and vitality that it will spill over to those in your presence."

To use Jesus' own words, this is what it means to be spiritual: to have our parched souls filled to overflowing with the living water of God's Spirit.

According to St. Basil a spiritual person is one who has become the temple of the Most Holy Spirit.

In Alexander Solzhenitsyn's extensively reported and famous sermon to America, delivered in 1978 at Harvard University, he said, "We have placed too much hope in politics and social reforms, only to find out that we were being deprived of our most precious possession: our spiritual life. It is trampled by the party mob in the East, by the commercial one in the West."

This is the spirituality the world needs today for its redemption.

Dr. Glenn Loury, who taught at Harvard, emphasized the need for spirituality today when he wrote, "The mention of God may seem quaint, but it is clear that the behavior problems of the ghetto (and not only there) involve spiritual issues . . . One cannot imagine effectively teaching sexual abstinence, or the eschewal of violence, without an appeal to spiritual concepts. The most effective substance-abuse recovery programs are built around spiritual principles."[*]

In Part Two of this book we shall describe the Orthodox spirituality of the Fathers of the *Philokalia*.

---

[*] "Finding God at Harvard." Edited by Kelly Monroe. Zondervan Publishing House. Grand Rapids, MI. 1966. pp. 69-70.

From the Philokalia

The heart itself is but a small vessel, yet dragons are there, and there are also lions; there are poisonous beasts and all the treasures of evil. But there too is God, the angels, the life and the kingdom, the light and the apostles, the heavenly cities and the treasuries of grace—all things are there.

– Pseudo-Macarius

CHAPTER FOUR

The Orthodox Spiritual Life: Maturing

To be mature in Christ means in its negative aspect to put away childish things: self-centeredness, insistence on having one's own way, anger, blaming others, envy, jealousy. To be a mature Christian in its positive aspect means to be more and more like Christ. Merely growing up is not enough. We are to grow up into something that is perfectly mature, and that for us Christians, is Christ. "Be ye perfect as I am perfect," said Jesus. Lecomte du Nouy, the French physicist, once wrote, "The perfect man is not a myth: he has lived in Christ." To be mature is to grow by the power of the Holy Spirit more and more like unto that perfect man: Jesus. "That you may grow up in all things into Him who is the head, even Christ" (Ephesians 4:15). To be mature in Christ is part of what it means to be spiritual. It is a life-long task that is accomplished by the Holy Spirit through daily repentance.

CHAPTER FOUR

The Orthodox Spiritual Life: Christian Maturing

Until we all attain to...mature manhood, to the measure of the stature of the fullness of Christ (Ephesians 4:13).

A novel a few years ago, *Second Growth*, dealt with life in a small town in Vermont, where there was very little opportunity for young people. A good teacher who was interested in a boy of fine promise, said to him, "I'd take this chance to go to college, if I were you. There won't be much else I could teach you around here. *You would stay the same size all your life.*"

"You would stay the same size all your life." An arresting sentence! It applies to many realms of life, besides that of a little town. We know that is just what happens to many people. They stay "the same size all their lives." Contrast this with the words of St. Paul, "And his gifts were that some should be apostles, some prophets, some evangelists...for building up the body of Christ. Until we all attain...to mature manhood, to the measure of the stature of the fullness of Christ" (Ephesians 4:13). In our Christian life we are not to remain the same size. We are to grow "to mature manhood" in Christ. As one quip put it: "Our pressing need today is for less publicity on how to stay young and more on how to grow up." To be spiritual means to keep "growing up" in our faith and in the life of Christ.

To be spiritual is to keep growing in love and understanding, to keep casting off the old and putting on the new in Christ. You are only young once, but you can stay immature indefinitely. To remain immature is to be unspiritual. Spirituality implies growth toward maturity in Christ.

Mature in Christ

To be mature is not enough for us Christians. The word of God calls on us to be mature *in Christ*. What does maturity in Christ mean? Negatively it means: putting away childish things, childish traits, and childish qualities of mind. As St. Paul said in the 13th chapter of First Corinthians, "When I was a child, I spoke as a child, I understood as a child, I thought as a child: but when I became a man, I put away childish things."

When St. Paul learned that divisions had sprung up in the Corinthian church causing dissension, envy and jealousy, he wrote them his first epistle in which he said that he could not address them as mature Christians. "You are babes in Christ," he said. "You haven't been developing into Christian maturity. Consequently I have fed you with milk, not solid food, because you are not ready for stronger food. While there exist among you envying, strife and divisions, are you not immature?" To be spiritual means to cast off the childish traits within us as we strive by God's grace to attain "the measure of the stature of the fullness of Christ."

The Perfect Man

To be mature in Christ means in its negative aspect to put away childish things: self-centeredness, insistence on having one's own way, anger, blaming others, envy, jealousy. To be a mature Christian in its positive aspect means to become more and more like Christ. Merely growing up is not enough. We are to grow up into something that is perfectly mature, and that for us Christians, is Christ. "Be ye perfect as I am perfect," said Jesus. Lecomte du Nouy, the French physicist, once wrote, "The perfect man is not a myth: he has lived in Christ." To be mature is to grow by the power of the Holy Spirit more and more like unto that perfect man: Jesus. "That you may grow up in all things into Him who is the head, even Christ" (Ephesians 4:15). To be mature in Christ is part of what it means to be spiritual. It is a life-long task that is accomplished by the Holy Spirit through daily repentance.

The person who is mature in Christ is not the person who goes through life expecting to receive love, like a child, but the person who gives love. The person who is mature in Christ is the person who understands, who forgives, who accepts responsibility for his failures, who disciplines himself, who is humble, realizing that without God he is nothing.

St. Paul singles out love as the most important ingredient of maturity and spirituality when he writes to the Colossians: "Above all put on love, which binds everything together in perfect harmony." It is when we allow the Trinity to come and live in us that we can achieve this kind of Godly maturity in our lives. This is what it means to be spiritual: to keep growing in Christ.

The Greatest Power in the World

There is a phrase in the Talmud which says, "Every blade of grass has its own angel that bends over it and whispers, 'Grow! Grow!'" The greatest power in the world is the power to grow. Look at the tiny acorn! For us this means not just physical growth. It means to channel this power to grow so that we may grow as Jesus grew: "in wisdom and stature and in favor with God and man." It means to grow mentally, physically, spiritually, socially and emotionally. It means to grow by God's grace from the image of God, in which we have been created, into the likeness of God which is Jesus. Through baptism we were born into the life of God. Now that we are born, we must grow in that life. Such growth "to mature manhood, to the measure of the stature of the fullness of Christ," can occur after baptism only through a dynamic personal relationship with Christ in the Church whereby He lives in us and we in Him. The essence of maturity is Jesus Christ, the most mature Person Who ever lived. To be spiritual is not just to be baptized but to keep growing in that new life—the life of Christ—that we received in baptism.

How Spiritual Growth Takes Place According to Macarius

Macarius uses the image of a newborn baby to describe how growth occurs after baptism. Possessing all the limbs it will ever have, the baby is already complete. Yet it still has to grow. Thus it is quite true to say that we receive the life of the Spirit through baptism. Baptism is indeed valid and true. Yet we still have to make progress by growing in the new life. Only so will the Spirit grow in us and become manifest as He makes us perfect.

Grace, continues Macarius, works in our souls as a kind of leaven. It does not immediately eliminate sin, but it does allow us progressively to recognize it for what it is: a foreign body which needs to be excised from the soul. Even if we remain in a largely helpless state, writes Macarius, we can begin to want to love the Lord, to want to pray, to want to believe in Him. The struggle that ensues from this is proof that we are not totally dead in sin but alive and growing slowly through struggle. Growth occurs not solely through our effort but only as we cooperate with the Spirit.

From One Degree of Glory to Another

"Grow," says Paul. Grow "to mature manhood, to the measure of the stature of the fullness of Christ." "Grow in the grace and knowledge of our Lord and Savior Jesus Christ" (II Peter 3:18). The result of this growth is described in II Cor. 3:18, "And we all, with unveiled face, beholding the glory of the Lord, are being changed into His likeness from one degree of glory to another; for this comes from the Lord..."

To be spiritual is a dynamic process of constant growth as we, "beholding the glory of the Lord... are being changed into His likeness from one degree of glory to another."

CHAPTER FIVE

The Orthodox Spiritual Life: Renewal

Many times the Church Fathers compare the church to Noah's ark. As those who entered the ark were saved from destruction, so those who enter the Church today are saved from the universal destruction of sin and death. But the work of the Church is higher and more positive than that of Noah's ark. Because under Noah's direction, the ark took in brute animals and brute animals it released. But the Church, wrote St. John Chrysostom, under the leadership of Christ, takes sinners and turns them into saints. The cock entered the ark a cock, and a cock he departed. The wolf entered the ark a wolf, and a wolf he departed. But when someone enters the ark of the Church, he enters a cock and departs a dove. He enters a wolf, and departs a lamb. He enters a caterpillar and departs a butterfly (St. John Chrysostom).

CHAPTER FIVE

The Orthodox Spiritual Life: Renewal

For neither circumcision counts for anything, nor uncircumcision, but a new creation (Galatians 6:15).

There is an old fable about a saloonkeeper who sold the old tavern building he had occupied for many years to a local church. The enthusiastic members removed the bar, added some lights, gave the whole place a fresh coat of paint, and installed some pews. Then they opened the doors for weekly services. Because of an oversight, however, a parrot belonging to the saloonkeeper was left behind. On Sunday morning the wise old bird was watching from the rafters. When the minister appeared he squawked, "New proprietor!" As the choir marched in, he quipped, "New floor show!" But when he looked out over the congregation, he was heard to exclaim, "But the same old crowd."

This imaginary tale brings a smile. But when we stop to consider the truth it suggests, perhaps it should move us to tears. It shows that there is hardly a difference between believers and unbelievers, Christians and non-Christians. In fact, it's "the same old crowd."

What Difference Does It Make?

An American bishop who attended a number of church services in the Soviet Union was asked by a young girl about the churches in America. After the bishop gave her as complete a picture as he could, she asked him, "But what difference does it make?"

This is the question the world is always asking of us Christians: What difference does Christ make in people? How are you Christians different from others, if you are at all different?

The difference is explained by St. Paul in Galatians 6:15, "For neither circumcision counts for anything, nor uncircumcision, but a new creation." It is not something external on our bodies that sets us apart as Christians. It is something internal, i.e., that through Christ, through repentance and the Holy Spirit, we have become a "new creation." As Paul says elsewhere, "If any person is in Christ he becomes a new person altogether—the past is finished and gone, everything has become fresh and new." "Behold, I make all things new," said Jesus. He established the *New* Testament. His people were to be a *new* people who had put off the old Adam and put on the new. "Put off your old nature which belongs to your former manner of life...and put on the new nature, created after the likeness of God in true righteousness and holiness" (Eph. 4:22-24). To be spiritual is to be in the process of becoming a new creation in Christ.

When Columbus returned to Spain he had to prove he had reached another world. His evidence was a new kind of people he had brought back with him—American Indians. The evidence of Christianity, says St. Paul, is a new kind of people, a "new creation."

A New Creation

The Arabs have an old saying: "Tell me that the leopard has changed its spots and I will believe it. Tell me that a man has changed his character and I will not believe it." This is not what Christ teaches. The fundamental principle of Christianity is that we can be changed in Christ.

St. John of the Ladder wrote, "You will be careful not to condemn sinners if you remember that...the thief (on the cross) was one of a band of murderers; but in one moment the miracle of regeneration took place in him." He became a new creation!

Amazing changes have occurred in science in the past few years. In fact, there have been more changes in the past 40 years than there have been in the past 4000 years. But it seems that in the words of Norman Cousins "man has exalted change in everything but himself."

The Most Needed Change

The most needed change today is in man himself. Unless man changes inside; unless he is born from above; unless he replaces selfishness with love, all the changes of science will be of no avail. Indeed they will only hasten his destruction.

A person once looked at a dinosaur in a museum and said "What happened to them? Why aren't there any dinosaurs living today? What could kill a thing as big as that?"

The guide answered, "Nobody killed them off. They just weren't able to change with their changing environment. When the climate and the environment changed, the conditions were so different they gradually died off."

Man's external environment has changed immensely; he has so many weapons of destruction at his disposal that unless he changes within, he may well suffer the fate of the dinosaur.

We may hear some optimistic voices like Carl Sandburg saying, "God made man a changer. He can change himself into a fish and dive deep and stay under water unafraid of any sea animals. He can change into a bird and travel farther with heavier cargo, wider wings, fiercer claws and beaks than any bird. God must have wanted man to be a changer. God wouldn't have put that awful unrest in him."

But the essential change is not for man to change into a bird and fly, but to change the wolf in him into a lamb. This is precisely what man cannot do. This is where he encounters the greatest difficulty. This is the condition St. Paul described as existing in himself: "I do not understand my own actions. For I do not do what I want, but I do the very thing I hate...I can will what is right but I cannot do it...I delight in the law of God, in my inmost self, but I see in my members another law at war with the law of my mind and making me captive to the law of sin which dwells in my members. Wretched man that I am: Who will deliver me from this body of death?" (Rom. 7:15-24).

The trouble, says Paul, is me. I've had more trouble with this self of mine than with anyone else I've ever met. He gets in my way. He drags me down, messes up things for me. He makes a fool of me. The only reason I hang around with him is that I'm stuck with him. I can't get away from him. Wretched man that I am, who will deliver me? This is not only Paul's problem, it is also our problem.

"It's My Character!"

There is an interesting story of a scorpion who, being a very poor swimmer, asked a turtle to carry him on his back across a river. "Are you mad?" exclaimed the turtle. "You'll sting me while I'm swimming and I'll drown."

"My dear turtle," laughed the scorpion, "If I were to sting you, you would drown and I would go down with you. Now where is the logic in that?"

"You're right," cried the turtle. "Hop on!"

The scorpion climbed aboard. Halfway across the river he gave the turtle a mighty sting. As they both sank to the bottom, the turtle said, "Do you mind if I ask you something? You said there'd be no logic in your stinging me. Why did you do it?"

"It has nothing to do with logic," the drowning scorpion replied sadly. "It's just my character."

The One Who Makes All Things New

This is where change is needed: in man's character, in man's nature. Psychiatry has never brought about this change. Neither has psychology or sociology or education or government or communism or socialism or anything else. Only Christ can produce this kind of a radical change, so as to make man a "new creation".

Regardless of what your parents or anyone else did to you in the past, you are responsible now to make the right choices to alter your way of life. If you make the choice to repent and commit your life to Christ as God, you can become a new creation. To be spiritual is to be a "new creation" in Christ Jesus, to keep growing by God's grace toward the likeness of God.

"Your self on your own hands is a problem and a pain," someone said, "but your self in the hands of God is a possibility and a power."

The only one who can recreate us is the One Who created us in the first place. He created us in His own image. He can also recreate us in the likeness of His Son and make us partakers of His life.

The Bible is a record not of theories of change but of changed lives. It tells of Jacob the cheater who became Jacob the righteous patriarch of his people. It tells of Moses, the hot-tempered murderer of an Egyptian, who was changed into Moses the patient leader of a chaotic crowd through the wilderness. It tells of unstable Simon who was changed into Peter, the bold herald of the risen Christ. It tells of Saul of Tarsus "breathing out fire and slaughter" against the Christians, who was changed into Paul, the author of the most beautiful description of love ever written: "Love bears all things...believes all things... endures all things. Love never ends." A totally new creation in Christ!

The True Ark

Many times the Church Fathers compare the Church to Noah's ark. As those who entered the ark were saved from destruction, so those who enter the Church today are saved from the universal destruction of sin and death. But the work of the Church is higher and more positive than that of Noah's ark. Because under Noah's direction, the ark took in brute animals and brute animals it released. But the Church, wrote St. John Chrysostom, under the leadership of Christ, takes sinners and turns them into saints. So, he says, the cock entered the ark a cock, and a cock he departed. The wolf entered the ark a wolf, and a wolf he departed. But when someone enters the ark of the Church, he enters a cock and departs a dove. He enters a wolf, and departs a lamb. He enters a caterpillar and departs a butterfly (St. John Chrysostom).

A Fresh Start

An irate subscriber stormed into a newspaper office waving the current edition, asking to see who wrote the obituary column. He was referred to a cub reporter to whom he showed the column, including his obituary. "You can see I am very much alive. I demand a retraction!" Replied the reporter, "I never retract a story. But I'll tell you what I'll do; I'll put you in the birth column and give you a fresh start!"

"If only I could begin all over again. If only I could have a fresh start." This has been our plea since Adam. Jesus is God come to earth in answer to this plea.

Let a man go to a psychiatrist, but what can he become? An adjusted sinner. But let him go in sincere repentance and faith to the foot of the cross, and what does he become? A new creature in Jesus Christ, forgiven, reconciled, with meaning and purpose in his life and on the way to heaven.

A New Man

God's eternal Son became man, and something happened to change the whole world. He is not just a new man, a new specimen of the species. He is the new Man—God's own man to produce a whole crop of new men—men and women with a new mind and a new heart ready to go God's way at whatever cost to themselves. New persons in Christ are like Christ Himself, new people with a whole new attitude toward life. "If any man is in Christ, he is a new creation—the old is past and gone, and everything is become fresh and new."

As C.S. Lewis wrote in his book, *Beyond Personality*, "Mere improvement is no redemption, though redemption always improves even here and now, and will, in the end, improve them to a degree we cannot yet imagine. God became Man to turn creatures into sons; not simply to produce better men of the old kind but to produce a new kind of man."

A New Kind of People

Listen to this description of the early Christians as a new kind of people, written by the Athenian orator, Aristides, to the Roman Emperor Hadrian (117-138 A.D.):

"The Christians know and trust God...They placate those who oppress them and make them their friends; they do good to their enemies. Their wives are absolutely pure, and their daughters modest. Their men abstain from unlawful marriage and are free from all impurity. If any of them have bondwomen or children, they persuade them to become Christians for the love they have toward them; and when they become so, they call them without distinction brothers...They love one another. They do not refuse to help the widows. They rescue the orphan from him who does him violence. He who has, gives ungrudgingly to him who has not. If they see a stranger, they take him to their dwellings and rejoice over him as over a real brother; for they do not call themselves brothers after the flesh, but after the Spirit and in God...If any one among them is poor and needy, and they do not have food to spare, they fast for two or three days, that they may supply him with necessary food. They scrupulously obey the commands of their Messiah. Every morning and every hour they thank and praise God for His loving-kindness toward them...Because of them there flows forth all the beauty that there is in the world. But the good deeds they do, they do not proclaim in the ears of the multitude, but they take care that no one shall perceive them. Thus they labor to become righteous...Truly, *this is a new people and there is something divine in them.*"

How?

How does one become a new creation? Paul gives us the answer when he says, "If any man be in Christ, he is a new creation." It begins with a new birth in Christ. "Truly, truly, I say to you," said Jesus, "unless one is born from above, of water and the Spirit, he cannot see the kingdom of God" (John 3:3). This new birth was given to us in baptism. The line of our heredity was transferred from the old Adam line to the new Christ line. Life found a new origin, a new beginning, a new heredity in this new birth. The blood of Jesus now flows in our very veins through the Eucharist. We have become a new people: God's people.

But this new birth in Christ, because it happened when we were children, must be followed by a personal acceptance of Christ as our Lord and Savior.

This is followed by repentance for our sins and a complete forsaking of the old life, after which our life is placed under new management. There is no better manager in this universe than the Lord Jesus Christ. The wisest and the best thing I can do with the life He gave me is to place it under His management. Then it will become truly new and a blessing to humanity.

Not Always Instant

"We may be damned alone," said Alexei Khomiakov, "but we are saved together." We are saved in that *koinonia* which is the Body of Christ. We Orthodox believe that to be saved it is necessary for every human creature to find fellowship in the Church of Jesus Christ. She is "the Body of Christ." She is "the Vine," "the Sheepfold," "the Temple of the Holy Spirit," "the Ark of Salvation." The Church is the life of Christ extended to humankind. The New Life, initiated by Baptism and sustained by the Eucharist, becomes the way to follow as one walks through this world. This means that salvation, as a rule, is not instant. It begins on the day of our Baptism and Chrismation when we renounce the devil, receive Christ, and accept the gift of the Holy Spirit. From that moment we begin a process of slow spiritual growth. The sacraments of the Church provide us with the grace we need to become gods by grace, deified, "partakers of divine nature" as St. Peter says.

Are You Saved?

No Orthodox Christian may say what some non-Orthodox Christians say, namely, "I believe that I am absolutely saved once and for all and that I cannot ever fall away from Christ." Not even St. Paul would make such a statement. Not when he himself wrote, "I do not run aimlessly (lest) after preaching to others, I myself be rejected" (I Cor. 9:27). As an Orthodox Christian I am walking in the path of Christ, but He has given me free will which means that I can choose to deny Him at any time. To say that I am saved once and for all, and cannot ever fall away from Christ is tantamount to God's taking away my free will and making me a robot.

Our Salvation...A Journey Not a Destination

The Orthodox Church teaches that our salvation (deification) begins at baptism and continues throughout life. It is a process of unending spiritual growth. *Keep on working with fear and trembling to complete your salvation* writes the Apostle Paul (Phil. 2:12). God's grace plus our human cooperation lead to salvation. Some of our Protestant brethren believe and vigorously teach that a person is "saved" instantly by merely making a confession of faith in Jesus Christ. Our Orthodox Church does not agree with them. The next time someone asks if you are saved, be prepared to share the Orthodox understanding and teaching of salvation. We are *regenerated* (reborn) in baptism by the grace of God, *justified* or made acceptable to God as righteous and worthy of salvation by the grace of Christ, *sanctified* or made free from sin by the Holy Spirit. All this leads to *deification*. It happens not immediately at one moment, but gradually as we grow in grace through the sacraments of the Church and in a fuller acceptance of the life of Christ. To be spiritual is to be growing in grace.

We are Called to Be Partakers of Divine Nature

The Orthodox Church's doctrine of salvation teaches that Christ the Savior came to save not only *from* but also *for*. He came to save us *from* sin *for* participation in the life of God. This exalted vision of the Christian life was expressed by St. Peter when he wrote that we are called "to become partakers of the Divine Nature" (II Peter 1:4). It was also affirmed by St. Basil the Great when he described man as "the creature who has received an order to become god." The whole emphasis of the Orthodox way of life is on "putting on Christ" and receiving the Holy Spirit through prayer and the sacraments so that we may begin to live a new life in union with Christ and in communion with the Holy Spirit, becoming not simply "good," "ethical" people but achieving gradually a new level of being, becoming a "new creation in Christ Jesus." The Fathers of the *Philokalia* have much to say on this subject as we shall see in the second part of this book.

CHAPTER SIX

The Orthodox Spiritual Life: The Jesus Prayer

At first this saving prayer is usually a matter of strenuous effort and hard work. But if one concentrates on it with zeal, it will begin to flow of its own accord, like a brook that murmurs in the heart. This is a great blessing, and it is worth working hard to obtain it.

– St. Theophan the Recluse

CHAPTER SIX

The Orthodox Spiritual Life: The Jesus Prayer

As Jesus drew near to Jericho a blind man was sitting by the roadside begging...

To catch the true meaning of these words, one must remember that the "roadside" by which the blind man was sitting was the gutter of some street in Jericho. He was blind, and he was a beggar sitting in the gutter. To the people of Jericho he was the lowest of the low.

...and hearing a multitude going by, he inquired what this meant. They told him, "Jesus of Nazareth is passing by." And he cried, "Jesus, Son of David, have mercy on me!" And those who were in front rebuked him telling him to be silent.

He knew of Jesus. He believed in Him. He cried out to Him with faith. But those around him rebuked him, "Quiet! The Master is busy! He's teaching a crowd of people. Do you think He would pay attention to you, a dirty, blind beggar wallowing in the gutter? How dare you trouble the Master; you—a nobody; you—the lowest of the low; you—the scum of the earth!"

...but he cried out all the more, "Son of David, have mercy on me!"

He didn't give up. No obstacles, no discouragement could stop him. He had heard what Jesus could do and had done. And nothing was going to stop him from making contact with Jesus. He cried out even louder than before, *Son of David, have mercy on me!*

Jesus Stopped

And Jesus stopped.

Above all the noise of the multitude Jesus heard the lonely prayer of the blind beggar and *He stopped*. The Almighty Lord and Master of the universe is stopped by the prayer of a poor, blind, forgotten beggar sitting in the gutter—a nobody! He commands the beggar to be brought to Him.

"What do you want me to do for you?" He asks. "Lord, let me receive my sight." And Jesus said to him, "Receive your sight; your faith has made you well." And immediately he received his sight and followed him, glorifying God; and all the people, when they saw it, gave praise to God.

This is the prayer that stopped Jesus, *Jesus, Son of David, have mercy on me.* Certainly if this prayer stopped Jesus then, it can stop Him today.

The Blind Man's Prayer Today

The blind man's prayer, altered but slightly, is known today as the Jesus Prayer: "Lord Jesus Christ, Son of God, have mercy on me, the sinner." It is one of the most commonly used prayers in the Orthodox Church. The Jesus Prayer holds in itself the whole Gospel truth. It is a summary of the Gospels. We read about it in that classic of Orthodoxy, *The Way of a Pilgrim,* the writing of which was greatly influenced by the *Philokalia*. This book is the story of an unnamed peasant who seeks out someone who will teach him how to fulfill the Biblical command to "pray without ceasing."

He wanders through Russia and Siberia with a knapsack of dried bread for food and the charity of people for shelter. He asks many church authorities and religious people, but none can teach him how to pray without ceasing. He is about to come away from his journey empty-hearted when at last he meets a holy man who teaches him the Jesus Prayer: "Lord Jesus, have mercy on me, the sinner." From this man he learns that to pray without ceasing is "a constant, uninterrupted calling upon the divine name of Jesus during every occupation, at all times, at all places, even during sleep." He learns to repeat it as many as 12,000 times a day without effort. The Jesus Prayer becomes a constant, warming presence within him, and brings him great joy.

St. Theophan the Recluse writes,

At first this saving prayer is usually a matter of strenuous effort and hard work. But if one concentrates on it with zeal, it will begin to flow of its own accord, like a brook that murmurs in the heart. This is a great blessing, and it is worth working hard to obtain it.

What is Different About This Prayer

What is so different about the Jesus Prayer?

Prayer, to the average person, is asking God for something. The Jesus prayer is not this. It is an attempt to change the one who prays.

St. John Chrysostom explains how this can happen:

I implore you, brethren, never to break or despise the rule of this prayer: A Christian when he eats, drinks, walks, sits, travels or does any other thing must continually cry: "Lord Jesus Christ, Son of God, have mercy upon me." So that the name of the Lord Jesus descending into the depths of the heart, should subdue the serpent ruling over the inner pastures and bring life and salvation to the soul. He should always live with the name of the Lord Jesus, so that the heart swallows the Lord and the Lord the heart, and the two become one. And again: do not estrange your heart from God, but abide in Him, and always guard your heart by remembering our Lord Jesus Christ, until the name of the Lord becomes rooted in the heart and it ceases to think anything else.

Another Father of the Church says:

Continue constantly in the name of the Lord Jesus that the heart may swallow the Lord and the Lord the heart, and these two may be one. However, this is not accomplished in a single day, nor in two days, but requires many years and much time.

By constant, almost incessant repetition, we make the reality of mercy, both receiving it from God and passing it on to others, the foundation of our lives.

We Become Prayer

As we pray the Jesus Prayer again and again, it becomes established in our hearts. In time the prayer rises to consciousness without effort on our part. In the midst of trouble, temptation, pain, anger, or frustration, this prayer makes us aware of God's presence. As a result, we *become* prayer. We begin to worship and pray, not in our own words, nor in our own minds, but in the Spirit.

The Power is in the Name

There is tremendous power in the name of Jesus. St. Paul says: "Everyone who calls upon the name of the Lord will be saved"

(Rom. 10:13). "Christ Jesus...humbled himself and became obedient to death, even death on a cross. Therefore God has highly exalted him and given him the name that is above every name, that in the name of Jesus every knee should bow, of things in heaven, and things on earth and things under the earth" (Phil 2:5-10). Jesus says in John 14:13, "If you ask anything in my name, I will do it." St. Peter says, "And there is salvation in no one else, for there is no other name under heaven given among men by which we must be saved" (Acts 4:12). The power of the Jesus Prayer, then, lies in the name Jesus, "the name that is above every name." Thus, the name *Jesus* alone can fulfill the whole need of the one who prays when it is prayed with faith and with a life that is lived in obedience to Christ. For, as our Lord said, "Not everyone who says to me, 'Lord, Lord,' shall enter the kingdom of heaven but he who does the will of my father who is in heaven" (Matt. 7:21).

There are some who see a close connection between the practices of Orthodox spirituality and some non-Christian Eastern religions. Yet the difference between them is enormous, "as far as the east is from the west" (Psalm 102:12). The Jesus Prayer serves as an example. When Orthodox Christians pray the Jesus Prayer, we are praying, repeating continuously, and calling upon the almighty name of the Lord of the Universe, Jesus Christ. But in yoga or zen, the person practicing this kind of prayer repeats continuously a word that is incomprehensible to him. And, as Archimandrite Ephraim, Abbot of Xeropotanou Monastery, states, if one inquires about the meaning of that incomprehensible word, one will discover that it is the name of some idolatrous deity, that is, some demon. "What accord has Christ with Belial?" asks St. Paul (2 Cor. 6:15).

The Early Martyrs

Many times we wonder how the early Christian martyrs marched to their death so courageously. We cease to wonder about the source of their courage, however, when we consider the life of St. Ignatius, the God-bearer, Bishop of Antioch, who was crowned in Rome with a martyr's death under the emperor Trajan. We read about him:

When they were taking him to be devoured by wild beasts and he had the name of Jesus constantly on his lips, the pagans asked him why he unceasingly remembered that name. The saint replied that he had the name of Jesus Christ written in his heart and that he confessed with his mouth Him whom he always carried in his heart.

The Jesus Prayer gave him the power to face death victoriously.

Power to Resist Evil

The Jesus Prayer can give us the power to resist every evil thought and temptation with which Satan attacks us. For example, when Satan knocks on the door of the mind seeking entrance through some evil thought, send Jesus to the door and he will flee. Resist every temptation with the Jesus Prayer. As soon as you feel that the stronghold of your soul is being assaulted by Satan, start praying the Jesus Prayer constantly and with faith. Satan will flee. St. John Climacus says, "With the name of Jesus flog the foes, because there is no stronger weapon in heaven or earth."

Astronauts carry their own atmosphere with them when they enter outer space. In like manner it is possible for us as Christians to create our own atmosphere or climate in the soul by the constant use of the Jesus Prayer. Thus even though we live in a sinful world, we can have the power in Christ to resist the world of sin which surrounds us.

St. Gregory of Sinai on the Jesus Prayer

St. Gregory of Sinai (1255-1346) describes the importance of the Jesus Prayer:

The gift which we have received from Jesus Christ in holy baptism is not destroyed, but is only buried as a treasure in the ground. And both common sense and gratitude demand that we should take good care to unearth this treasure and bring it to light. This can be done in two ways. The gift of baptism is revealed first of all by a painstaking fulfillment of the commandments; the more we carry these out, the more clearly the gift shines upon us in its true splendor and brilliance. Secondly, it comes to light and is revealed through the continual invocation of the Lord Jesus, or by unceasing remembrance of God, which is one and the same thing. The first method is powerful but the second is more so; so much so that even fidelity to the commandments receives its full strength from prayer.

Test It In the Laboratory of Life

In science almost every theory is tested in the laboratory. So it is with our Christian faith. It must be tested in the laboratory of life. Try this experiment. Let the last words you utter each night be the Jesus Prayer. Fall asleep with these words on your lips. What better way to end a day than with Jesus? During the day, whether you are talking, sitting, walking, making something, eating or occupied in some way, repeat the Jesus Prayer, or the name of Jesus alone in love and adoration. Try this experiment and discover for yourself what countless others have discovered, among them Princess Illeana of Romania. She wrote:

Prayer has always been of very real importance to me, and the habit formed in early childhood of morning and evening prayer has never left me; but in the practice of the Jesus Prayer I am but a beginner. I would, nonetheless, like to awaken interest in this prayer because, even if I have only touched the hem of a heavenly garment, I have touched it—and the joy is so great I would share it with others.

Praying While Asleep

She tells how the Jesus Prayer had been helpful to her in surgery. Jesus, she says, had been her last conscious thought before she went under anesthesia, and the first word on her lips when she came out of surgery. It was marvelous to know, she writes, that even during the surgery her unconscious mind had been praying the Jesus Prayer: "Lord Jesus, Son of God, have mercy upon me the sinner." For if we fall asleep with the Jesus Prayer, our unconscious mind (which never sleeps) will continue to pray and we will find ourselves waking up with this prayer on our lips. This is what had happened to Princess Illeana during her surgery. She concludes,

When I arise in the morning, it (the Jesus Prayer) starts me joyfully upon a new day. When I travel by air, land, or sea, it sings within my breast. When I stand upon a platform to face my listeners, it beats encouragement.... At the end of a weary day, when I lay me down to rest, I give my heart over to Jesus: "(Lord), into thy hands I commend my spirit.' I sleep, but my heart, as it beats, prays on: "Jesus."

St. Isaac the Syrian describes the phenomenon of praying during sleep as follows:

When the Spirit takes its dwellingplace in man he does not cease to pray, because the Spirit will constantly pray in him. Then, neither when he sleeps nor when he is awake, will prayer be cut off from the soul; but when he eats and when he drinks, when he lies down or when he does any work, even when he is immersed in sleep, the perfumes of prayer will breathe in his heart spontaneously.

Placing Ourselves in God's Presence

The practice of keeping the Name of Jesus ever present in the ground of one's being was, for the ancient monks, the secret of the "control of thoughts," and of victory over temptation. It accompanied all the other activities of the monastic life imbuing them with prayer. It was the essence of monastic meditation, a special form of the practice of the presence of God.

In calling upon the name of Jesus in the Jesus Prayer, we are placing ourselves in His very presence, confessing with the Apostle Peter that He is truly the Christ, and seeking like the woman with the flow of blood to touch the hem of His robe in faith and love.

Ruminating on the Blessed Name

St. Macarius describes the effect of the Jesus Prayer,

I remember that in my childhood, when I was in my father's house, I noticed that the old women and young girls had something in their mouth, some chewing-gum, that they masticated in order that it might sweeten the saliva in their throat and the bad smell in their mouth, and so moisten and refresh their lives and all their inward parts. If this material thing can obtain so much sweetness for those who chew it, how much more can the food of life, the fountain of salvation, the source of living waters, the sweetness of all sweet things, our Lord Jesus Christ, whose precious and blessed name makes demons disappear like smoke when they hear it in our mouth. This blessed name, if we ruminate on it and chew it constantly, obtains a revelation for the intellect, the driver of soul and body, chases all evil thoughts away from the immortal soul and shows her the things of the heavens, above all him who is on high, our Lord Jesus Christ, King of kings, Lord of lords, the heavenly reward of those who seek him with their whole heart.

Thoughts to Ponder on the Jesus Prayer

Through the remembrance of Jesus Christ, gather together your disintegrated mind that is scattered abroad.
-Philotheos of Sinai

The prayer continues to pray within me even when I am talking with others or concentrating on manual work. The prayer has become the active presence of God's Spirit guiding me through life. Thus we see how through...the activity of the Jesus Prayer in our heart, our whole day can become a continual prayer.
-Henri Nouwen

Make it your habit to pray these words with your mind in your heart: "Lord Jesus Christ, Son of God, have mercy on me." And this prayer, when you have learned to use it properly, or rather, when it becomes grafted to your heart, will lead you to the end which you desire: it will unite your mind with your heart, it will quell the turbulence of your thoughts, and it will give you power to govern the movements of your soul.
-St. Theophan the Recluse

Why is the word "sinner" included in the Jesus Prayer? St. Isaac the Syrian repeats the following saying of another spiritual father: "If anyone does not recognize himself as a sinner, his prayer is not acceptable to God."
-Anonymous

In the Christian East the Jesus Prayer is the prayer of one who, like the prodigal son, is on his way home.
-Gabriela Winckler

The surest way to union with the Lord, next to Communion of His Flesh and Blood, is the inner Jesus Prayer.
-Bishop Justin

Communion must come first, and then the Prayer: the Invocation of the Name is not a substitute for the Eucharist, but an added enrichment.
-Igumen Chariton of Valamo

Every Christian should be united with the Lord in his heart, and the best means to achieve such a union is precisely the Jesus Prayer.
-Bishop Justin

After having purified and unified our minds by the Jesus Prayer, our thoughts swim like happy dolphins in a calmed sea.
-St. Hesychius (+450)

God's name is not known; it is wondered at.
-St. Gregory of Nyssa

When I prayed in my heart, everything around me seemed delightful and marvelous. The trees, the grass, the birds, the air, the light seemed to be telling me that they existed for man's sake, that they witnessed to the love of God for man, that all things prayed to God and sang his praise.
-From The Way of a Pilgrim

Again I started off on my wanderings. But now I did not walk along as before, filled with care. The invocation of the Name of Jesus gladdened my way. Everybody was kind to me. If anyone harms me I have only to think, "How sweet is the Prayer of Jesus!" and the injury and the anger alike pass away and I forget it all.
-From The Way of a Pilgrim

You can say the Jesus Prayer for persons who are depressed or ill, simply by adding the words, "Lord Jesus Christ, Son of God, have mercy on your servant _____ or your servants _____."
-A.C.

St. Paul writes, "...no one can say, 'Jesus is Lord' except by the Holy Spirit" (I Cor. 12:3). When one is praying the Jesus Prayer, the

Holy Spirit descends like the cloud on Mount Tabor.
                                            -Archimandrite Hierotheos Vlachos

A monk, whether he eats or drinks, whether he sits or serves, travels, or does anything else, must cry out unceasingly: "Lord Jesus Christ, Son of God, have mercy upon me." In this way the Name of the Lord Jesus, descending into the depths of the heart, will tame the dragon that guards the pastures of the heart, and will save the soul and quicken it. Dwell unceasingly with the Name of the Lord Jesus, so that your heart may absorb the Lord, and the Lord absorb your heart, and the two be one. Do not sever your heart from God, but dwell with Him. Always guard your heart with the remembrance of our Lord Jesus Christ, until the Name of the Lord is deeply rooted there and you cease to think of anything else: and so Christ will be glorified in you.
                                            -Kallistos and Ignatios Xanthopoulos

Call to him with fervor: "Lord Jesus Christ, Son of God, have mercy upon me the sinner." Do this constantly in church and at home, traveling, working, at table, and in bed: in a word from the time you open your eyes till the time you shut them. This will be exactly like holding an object in the sun, because this is to hold yourself before the face of the Lord, who is the Sun of the spiritual world.
                                            -Abba Philemon

Sometimes, there was such a bubbling up in my heart and a lightness, a freedom, a joy so great that I was transformed and felt in ecstasy. Sometimes I felt a burning love for Jesus Christ and for the whole divine creation. Sometimes my tears flowed all on their own in thanksgiving to the Lord who had mercy on me, such a hardened sinner. Sometimes the sweet warmth of my heart spilled over into all my being, and I felt the presence of the Lord with great emotion. Sometimes, I felt a powerful and deep joy on invoking the name of Jesus Christ, and I understood the meaning of his saying, "The Kingdom of God is within you."
                                            -From *The Way of a Pilgrim*

Prayer, then, is to become what we already are, to gain what we already possess, to come face to face with the One who dwells even now within our innermost self.

-Bishop Kallistos Ware

Paul Evdokimov states that the Name of God is a form of his presence. He writes,

This is why his name could be pronounced only by the high priest on the day of Yom Kipur, in "the holy of holies" of the temple in Jerusalem. The Incarnation makes each of us a high priest, but at every moment we are the bearers of the name. The name of Jesus ... contains the power of salvation...for he is present there and we adore him in his name...The beginning and the end are gathered here in a single word charged with the sacramental presence of Christ in his Name.[*]

---

[*] "Ages of Spiritual Life." Paul Evdokimov. SVS Press. Crestwood, NY. 1998. p. 212.

CHAPTER SEVEN

The Orthodox Spiritual Life: The Power of Jesus' Name

Jesus, sweet-scented Flower, make me fragrant!
Jesus, Eternal Temple, shelter me!
Jesus, Garment of Light, adorn me!
Jesus, Pearl of great price, beam on me!
Jesus, Holy Light, make me radiant!
Jesus, Son of God, have mercy on me!

– from the Orthodox Akathist
Hymn to Jesus

CHAPTER SEVEN

The Orthodox Spiritual Life: The Power of the Name "Jesus"

The Jesus Prayer can be shortened in many ways. It can become seven words in English: "Lord Jesus Christ, have mercy on me," or two words in Greek, *Kyrie eleison*, "Lord have mercy", or "Lord Jesus" or simply "Jesus," repeated prayerfully.

The power of the Jesus Prayer lies in the Most Sweet Name of Jesus. Father Lev Gillet who wrote under the name of "A Monk of the Eastern Church" says, "This name (Jesus) has in it God's presence and power." Gregory of Sinai (+1346) wrote, "By pronouncing Jesus' name we feed on it, it becomes our nourishment." St. John Kronstadt believed that the name of Jesus, invoked in prayer with faith, already contains God's presence.

Thus, the power of the Jesus Prayer lies in the name, "Jesus", the name that is above every name. Devils are cast out and people are healed through the Name of Jesus, for the Name is power. Jesus Himself said, "Whatever you shall ask the Father in My Name, he will give it to you" (John 16:23). "Flog your enemies with the Name of Jesus," urges St. John Climacus, "for there is no weapon more powerful in heaven...or on earth..."

St. Theophan the Recluse wrote,

The Jesus Prayer is like any other prayer. It is stronger than all other prayers only in virtue of the all-powerful Name of Jesus, our Lord and Saviour. But it is necessary to invoke His Name with a full and unwavering faith—with a deep certainty that He is near, sees and hears, pays whole-hearted attention to our petition, and is ready to fulfill it and to grant what we seek.

Fr. Lev Gillet adds,

Jesus' name is a concrete and powerful way of transfiguring men in their deepest and most divine reality. The men and women we meet in the street, factory, office, and especially those who seem to be irritating and unlikable, let us go toward them with Jesus' name in our heart and on our lips.... If we see Jesus in each man, if we say "*Jesus*" *over each person, we will go through the world with a new vision and with a new gift in our heart. We can thus transform the world, as much as it is within us, and make our own the word Jacob spoke to his brother: "I saw your face and it was like seeing God's face" (Gn. 33:10).*

Wherein Does the Power of the Name of Jesus Lie?

We begin by looking at Matthew 1:21:

Joseph, son of David, do not fear to take Mary your wife, for that which is conceived in her is of the Holy Spirit; she will bear a son, and you will call his name Jesus, for he will save his people from their sins.

Note well that *Jesus* is the name given to God's Son by God Himself—not by us! It is divinely revealed: *"You will call His name Jesus for He will save His people from their sins."*

And that is exactly what the name "Jesus" means, i.e., *God is salvation, God saves*. When we put the two words together *Jesus* and *Christ*, we come up with a confession of faith which is one of the earliest creeds of the Church. In saying Jesus Christ, we are, in effect, confessing that Jesus is the Christ, the Messiah, the One anointed by God to save the world.

Jesus! By this name St. John Chrysostom writes:

> *Death is destroyed,*
> *Demons bound,*
> *Heaven opened,*
> *The gates to paradise unlocked,*
> *The Holy Spirit sent,*
> *Slaves are freed,*
> *Enemies become sons,*
> *Strangers become heirs,*
> *And men become angels.*

Jesus is the Whole Truth About God

We read in the Book of Hebrews, "In many and various ways God spoke of old to our fathers by the prophets; but in these last days he has spoken to us by a Son, whom he appointed heir of all things, through whom also he created the world" (Hebrews 1:1-2). The revelation of God that came through the prophets was *in many parts* (polymeros) and *in many ways* (polytropos). In the Old Testament God spoke through many prophets. Yet the prophets grasped only part of the mind of God; Jesus was the mind of God. Each prophet had grasped a *part* of the truth of God. Jesus was the *whole* truth.

Jesus is the *apaugasma* of God's glory, i.e., the shining forth of God's glory among men, the exact image and expression of God. The prophets had a message from God Himself. Indeed, they had the word of God but they themselves were not the Word. Jesus was and is the Word of God, the same "yesterday, today, and forever."

St. John Chrysostom on Jesus

He is the Head; we are the body.
He is the foundation; we are the building.
He is the vine; we are the branches.
He is the Bridegroom; we are the bride.
He is the Shepherd; we are the sheep.
He is the Way; we are they who walk therein.
He is the indweller; we are the temple.
He is the Heir; we are the co-heirs.
He is the Resurrection; we are those who rise with Him.
He is the Light; we are the enlightened.

He was Conceived of the Holy Spirit

"For that which is conceived in her is of the Holy Spirit."

In these words, God shows that He alone is Master and Lord. Humanity cannot take credit for Jesus. Our culture produces great people, but it did not, and could not, produce Jesus. He is the work of God. He is the only begotten Son of God. This is what God's word means when it says that Jesus was conceived of the Holy Spirit. As St. Ambrose wrote,

When we speak about wisdom, we are speaking of Christ.
When we speak about virtue, we are speaking of Christ.
When we speak about justice, we are speaking of Christ.

When we speak about peace, we are speaking of Christ.
When we speak about truth and life and redemption, we are speaking of Christ.

"The Way of the Pilgrim"

The spiritual classic *The Way of a Pilgrim* is the story of a young monk's pilgrimage, walking from monastery to monastery searching for life's answers. As he progresses he learns *The Jesus Prayer*, which he prays thousands of times until it becomes like breathing in and breathing out: *Lord Jesus Christ, have mercy on me, the sinner.* Through this prayer he finds inner peace and strength. His whole life is changed. For, there is power in the name of Jesus. It can dispel depression. It can lift our spirit to the throne of God. A contemporary monk of the Coptic Church wrote,

My doctor is Jesus Christ. My food is Jesus Christ. My fuel is Jesus Christ.

The Image of the Invisible God

He is the image of the invisible God, the first-born of all creation; for in him all things were created, in heaven and on earth, visible and invisible..... all things were created through him and for him. He is before all things, and in him all things hold together. He is the head of the body, the church; he is the beginning, the first-born from the dead, that in everything he might be pre-eminent. For in him all the fullness of God was pleased to dwell, and through him to reconcile to himself all things, whether on earth or in heaven, making peace by the blood of his cross (Col. 1:15-20).

For in Him (Jesus) the whole fullness of deity dwells bodily, and you have come to fullness of life in Him..." (Col. 2:9-10).

No matter how much we may have read and heard about Jesus, we need to remember that He is far greater than anything we have ever read or heard about Him.

Theophany

When Jesus was about thirty years old, He came to the Jordan River to His Forerunner, John the Baptist, to be baptized. Without hearing Him speak a word, John immediately identified Him as "the

Lamb of God that takes away the sin of the world" (John 1:29). When he was baptized, the heavens opened and a voice was heard to say: "This is my beloved Son, with whom I am well pleased" (Matt. 3:17). The Holy Spirit in the form of a dove descended and remained on Him.

With good reason the Tradition of the Church singles out this event as a great Feast. It is called Theophany—the revelation—the showing forth—of God. At the very beginning of His public ministry Jesus is fully authenticated as the Messiah. The voice of the Father and the descent of the Spirit confirm that the man Jesus is simultaneously the Son of God. Jesus is anointed by the Spirit. This anointing reveals Him as the Christ, the Anointed One.

And you shall call his name Jesus: for he will save his people from their sins. He breaks down the barrier of sin that He may lead us into the very presence of God. This is expressed in the Book of Hebrews with those words that are so full of meaning, *Let us draw near... to the throne of Grace.*

Therefore, brethren, since we have confidence to enter the sanctuary by the blood of Jesus, by the new and living way, which he opened for us through the curtain, that is, through his flesh...let us draw near with a true heart in full assurance of faith.... (Hebr. 10:19-22).

Let us with confidence draw near to the throne of grace, that we may receive mercy and find grace to help in time of need (Hebr. 4:16).

In the words of Melito, second century Bishop of Sardis:

Jesus is everything:
in that He judges He is law,
in that He teaches He is gospel,
in that He saves He is grace...
in that He is begotten He is Son,
in that He suffers He is sheep,
in that He is buried He is man,
in that He comes to life again He is God.
Such is Jesus Christ,
to Whom be glory forever.

"Lord, To Whom Shall We Go?"

One day when many of His disciples left Him, Jesus turned to those who were left and asked, "Will you also go away?" And Simon Peter answered quickly, "Lord, to whom shall we go? Where is there another teacher who can give us what You have given us? If we leave You, we leave everything. You have words of eternal life."

To whom shall we go with our great burning social problems? To whom shall we go for the answer to war? To whom shall we go for the answer to broken homes? To whom shall we go for the answer to hatred and prejudice?

To whom shall we go if not to Christ? To whom do people go when they turn their backs on Christ? To drugs, to fortune tellers, to gurus, to black magic, to devil worship, to astrology, to the agnostic, to the atheist.

To whom shall we go?

Not to drugs. Not to education. Not to science. Not to astrology. Not to New Age. Not to gurus. Not to black magic. Not to the atheist or the agnostic, but to Jesus. He alone has the answer. He alone is the answer. He alone has the power. He alone is the way, the truth, the life. Where is there another Teacher Who can give us what He has given us? Where is there another God Who can do for us what He has done for us?

"Will you also go away?" asked Jesus.

And Peter answered, "To whom shall we go? You alone have words of eternal life."

Melito, Bishop of Sardis, in the second century put these words in the mouth of Christ:

I am the Christ.
I am the one who destroyed death,
and triumphed over the enemy
and trampled Hades under foot,
and bound the strong one,
and carried off man
to the heights of heaven,
I, He says, am the Christ...
I am your forgiveness,
I am the passover of your salvation,

I am the lamb which was sacrificed for you,
I am your ransom,
I am your light,
I am your saviour,
I am your resurrection,
I am your king,
I am leading you up to the heights of heaven,
I will show you the eternal Father,
I will raise you up by my right hand.

Malcolm Muggeridge

Malcolm Muggeridge, the famous British journalist, once put his faith for his nation in the Labor Party of England. He thought this was the new messiah and he worked tirelessly for it. But after years of frustration, he gave up.

He moved to Russia, seeking another messiah to soothe his troubled spirit—something that would bring peace in international affairs. As he got into communism, he thought it might be the answer to the world's problems. But eventually he became disillusioned with that, too, seeing it could never bring the peace the world needed.

After a process of elimination Malcolm Muggeridge came to the conclusion that the one thing that could save the world was love. And what is the greatest embodiment of love this world has ever known? His mind went back to Jesus Christ. Quietly, at an elderly age, Muggeridge gave his life to Jesus Christ and found in Him the joy of his life. Our hearts are restless till they find their rest in Him: Jesus!

And there is salvation in no one else; for there is no other name under heaven given among men by which we must be saved (Acts 4:12). Jesus!

Jesus, the Truth, dispelling falsehood!
Jesus, the Light above all lights!
Jesus, the King, surpassing all in strength!
Jesus, the Bread of Life...
Jesus, Source of Knowledge...
Jesus, Garment of Gladness...
Jesus, Veil of Joy...

Jesus, Giver to those who ask...
Jesus, Opener to those who knock...
Jesus, Redeemer of sinners...
Jesus, Son of God, have mercy on me!
                    -From *The Orthodox Akathist*
                         Hymn to Jesus

The Messiah Has Come

A Jewish soldier who had attended Christian services during World War II went to a rabbi and asked him the difference between the Messiah of the Jews and the Jesus of the Christians. The rabbi explained, "The difference is that we Jews believe the Messiah is still to come, whereas Christians believe he has already come in Jesus." To this, the soldier asked what was an unanswerable question, "But, rabbi, when our Messiah does come, what will he have that Jesus does not have? Will he have more love? more miraculous power? more purity of life? more divine forgiveness? more perfect righteousness?"

Jesus, True God!
Jesus, Glorious King!
Jesus, Innocent Lamb!
Jesus, Wonderful Shepherd!
Jesus, my Hope after death!
Jesus, my comfort at Thy Judgment!
Jesus, Son of God, have mercy on me!
                    -From *The Orthodox Akathist*
                         Hymn to Jesus

Two Mountain-Top Events

The scene is Mt. Sinai. Moses has been called there by God to receive the ten commandments. The mountaintop suddenly blazes with fire. Clouds of black smoke boom over the great rocks and fill the deep ravines. Lightning splits the dark sky. The sound of thunder threatens to send the heavens tumbling down. The earth quakes and threatens to swallow the whole of creation. Then out through the dark clouds, in an atmosphere of fear and trembling, within the mist and smoke that cover the mountain, under the noise of a thunderstorm and the blowing of trumpets, Moses receives the law from God:

I am the Lord your God...You shall have no other gods before me...You shall not kill...You shall not commit adultery...You shall not steal ...

Now the scene changes. We are on another mountain many centuries later—this time a lovely hillside. There is no lightning, no thunder, no clouds, no earthquake. It is a warm summer afternoon. The sun is shining brightly. There is no longer any distance between man and God, because God is now with man. Jesus sits upon a rock. The people are seated around Him. He opens His mouth and teaches the people He loves the beatitudes:

Blessed are the pure in heart, for they shall see God...Blessed are the peacemakers, for they shall be called sons of God...Blessed are the merciful, for they shall obtain mercy ...

He is the same God who gave Moses the law on Mt. Sinai. Only now there is no cloud to hide Him from His people, no feeling of fear and trembling. All this is replaced by love: the Master sits down and speaks to His children in love. This is one of the great differences between the Old and the New Testaments. The One Who accounts for the difference is Jesus!

> *Jesus, invincible strength,*
> *Jesus, boundless mercy,*
> *Jesus, unsurpassable in beauty,*
> *Jesus, unspeakable in love,*
> *Jesus, Son of the Living God,*
> *Jesus, have mercy on me, a sinner.*
>
> -From *The Akathist Orthodox Hymn to Jesus*

"I Knew Him!"

Even in the dark solitude of her blindness and deafness, Helen Keller became aware of the existence of God. When her teacher, Annie Sullivan, had at last found a way to communicate with Helen, Philips Brooks was asked to share the message of God's love with her.

She placed her fingertips on the famous preacher's lips as he talked in simple language about God and his revelation in the person of Jesus Christ. After a while, her body began to tremble with suppressed emotion. Finally, she could stand it no longer. *I knew Him!* she cried out. *I knew Him! I didn't know His name, but I knew Him!*

> *Jesus, Uncontrollable Word!*
> *Jesus, Inscrutable Intelligence!*
> *Jesus, Incomprehensible Power!*
> *Jesus, Inconceivable Wisdom!*
> *Jesus, Boundless Dominion!*
> *Jesus, Supreme Strength!*
> *Jesus, Eternal Power!*
> *Jesus, my Savior, save me!*
> -From *The Orthodox Akathist Hymn to Jesus.*

Because of Jesus

When a famous musician, theologian and medical doctor, left everything to go to Africa as a missionary doctor, he was asked, "Why are you here? Why do you do this?" He replied, "Because Jesus sent me."

When Mother Teresa was asked why she spent her life serving the poor, she replied, "Because I love Jesus."

Ask St. Paul what made him the greatest Christian missionary who ever lived and you will hear him say, *I count all things but loss for the excellency of the knowledge of Christ Jesus my Lord* (Phil. 3:8). This knowledge of Jesus was not only a sound theological belief about Jesus in Paul's mind, it was also a deep personal love relationship with Jesus in his heart, so deep and so total that he could only say that Christ was his life. *For me to live is Christ.* To know Christ is to live in Him and He in us.

> *Jesus, sweet-scented Flower, make me fragrant!*
> *Jesus, Eternal Temple, shelter me!*
> *Jesus, Garment of Light, adorn me!*
> *Jesus, Pearl of great price, beam on me!*
> *Jesus, Holy Light, make me radiant!*
> *Jesus, Son of God, have mercy on me!*
> -From *The Orthodox Akathist Hymn to Jesus*

Your Treasure and Glory

St. Nicodemos of Mount Athos wrote:

Your treasure is Jesus Christ. Your glory is Jesus. Your pleasure is Jesus. Your whole life is Jesus. Because by suffering for Jesus, you have Jesus. And by having Jesus, you have gained all earthly and heavenly things, you have gained everything.

One who was brought up from the gutter by Jesus and was now engaged in a ministry to help bring others to the Savior said, "It doesn't matter what you're going through, I know the answer and His name is Jesus."

It has been said that the perfect friend is one who knows the worst about you and loves you all the same. There's only One Who loves like that, and His name is Jesus.

He doesn't just forgive your sins, He forgets as well (Jer. 31:34). He doesn't just give you words of truth, He is Truth (John 14:6). He doesn't just tell you which way to go, He is the Way (John 14:6). He doesn't just tell you what life is all about, He becomes your life (John 14:6). He doesn't just know your future, He holds it in His hand (Psalm 31:15).

A Testimony of Power

Listen to this testimony from a person for whom the kingdom of God had indeed come with power. He writes,

Jesus is that in me which holds me steady and calm in the midst of confusion. Jesus is that in me which undergirds my efforts and strengthens my will. Jesus is that in me which says, "Keep on. Take one step more." Jesus is that in me which speaks through me in words that convey feelings of peace, trust, and understanding. Jesus is that in me which banishes fear. Jesus is that in me which rises triumphant out of every trial. Jesus is that in me which never accepts defeat. I can do all things through Christ Who strengthens me.

What Jesus Brings With Him

If someone were to ask you the question: "What does Jesus bring with Him when we open the door and let Him come into our lives?" what would you answer? Well, here are some of the treasures He brings:

1. The kingdom of God come with power; He brings that!
2. Forgiveness of sins; He brings that!
3. Inward cleansing; He brings that!
4. Peace with God; He brings that!
5. Eternal life; He brings us that!
6. The gift of the Holy Spirit; He brings that!
7. Love.
8. Joy.
9. Victory over temptation.
10. Resurrection from the dead.
11. A glorified body.
12. Immortality.
13. A dwelling place in the house of the Lord forever.

If the kingdom of God has come with power for you, then you have received, are receiving, and one day will receive in full all these blessings and more.

The Great Question

The most important question in life is this: on which side of the door of your life is Jesus? Is He inside or outside? We are not really living until we open the door to Him. To open the door to Jesus is to experience the kingdom of God come with power. To close the door on Him is death. As the Apostle John writes, *He who believes in the Son has eternal life; he who does not obey the Son shall not see life...* (John 3:36).

When we open the door through faith, prayer and Communion, He enters. What happens when He enters? Does He find our soul blackened with sin? He makes it whiter than snow. Does He find us naked? He clothes us with the royal robes of a prince or princess. Does He find us thirsty and starving? He places us before the Messianic banquet table overflowing with manna from heaven. Does He find us living in a filthy hovel? He transforms the hovel into a sacred temple. *Do you not know that you are temples of the Holy Spirit and that God's Spirit dwells in you?* (St. Paul).

This is what happens to you when you open the door each day through prayer to let Jesus in. The kingdom of God comes to you with power.

Blaise Pascal

Blaise Pascal, one of the greatest thinkers who ever lived, said of Jesus:

"He who knows not Him (Jesus) knows nothing either in the order of the world or in himself. For not only do we know nothing of God but by Jesus Christ; but we know nothing of ourselves also but by Jesus alone... In Him is all our happiness, our virtue, our life, our light, our hope."

> *Jesus, Sweetness of the heart!*
> *Jesus, Strength of the body!*
> *Jesus, Purity of the soul!*
> *Jesus, Brightness of the mind!*
> *Jesus, Gladness of the conscience!*
> *Jesus, Son of God, have mercy on me!*
> -From *The Orthodox Akathist Hymn to Jesus*

Testimonies About Him from Scripture

The Pharisees said of Him: *This man receives sinners.*

Pilate said of Him: *I find no fault in Him.*

Judas said of Him: *I have condemned innocent blood.*

The Roman Centurion who was present at the crucifixion said of Him: *Truly this was the Son of God.*

The thief who at first reviled Him, finally prayed to Him, *Remember me, Lord, when You come into Your kingdom.*

The unclean spirit said of Him: *Jesus, Thou Son of the most high God.*

John the Baptist said of Him: *Behold the Lamb of God who takes away the sin of the world.*

The Apostle John said of Him: *In the beginning was the Word, and the Word was with God, and the Word was God.*

Thomas said of Him: *My Lord and my God.*

The angels said of Him: *Unto you is born this day a Savior Who is Christ the Lord.*

God the Father said of Him: *This is my beloved Son in whom I am well pleased... This is my beloved Son; listen to Him.*

Who is This Jesus?

Who is this Jesus?
St. Gregory the Theologian answers:
- *He was born, but He was already begotten;*
- *He issued from a woman, but She was a virgin...*
- *He was wrapped in swaddling bands, but He removed the swaddling clothes of the grave when He rose again.*
- *He was laid in a manger, but He was glorified by angels, and proclaimed by a star, and worshipped by the Magi.*
- *He had no form nor comeliness in the eyes of the Jews, but to David He was fairer than the children of men. And on the mountain He was bright as the lightning, and became more luminous than the sun, initiating us into the mysteries of the future...*
- *He was baptized as man, but He remitted sins as God.*
- *He was tempted as man, but He conquered as God.*
- *He hungered, but He fed thousands.*
- *He thirsted, but He cried: "If any man thirst, let him come unto me and drink."*
- *He was weary, but He is the peace of them that are sorrowful and heavy-laden...*
- *He prays, but He hears prayer.*
- *He weeps, but He puts an end to tears.*
- *He asks where Lazarus was laid, for He was a man; and He raises Lazarus, for He is God...*
- *As a sheep He is led to the slaughter, but He is the Shepherd of Israel and now of the whole world...*
- *He is bruised and wounded, but He heals every disease and every infirmity.*
- *He is lifted up and nailed to the tree, but by the tree of life He restores us...*
- *He lay down His life, but He has the power to take it again; and the veil is rent, for the mysterious doors of Heaven are opened; the rocks are cleft, the dead arise.*
- *He dies, but He gives life, and by His death destroys death.*

- *He is buried, but He rises again.*
- *He goes down to Hell, but He saves the damned.*

(Oratio, XXIX: 19, 20).

This is the Jesus we love. This is the Jesus we worship. This is the Jesus whose name the heart prays constantly, "Jesus, Son of God, have mercy." *Thirst for Jesus*, wrote St. Isaac of Syria, *so that He may inebriate you with His love.*

Let us run with determination the race that lies before us. Let us keep our eyes fixed on Jesus, on Whom our faith depends from beginning to end (Hebrews 12:1-2).

> *Jesus, Most Wonderful, Forefathers' deliverance!*
> *Jesus, Most Sweet, Patriarchs' Exaltation!*
> *Jesus, Most Beloved, Prophets' Fulfillment!*
> *Jesus, Most Marvelous, Martyrs' Strength!*
> *Jesus, Most Tender, Saints' Rejoicing!*
> *Jesus, Everlasting, Sinners' Salvation!*
> *Jesus, Son of God, have mercy on me!*
> -From *The Orthodox Akathist Hymn to Jesus*

We close this chapter with a meditation on the power of the Name of Jesus written by a pilgrim after a visit to Mount Athos:

> *Jesus, Thou who art*
> *Love beyond our comprehending*
> *glory to Thee*
> *Who dost sustain the universe*
> *by Thy power.*
>
> *Jesus, Thou Who art*
> *the Way, the Truth, the Life*
> *I thank Thee*
> *for showing me the truth,*
> *in life-giving words.*
>
> *Jesus, Thou Who art*

Light beyond all light,
I confess to Thee
that I walk in darkness,
the darkness of sin.

Jesus, Thou Who art
final judge of all
I confess to Thee
that I have never been pierced
by Thy love, as I should have been.

Jesus, Thou Who art
Life-giving and sweetest warmth,
rekindle my frozen heart.
Jesus, Thou Who art
garment of light,
worn by the stars,
clothe my nakedness.

Jesus, Thou Who art
all in all:
purify my heart
that I may see Thee.

Jesus, Thou Who art
in all and beyond all, my God:
show me Thy face
and I shall be saved.
Jesus, Son of God, have mercy on me.

>   -by Archim. Ierotheos Vlachos in his book
>   *A Night in the Desert of Mt. Athos.*

"Jesus" this is the Name above every name. It is from this Name that the Jesus Prayer receives its power. It is this prayer that creates "a small murmuring stream" in the heart from which flow the waters of everlasting life. In the words of St. Theophan the Recluse:

I will remind you of only one thing: one must descend with the mind into the heart, and there stand before the face of the Lord, ever present, all seeing within you. The (Jesus) prayer takes a firm and steadfast hold, when a small fire begins to burn in the heart. Try not to quench this fire, and it will become established in such a way that the prayer repeats itself: and then you will have within you a small murmuring stream.

CHAPTER EIGHT

The Orthodox Spiritual Life: The Call to Perfection

Aiming at perfection reflects who we will be. For we are now in the process of being perfected (II Cor. 7:1). St. John Climacus wrote, "The perfect but still unfinished perfection of the perfect." We are being continuously cleansed and perfected through repentance as we go through life. When Jesus returns, that process will be completed. As the Apostle John writes, "Beloved, we are God's children now; it does not yet appear what we shall be, but we know that when He (Jesus) appears we shall be like Him, for we shall see Him as He is" (I John 3:2). Nicholas Cabasilas writes, "The life in Christ originates in this life ... It is perfected, however in the life to come." Thus, as children of God, we should always be aiming at perfection. But demanding it with a perfectionism that cannot accept failure misses the point of who we still are.

CHAPTER EIGHT

The Orthodox Spiritual Life: The Call to Perfection

In a conversation with some friends, a person was criticized for some failure. The person who was criticized quickly replied, "Well, I can't be perfect at everything."

John Henry Newman said once, "Nothing would be done at all if a person waited till he could do it so well that no one would find fault with him." "He who makes no mistakes never makes anything," says a proverb.

We are told not to expect perfection from ourselves or from others. Bruce Barton said once, "If you expect perfection from people, your whole life is a series of disappointments, grumblings and complaints. If, on the contrary, you pitch your expectations low, taking folks as the inefficient creatures which they are, you are frequently surprised by having them perform better than you had hoped."

Mickey Mantle became a great ball player because he made three of every ten hits. In other words, he missed seven out of every ten hits!

Excellence Versus Perfection

Dr. DeBakey, the famous heart surgeon, said, "I plead guilty to being a perfectionist. That patient on the table is a living human being. His heart, his life is in our hands, and a single mistake can kill him. I have to be a perfectionist."

One cannot but admire such a surgeon. Yet the truth is that there is a difference between striving for excellence and striving for perfection. The first—striving for excellence—is attainable, gratifying, and healthy. The second—striving for perfection—is often unattainable, frustrating and neurotic. It is unrealistic to expect anyone—even Dr. DeBakey—to be perfect all the time.

The stenographer who retypes a lengthy letter because of a trivial error, or the boss who demands such retyping, might profit from examining the Declaration of Independence. When the writer of that document made two errors of omission, he inserted the missing letters between the lines. If this is acceptable in the document that gave birth to American freedom, surely it should be acceptable in a letter that will be briefly glanced at en route to someone's wastebasket.

Socrates was wryly realistic when he said, "I have discovered Utopia, but I can find no perfect person to bring into it."

Someone said, "It's true that nature didn't make us perfect, but she did the next best thing, she made us blind to our faults. Thus, some of us go through life thinking we're perfect."

There is no such thing as a perfect family. There are no perfect parents and there are no perfect children. How much we need to heed that child's motto which says, "Please be patient with me, God isn't finished with me yet." He isn't finished ever with any one of us whether we are children or adults.

Too Much Insistence on Perfection

A sixteen-year-old girl took an overdose of medication to kill herself because she could not stand herself. A wise counselor discovered that she was trying to live up to the expectations of a mother who was a perfectionist. The girl tried to earn her mother's approval, and never got it.

Too much insistence on perfection can be destructive. Every child should grow up feeling it's not a tragedy to make a mistake.

"Have you Ever Made a Mistake?"

A person who had opened her own decorating shop went to call on a prospective client—a very rich, but crusty, old lady. "I doubt I'll get the job," she said to a friend, "I know she's already turned down every other shop in town."

Nevertheless she visited her and gave her the estimate. The old lady fixed her with a sharp stare and said, "Have you ever made a mistake?"

"Why, of course!" replied the decorator rather startled.

"Fine," the old lady said, "You can take the job. I didn't want to fool with someone who hadn't had a chance to benefit from previous mistakes."

No Perfect Marriages

There are no perfect heart surgeons, no perfect presidents, no perfect parents, no perfect children, and there are no perfect marriages. Many couples enter marriage with expectations that are altogether too idealistic. Imperfect people marry imperfect people and then begin to expect perfection from one another. We expect from our spouse the kind of perfection that belongs only to God. A husband said to his wife one day, "Young lady, you made a grave mistake. You married a man instead of an archangel." No marriages are made in heaven. They come in kits and we have to put them together. A perfect wife is one who doesn't expect a perfect husband. One wife said to her husband one day, "If you weren't such a perfectionist, you'd be a perfect husband." I guess we need to remember that love has eyelids as well as eyes.

No Perfect Christians

Just as there are no perfect families or marriages, so there are no perfect Christians.

A stranger came into town on a Sunday morning and looked around for a church to attend. While standing outside one church he heard the minister and the congregation praying together: "We have left undone the things we ought to have done, and we have done the things we ought not have done."

He hesitated no longer, went inside, and dropped into a seat, sighing: "Thank goodness, I've found my kind of people at last."

In all other religions one has to be perfect in order to come to God. In Christianity one does not. One comes admitting he is a sinner but not wanting to remain one. He comes to the Savior asking to be forgiven and cleansed. Christ did not die for us because we are perfect but because we are not. The perfect person needs no Savior. We cling to God's grace. He loves us in spite of our sins. "The saints," someone said, "are the sinners who keep on trying." The Church has never been a museum for the exhibition of perfect Christians, but always a hospital for the healing of ailing and imperfect Christians.

The Lord did not commit Himself to loving only perfect people. Just the opposite! He said, "I came not to call the righteous (the perfect), but sinners to repentance." He served those who desperately needed to grow up in the knowledge of God. Not only did He not despise them but He said, "There is more joy in heaven over one sinner who repents than over ninety-nine who do not."

Someone wrote,

Since the entire world after the Fall was not the perfect world that God had created or intended, but is the world that God loves nevertheless, we can paraphrase John 3:16: "For God so loved the less-than-perfect people of the world that he gave his only begotten Son that no matter how less-than-perfect we are, if we believe in him, we will not perish but have everlasting life."

Is There No Hope for the Less Than Perfect?

Many people are bothered by Christ's words on perfection. They seem to think that Jesus was saying, "Unless you are perfect, I will not help you." Since they cannot be perfect, they feel that their situation is hopeless. This, of course, is not what Jesus is saying. What He is saying is that the only help He will give us is help to assist us on our journey toward perfection. We may want something less: but He will give us nothing less. The words are clear: "You shall be perfect as your heavenly Father is perfect."

Who's Perfect?

If there are no perfect people, no perfect families, no perfect marriages, no perfect Christians, is there such thing as perfection? There most certainly is. We read in Hebrews 7:26-27, "For it was fitting that we should have a high priest, holy, blameless, unstained, separated from sinners, exalted above the heavens. He has no need, like those high priests, to offer sacrifices daily, first for His own sins and then for those of the people; He did this once for all when he offered up himself." Jesus was the only High Priest Who was "holy, blameless, unstained, separated from sinners, exalted above the heavens," Who had no need to offer sacrifices for His own sins, for He had none. So, there is such a thing as perfection. Only it is not a thing but a Person. Jesus is the Perfect One—the only Perfect One.

We are to leave perfection to Christ. He is God. According to the ancient Greeks to "know thyself" meant to know that you are human; that you are not God.

Among the early monks, there was a group called the Messalians. These were monks who hoped to form an aristocracy of "perfect," "super-Christians." The tradition of the church at that time, especially St. Basil, rejected that false notion of perfection. In fact, Macarius defines a monk as follows: "a monk is called a monk because he converses day and night with God." And this same grace is granted not only to monks but to all Christians.

The early monks looked upon any idea of perfection as a form of pride. One story from the desert fathers describes satan as disguising himself as an angel of light and coming to a hermit to commend him on his spiritual progress. The hermit responded by saying, " You must be making a mistake; it is to someone else that you have been sent. I have not made any spiritual progress."

"You Must be Perfect..."

Jesus said, "You must be perfect even as your Father in heaven is perfect." Does He not thus expect us to be perfect? It is regrettable that the words of Jesus "You shall be perfect" were mistranslated by some as "You must be perfect." The Greek verb *eseste*, used in the original Greek, is a verb in the future tense. It is a promise which says very clearly that perfection is to be granted in the future by grace. It is an ongoing process of continued growth in the life of Christ of which perfection is the goal. In the English translation it is incorrectly translated in the present tense and in the imperative implying that we are expected to reach perfection now. It is not you *must* be perfect but you *shall be* perfect.

Perfection in this life according to Orthodox theology and spirituality is not the state of "I have arrived. I have made it. I am saved. Rather, it is the state of "I am on the way. I am moving. I am on a journey. I am growing." Man's life is never complete even in the Kingdom of God. We shall always be "on the way." Our very perfection is always to grow more perfect, more like unto Christ. And this is a never-ending process.

Epectasis

St. Gregory of Nyssa used the word *epectasis,* which means a "stretching out," striving to exceed one's capacity. It is based on

Paul's statement: "I strain ahead for what is still to come" (Phil. 3:13). The Holy Spirit plants a power in us that expands our capacity and makes us capable of possessing God in an unending process of greater and greater growth, both in this life as well as in the life to come. St. Gregory described true perfection as "never to stop growing toward what is better and never to place a limit on perfection."

Movement Toward Perfection

To be as perfect as God, is impossible for us. But to keep moving toward perfection is always within our possibility with the help of God. In Orthodox spirituality, salvation is not a state of being; it is the motion toward theosis, toward becoming like God, toward union with God, which can never be fully achieved here on earth. It is growth toward perfection. It is moving from sin to Christ, from slavery to freedom, from darkness to light, from falsehood to truth, from despair to hope, from death to life. And once we have reached truth, it is moving from truth to greater truth, from wisdom to greater wisdom, from joy to deeper joy, from understanding to deeper understanding, from all-embracing love to more all-embracing love. And this process goes on eternally. We can never reach the point where we can say, "Well, now I've made it. I just have to sit around and be perfect."

From the Lives of Saints

There was a very holy monk on Mt. Athos. All the monks revered him and tried to imitate his holiness. When asked about his holiness, the revered monk replied, "I've only just begun, my son. I've only just begun." "The love of God excludes all self-complacency," wrote Paul Evdokimov.

Abba Sisois, who had spent 80 years in the desert, was dying at age 100. He had lived a life of repentance. Tears of penitence had deeply scarred his radiant face. Yet at age 100, he was asking for time to repent. His disciples were amazed. "You are asking for time to repent, you who are the master of repentance." The old saint replied, "I'm only just beginning to learn that art." After 80 years of unprecedented spiritual growth, he had still not reached perfection. He was still excited about growing, realizing his unlimited possibilities in Christ.

He is Building a Palace

C.S. Lewis wrote,

I find I must borrow yet another parable from George MacDonald. Imagine yourself as a living house. God comes in to rebuild that house. At first, perhaps, you can understand what He's doing. He's getting the drains right and stopping the leaks in the roof and so on: you knew that those jobs needed doing and so you are not surprised. But presently he starts knocking the house about in a way that hurts abominably and which doesn't seem to make sense. What on earth is He up to? The explanation is that He is building quite a different house from the one you thought of—throwing out a new wing here, putting on an extra floor there, running up towers, making courtyards. You thought you were going to be made into a decent little cottage: but He is building a palace. He intends to come and live in it Himself.

The command "Be ye perfect" is not idealistic gas. Nor is it a command to do the impossible. He is going to make us into creatures that can obey that command. He said (in the Bible) that we were "gods" and He is going to make good His words. If we let Him—for we can prevent Him, if we choose—He will make the feeblest and filthiest of us into a god or goddess, a dazzling, radiant, immortal creature, pulsating all through with such energy and joy and wisdom and love as we cannot now imagine, a bright stainless mirror which reflects back to God perfectly (though, of course, on a smaller scale) His own boundless power and delight and goodness. The process will be long and in parts very painful; but that is what we are in for. Nothing less. He meant what He said.*

Reaching Higher Plateaus

About 400 years before Christ a gifted Greek named Timanthes took instruction in art from a well-known tutor. After several years the budding young painter created an exquisite picture. When he was commended for his accomplishment, he became so enraptured with what he had produced that he sat day after day just gazing at the portrait. He mistakenly believed he would never be able to advance beyond that point. One morning when he went to admire his work again, he discovered that the master had blotted it out. Angry, and in tears, Timanthes ran to him and asked him why he had destroyed his

---

* "Beyond Personality." C.S. Lewis. Macmillan Co. NY. 1948. pp. 48-49.

cherished possession. The wise man replied, "I did it for your own good. That painting was retarding your progress. While it was an excellent piece of art, it was not perfect—even though it appeared that way to you. Start again and see if you can do even better!" The student took his advice and produced his greatest masterpiece called *Sacrifice of Iphigenia*, which is regarded as one of the finest paintings of all antiquity.

Our heavenly Father never wants us to be content with our accomplishments, no matter how able or perfect they may appear to us. He would have us reach even higher plateaus of service and holiness. St. Paul recognized this. That is why he said, "Not that I...am already perfect; *but I press on...*" (Phil. 3:12).

Imperfect Disciples

Did Jesus choose His disciples because they were perfect? Did He not choose Judas who betrayed Him? Did He not choose Peter who denied Him three times? Did He not choose James and John who vied for first place in the kingdom?

It was not just the disciples of Jesus who were imperfect. We are all imperfect. Yet we see in the kind of people Jesus called to be His disciples that God uses weak and imperfect people to accomplish His exalted purposes. "God chose what is weak in the world to shame the strong" (I Cor. 1:27).

What is Perfectionism?

Perfectionism, which is not only a sin but also a disease, is basically the sin of pride. It assumes that we are not imperfect, but perfect. It reminds me of the person who said, "I never made a mistake. I thought I did once, but I was wrong." A very realistic person said once, "I never make the same mistake twice. Every day I make new ones."

Perfectionism has been defined as that personal tendency in many of us to expect perfect or nearly perfect performance from ourselves and others and to let relatively minor "imperfections" make someone or something totally unacceptable to us. This is not to say that all attempts to excel or achieve are perfectionistic. Perfectionism is an all-or-nothing mentality that demands unrealistically and inappropriately high standards. In view of this definition of perfectionism, I can appreciate why someone said once, "A clever man is one who believes in making a mistake now and then just so his friends will not accuse him of being perfect!"

Common feelings associated with perfectionism include: "I am indispensable;" "If I err, I'm a failure;" "If I don't do it, it won't be perfect; it won't succeed;" "What others think of me is most important;" "I am what I do;" "I can't forgive myself;" "I am unable to relax, must always be busy;" "I fear not being liked or loved," etc.

A Common Disease

Perfectionism is a disease common to all, including pastors. A retired Christian psychiatrist, in her nineties, said to her pastor one day: "Your trouble is obvious. You want to be God. You wonder if your counseling will help others; you want to straighten life out for them. You fret about the results of your preaching, and on and on. We cannot control the consequences of what we do or do not do" she said to the pastor. "That belongs to God. If we try to manage or manipulate the consequences of our actions, then we try to be God. We are called to do the best we can, and commit the consequences to God. We are to do our part but to let God be God. He is supreme. He is sovereign. He is perfect. He is all-knowing—not we."

This reminds me of a church where the pastor was ill and every week they would place a note on the outdoor church sign just under the sermon title, informing parishioners of the pastor's condition. One Sunday the sign read as follows: "God is Good"—"The pastor is better."

We are not perfect. In fact, Christianity is the only religion where one does not have to be perfect in order to come to God. The fact is that you will not come to God if you think you are perfect. The Pharisees were a good example of this. It was not the meticulously "religious" Pharisee but the humble tax collector who beat his breast and said, "Lord, be merciful to me, the sinner" whom God praised. There is wisdom in the bumper sticker which said, "Not perfect. Just forgiven." The Apostle John says to those who think they are perfect: "If we say we have no sin, we deceive ourselves and the truth is not in us" (I John 1:8). "Perfection," declared St. Isaac, "is the depth of humility."

Christ Did Not Die for the Perfect

Christ did not die for us because we are perfect but because we are not. The perfect person needs no Savior. And if Jesus said, "You shall be perfect, even as your Father who is in heaven is perfect" (Matt. 5:48), this call to perfection throws us back week by week, day by day, on the mercy and the grace of God, because none of us is perfect and never will be here on earth. If perfection is fulfilling our goal to be perfect reflections of the love of God, then we know that we are miserable sinners utterly dependent minute by minute on God's forgiveness and grace. Thus Christ's command to perfection keeps us humble and penitent knowing that we can never meet it: it keeps us constantly praying the Jesus Prayer, "Lord Jesus, Son of God, be merciful to me, the sinner."

The Perfect Church?

A self-righteous person once said to a pastor, "When I find a perfect church, I'll join it!"

The pastor replied, "Young man, there has never been a perfect church. I am sure my church is not perfect. If perchance you ever find a perfect church, I would advise you not to join it, for as soon as you join it, it will become an imperfect church."

Perfect Christians?

Presented with the claims of Christ, a Hindu replied devastatingly, "I would like to believe in Christ. We of India would like to believe in Christ. But we have never seen a Christian who was like Christ."

And, I would add, he never will see a Christian who is like Christ, because only Christ is sinless. He alone is perfect. We are not. Christianity does not offer us Christians, however saintly or unsaintly. It offers us Christ, a perfect, sinless and divine Christ: God in the flesh, the Savior of the world.

The great French preacher, Francois Fenelon said once, "The love of God never looks for perfection in created things. It knows that perfection dwells with Him alone. As it never expects perfection, it is never disappointed." God does not look for perfection, but He does look for repentance and holiness which is the desire to do God's will in all things.

Just as wise fathers do not expect perfection from their children, so our heavenly Father does not expect it from us. But He asks that we keep it as our goal (I Peter 1:15-16) and to accept our shortcomings as He patiently perfects us. All the while He expects us to aim at perfection as a goal, to be constantly growing toward perfection through daily repentance.

Aim at Perfection

Aiming at perfection reflects who we will be. For we are now in the process of being perfected (II Cor. 7:1). St. John Climacus wrote, "The perfect but still unfinished perfection of the perfect." We are being continuously cleansed and perfected through repentance as we go through life. When Jesus returns, that process will be completed. As the Apostle John writes, "Beloved, we are God's children now; it does not yet appear what we shall be, but we know that when He (Jesus) appears we shall be like Him, for we shall see Him as He is" (I John 3:2). Nicholas Cabasilas writes, "The life in Christ originates in this life... It is perfected, however, in the life to come." Thus, as children of God, we should always be aiming at perfection. But demanding it with a perfectionism that cannot accept failure misses the point of who we *still are*.

We Fall and Get Up Again

The Orthodox Christian belief regarding perfection is exemplified in the following story of the Desert Fathers that is found in the spiritual classic *Evergetinos* (volume one of the first book):

A certain brother asked Abba Sisoes:
"Counsel me, Father, for I have fallen to sin. What am I to do?"
The Elder said to him:
"When you fall, get up again."
With bitterness the sinning brother continued:
"Ah! Father I got up, yet I fell to the same sin again."
The Elder, so as not to discourage the brother, answered:
"Then get up again and again."
The young man asked with a certain despondency:

"How long can I do that, Father?"

The Elder, giving him courage, said to the brother:

"Until the end of your life, whether you be found in the commendable attempt of lifting yourself up from sin or falling again to it. For, whatever it is that a man is found at the last moment of his life on earth, whether it be in good things or evil, there he will be judged, proceeding either to punishment or to reward."

God's demand that we aim constantly toward perfection should never discourage us, because each time we fall, God will pick us up, provided we repent.

Repentance Has No End

Vladimir Lossky wrote in his classic book *Mystical Theology of the Eastern Church*,

Repentance, like the way of ascent towards God, can have no end. "Repentance," says St. Isaac the Syrian, "is fitting at all times and for all persons. To sinners as well as to the righteous who look for salvation. There are no bounds to perfection, for even the perfection of the most perfect is nought but imperfection. Hence, until the moment of death neither the time nor the works of repentance can ever be complete...the more perfect one becomes, the more one is aware of one's own imperfection."*

If it were not for repentance none of us would survive on the road to perfection. Truly, repentance as a way of ascent to God can have no end. Praise the Lord that "He has established repentance as the way of salvation" (St. Chrysostom). "A spiritual person," wrote Paul Evdokimov, "is a saint who confesses himself a sinner."

The Holy Gifts for the Holy

As the priest lifts the consecrated Bread he says, "The Holy Gifts for the holy (people of God)." He does not say, "The Holy Gifts for the *sinless*" or "The Holy Gifts for the *perfect*" because none of us is sinless or perfect. He says "...for the holy (people of God.)" "Holy," of course, means those who are in the process of separating themselves from the sinful world around them and within themselves and within themselves and conforming their lives to the will of the One Holy God. Such holiness can never be achieved with-

---

* "Mystical Theology of the Eastern Church." Vladimir Lossky. St. Vladimir's Press. Crestwood, NY. pp. 204-5.

out the power of the precious Body and Blood of Jesus in us. In fact, St. Nicholas Cabasilas wrote, "The faithful are called saints (*ayioi* or *holy*) because of the holy things of which they partake, because of Him whose body and blood they receive." We shall never succeed in our journey toward perfection without the presence of Jesus who is offered to us in the holy Eucharist and who enables us to say with St. Paul, "I can do all things in Christ who strengthens me."

Exhausting!

The sin of perfectionism is totally exhausting. Imagine the pressure one would live under if one had to be always perfect in everything. After the Romanian super-gymnast, Nadia Comaneci, won an unprecedented seven perfect scores at the 1976 Olympic Games, she was under constant pressure from the crowds who demanded perfection in everything she did and would boo her for any minor slip-up. She simply couldn't take it. It was too high a price to pay for winning seven perfect scores.

Goodness Matters

Although perfection is one of those impossible possibilities, it should be our spiritual aim in life—even though we always fall short. It makes a difference whether a Christian is moral or immoral, good or bad, loving or indifferent. But having said that, we must confess that Christians are not yet perfect. Even Paul said of himself, "Not that I have already obtained this or am already perfect... but I press on toward the goal..." It takes a lifetime and beyond to perfect real sinners—people like us who make up the Church.

We Are on the Way

Thus, we remain people who are on the way. None of us has yet arrived. We are "on the road," to be found at different locations, different levels of growth. And as long as we are on the road and moving forward toward the goal of perfection, we should be patient with ourselves and understanding of others. More than that, we need to link hands and help our weaker brothers and sisters. This is what the Church is all about. It is a redemptive fellowship of forgiven sinners who are in the slow, difficult process of being transformed into saints by the grace of God.

God: Easy to Please, Hard to Satisfy

C.S. Lewis suggested that God is easy to please but hard to satisfy. We are that way with our children. When our children come home from school and are able to read for the first time, we are *pleased* but we are not *satisfied* until they can read Plato, Aristotle, the newspaper and the Bible. We are not pleased until the riches of human history and culture are open to them. God is like that. He is pleased with our first infant, stumbling steps of Christian discipleship and with each stage of Christian growth. But He will not be satisfied until one day we are made perfect. He loves us the way we are; but He loves us too much to leave us the way we are.

One Day We Shall Be Made Perfect

And, thank God, one day we shall be made perfect. One day we will arrive at our goal. We shall reach our heavenly Father and our true home in heaven. Then there will be no more sick and weak bodies, no more battered psyches, no more broken relationships. We will be made whole. Our sins will have been washed away completely. There will no longer be a command to be perfect, but God will breathe upon us with His Holy Spirit and declare us perfect. Then we will truly be saints, redeemed children of the living God, who by grace have become "partakers of divine nature." Imperfect disciples now, but by God's grace growing to become one day perfected saints in God's Kingdom.

Please Note:

Now that we have concluded the general introduction to Orthodox spirituality, we shall enter Part Two to study the specific spirituality of the Fathers of the *Philokalia*.

Part Two

ORTHODOX SPIRITUALITY According to the Fathers of the Philokalia

CHAPTER NINE

Nepsis or Inner Attention

Prayer is not merely a gift, it is hard work. It demands constant vigilance, nepsis, and watchfulness. This is why Proverbs 4:23 says, "Watch over your heart with all diligence, for out of it flow the springs of life." Jesus commanded His disciples at the end of His apocalyptic warnings: "Watch! What I say to you, I say to all: Watch!" (Mark 13:33, 37). Such watchfulness blocks demonic thoughts from invading the heart, enabling the mind to concentrate on "the one thing needful" (Luke 10:42). "The mind of an attentive man is the sentry, the sleepless guardian, placed over the inner Jerusalem," wrote St. Seraphim. Such a heightened state of vigilance causes a person to be awake even when he sleeps, "Though I sleep, my heart keeps awake" (Song of Solomon 5:2).

CHAPTER NINE

Nepsis or Inner Attention

The authors whose works are included in the *Philokalia* are often called the "Wakeful Fathers" because of the great emphasis they placed on wakefulness and alertness in the spiritual life.

One of the major means of theosis according to the *Philokalia* is expressed by the Greek word *nepsis* which means vigilance, watchfulness, alertness, attentiveness.

The Bible on Watchfulness

Nepsis or inner attention is based on the words of Jesus. It is only through watchfulness and alertness that we can ever be ready for the hour the Lord addressed when His disciples asked,

Tell us, when will this be, and what will be the sign of your coming and of the close of the age? (Matt. 24:3).

Watch, therefore, for you do not know what hour the Lord is coming (Matt. 24:42).

The two greatest events in human history are: 1. When God became man in Jesus to save us from sin and death and raise us to heaven; and 2. the Second Coming of Christ. Although no one knows the year, the month, the day, or the hour; the exact date is on God's calendar, known only to Him.

It is interesting that the word calendar comes from the Latin word *kalendae* which in Roman society referred to the time when accounts became due. So, too, at Christ's Second Coming we will stand before His judgment seat and give an account of what we have done with our lives (II Cor. 5:10). Watchfulness, therefore, should be part of every Christian's lifestyle. Every Christian's middle name should be "Gregory" which in Greek means "the watchful or vigilant one."

"Blessed are those servants whom the Lord when He comes, shall find watching," said Jesus (Luke 12:37). The Day of the Lord is coming. To those who are not watching, He will come unexpectedly as "a thief in the night" (I Thess. 5:2), but to those who are watching He will come not as a thief but as the Bridegroom of our souls.

Preparing for God's Judgment

What an awesome moment it will be to stand before God's judgment seat. In one painful moment the whole of what we are will be exposed.

This awesome thought prompted Isaac of Syria to consider ways by which we can prepare for that Day:

When you approach your bed, say to it: "This very night, perchance, you will be my tomb, O bed; for I know not whether tonight, in place of a transient sleep, the eternal sleep of the future will be mine." And so, while you still have legs, follow the path of doing, before you are tied by bonds that can never be severed. While you still have hands, crucify yourself in prayer before death comes. While you still have eyes, fill them with tears, before they are covered by dust. As a rose wilts at a breath of the wind, so at a little puff on even one of the elements of which you are composed you will die. Establish, O man, in your heart the thought that instant departure confronts you, and constantly say to yourself: "There, already, at the door is the messenger come for me. Why am I idle? My removal is for ever; there will be no return."

St. Paul enjoins us to be watchful:

Besides this you know what hour it is, how it is full time now for you to rise from sleep. For salvation is nearer to us now than when we first believed; the night is far gone, the day is at hand. Let us then cast off the works of darkness and put on the armor of light..." (Rom. 13:11-12).

Jesus Speaks of Vigilance

Jesus often spoke to His disciples on the subject of vigilance:

Take heed that no one leads you astray. For many will come in my name, saying, "I am the Christ", and they will lead you astray (Matt. 24:4-5).

Watch therefore for you do not know on what day your Lord is coming. But know this, that if the householder had known in what part of the night the thief was coming, he would have watched and would not have let his house be broken into. Therefore, you also must be ready; for the Son of man is coming at an hour you do not expect (Matt. 24:42-44).

But take heed to yourselves lest your hearts be weighed down with dissipation and drunkenness and cares of this life, and that day come upon you suddenly like a snare; for it will come upon all who dwell upon the face of the earth. But watch at all times, praying that you may have strength to escape all these things that will take place, and to stand before the Son of man (Luke 21:34-36).

Watch, therefore, and pray at all times (Luke 21:36). Watch and pray that you enter not into temptation; the spirit indeed is willing, but the flesh is weak (Matt. 26:41).

"Watch!"

Prayer is not merely a gift, it is hard work. It demands constant vigilance, *nepsis*, and watchfulness. This is why Proverbs 4:23 says, "Watch over your heart with all diligence, for out of it flow the springs of life." Jesus commanded His disciples at the end of His apocalyptic warnings: "Watch! What I say to you, I say to all: Watch!" (Mark 13:33,37). Such watchfulness blocks demonic thoughts from invading the heart, enabling the mind to concentrate on "the one thing needful" (Luke 10:42). "The mind of an attentive man is the sentry, the sleepless guardian, placed over the inner Jerusalem," wrote St. Seraphim. Such a heightened state of vigilance causes a person to be awake even when he sleeps, "Though I sleep, my heart keeps awake" (Song of Solomon 5:2).

An elder was once asked, "In what way can the intellect be purified from impure and wicked thoughts?"

And he replied:

"By not knowing what it means to sleep!!!"

Watchfulness means that when we pray, we should pray with the lips and the heart. We should pay attention to each word of the prayer and deeply embrace the meaning of each word within our hearts. For, the devil is constantly trying to steal our prayers by distracting our thoughts. "Negligence (inattentiveness), like a dark night, kills the soul," wrote St. Gregory the Sinaite.

Controlling the Mind

Watchfulness means that when we pray the whole person is standing before God in full attention. We are completely present to

God as we pray to Him. The mind (*nous*) is not like a broken TV set that one cannot turn off, or switch channels, or lower the volume. The mind can be controlled. The mind (*nous*) has a control switch (*egemonikon*) which controls the thoughts (*logismoi*). The *egemonikon* (intellect or nous) is the helmsman of the soul. Without a helmsman, a ship would never reach the harbor. Specifically the *egemonikon* is "the mind of Christ" that we received in holy baptism. The intellect (*nous*) is "the eye of the soul" as Jesus said, "If therefore, thine eye be single, thy whole body shall be full of light. But if thine eye be evil, thy whole body shall be full of darkness" (Matt. 8:22-23). Evil thoughts are crowded out by the intellect (*nous*) through watchfulness, prayer, especially the Jesus Prayer, the Psalms, and Scripture in general. When someone asked a monk on Mt. Athos, "What do you do here all the time?" The monk replied, "We keep watch over the mind (*nous*) in vigil."

Do Not Provide A Landing Space for Logismoi

Two pilgrims once asked an ascetic monk of Mt. Athos:

"To what extent are we responsible for the thoughts that attack our intellect?" The Elder replied with a beautiful example,

"Airplanes pass over where I live. I cannot hinder the airplanes. I'm not responsible for that. I would be responsible if I began to build an airport. The acceptance of the attacks, which is consent, can be compared to the airport."

Some brothers once asked abba Silouan: "What kind of life did you lead, what struggles have you pursued so as to receive this wisdom?"

And he replied: "Never did I leave a thought in my heart that would offend God."

Such thoughts did come to him, but he did not entertain them.

An intellect that is pure and does not offend God is like an eye that does not accept even the smallest particle of dust. It is on the eye of the soul—the intellect—that all the other powers of the soul depend. This is why Jesus admonishes us, "If, therefore, your eyes be single (pure), your whole body will be full of light. But if your eye be evil, your whole body will be full of darkness" (Matt. 6:22-23).

How does one guard the mind?

The answer comes from the Cherubic Hymn: By laying aside all worldly cares which cloud and drown the intellect that we may receive the King of all invisibly escorted by angelic hosts.

Be Completely Tuned to God

There is in the mind a deep center where the whole person converges. This center is to be completely tuned in to God. To be completely present to God is the beginning of true prayer. The essential part of prayer is this inner attention to God as we speak to Him. St. Theophan said, "When praying to God, start as if you had never prayed before." John Ciardi said once, "A man is what he does with his attention."

The intellect is like a bridegroom. St. Ilias the Presbyter said, "The intellect that encloses itself within the mind during prayer is like a bridegroom conversing with the bride inside the bridal chamber."

"Again and Again Let Us Pray"

We are to watch over our scattered mind bringing it back again and again to the words we are praying. This is beautifully illustrated in the liturgy where the words "Again and again let us pray to the Lord" call on us to collect our scattered attention and re-focus it on God. This call to attention with the words "again and again" is addressed to us many times during the liturgy. It is a call to *nepsis*, attentiveness.

The radio operator on the *Titanic* kept receiving messages of icebergs ahead, but he placed them under a paperweight on his desk because he was too busy listening to the results of an international sailboat race. He never sent them on to the captain. God is constantly sending His word to us, urging us to prepare, warning us of icebergs ahead. We need to develop the virtue of attentiveness, of holy listening as God speaks to us.

Attentiveness United to Prayer

St. Symeon the New Theologian wrote of the importance of uniting attention with prayer:

Attention must be so united to prayer as the body is to the soul... Attention must go forward and observe the enemies like a scout, and it must first engage in combat with sin, and resist the bad thoughts that come to the soul. Prayer must follow attention, banishing and destroying at once all the evil thoughts which attention previously fought, because by itself attention cannot destroy them.

Jesus links watchfulness with prayer, "Watch, therefore, at all times praying..."

The sublime troparion of the Bridegroom Christ which is chanted contritely during Holy Week is a call to such watchfulness:

Behold, the Bridegroom comes in the middle of the night; and blessed is the servant whom He shall find watching, but unworthy is he whom He shall find in slothfulness. Beware, then, O my soul, and be not overcome by sleep, lest thou be given over to death and shut out from the Kingdom. But return to soberness and cry aloud: Holy, holy, holy art Thou, O God: through the Theotokos have mercy upon us.

Immediately following this troparion comes the Doxasticon, the hymn of doxology. Inspired by the parable of the ten virgins, the theme again is watchfulness:

Keep in mind that fearful day and be vigilant, my soul. Kindle thy lamp and cause it to burn brightly with the oil of compassion. For thou dost not know when thou shalt hear the cry, "Behold, thy Bridegroom!" Be watchful, then, my soul, and do not slumber, lest thou be left outside knocking at the door like the five virgins. But continue wakeful, and so with the rich oil of mercy in thy lamp go out to meet Christ thy God; and may He grant to thee the divine bridal chamber of His glory.

St. John Chrysostom in his divine liturgy prays for "watchfulness of the soul" (*eis nipsin psyhis*) in his prayer following the consecration of the Gifts. Such vigilance of soul is one of the blessed fruits of the Eucharist.

Archimandrite Ioannikios writes in his excellent book, "*Themes on the Philokalia: Watchfulness and Prayer*":

Watchfulness, like a general intelligence agency and at the same time the headquarters of military operations, knows how to urgently and unceasingly call upon the omnipotent alliance of divine mercy which immobilizes and disarms every internal and external enemy. But even after this disarmament, it does not rest. It remains the sleepless eye of the soul in its vigilant guard, the never-sleeping observa-

tion post, the penetrating searchlight which follows every movement of the world inside the soul, and searches to keep the field of the heart clean, fertile and receptive to the grace and operation of the Holy Spirit.

St. Isaac of Nineveh urges us to be watchful and prayerful:

Wake up, keep watch! If the thought that comes to you is a good thought you should know that God wants to open up a way of life for you... But if the thought is dark, if you are in two minds because you cannot see clearly whether it is to help you or deceive you—since an evil thought can be hidden under an appearance of good—keep watch night and day in the ardour and intensity of prayer so as to prepare yourself to fight it. Do not chase after it and do not accept it either, but pray about it earnestly. Do not cease to call on the Lord and he will show you whence it comes.

The Theme of Watchfulness in the Canon of St. Andrew of Crete

There is a great wealth of *nepsis* or vigilance in the penitential Canon of St. Andrew of Crete. Following are some prime examples:

Thou hast heard—O my soul, be watchful!—how Ishmael was driven out as the child of a bond-woman. Take heed, lest the same thing happen to thee because of thy lust.

Awake, my soul, consider the actions which thou hast done; set them before thine eyes, and let the drops of thy tears fall. With boldness tell Christ of thy deeds and thoughts, and so be justified.

Be watchful, O my soul, be full of courage like Jacob the great Patriarch, that thou mayest acquire action with knowledge, and be named "Israel," "the mind that sees God;" so shalt thou reach by contemplation the innermost darkness, and gain great profit.

Rise up and make war against the passions of the flesh, as Joshua against Amalek, ever gaining the victory over the Gibeonites, thy deceitful thoughts.

St. John Climacus

St. John Climacus describes vigilance as "the quenching of lust, deliverance from dream phantoms, a tearful eye, a softened heart, the guarding of thoughts, the subduing of passions, the taming of spirits, the chastisement of the tongue, the banishment of fantasies" (*The Ladder 20:5*). These words of John Climacus echo the words of Jesus, "Let your loins be girded and your lamps burning and be like men who are waiting for their master to come home from the marriage feast, so that they may open to him at once when he comes back and knocks" (Luke 12:35-36).

St. Cyril of Alexandria

Commenting on the watchfulness enjoined by our Savior, St. Cyril, Patriarch of Alexandria, wrote,

The lamp apparently represents the wakefulness of the mind... Christ, therefore, commands us to be awake; and to this His disciple also arouses us by saying: "Be awake, be watchful." The wise Paul writes, "Awake, O sleeper, and arise from the dead, and Christ shall give thee light."

St. Basil the Great

St. Basil the Great emphasized the importance of *nepsis* when he wrote:

We should watch over our heart with all vigilance not only to avoid ever losing the thought of God or sullying the memory of his wonders by vain imaginations, but also in order to carry about the holy thoughts of God stamped upon our souls as an ineffaceable seal by continuous and pure recollection...so the Christian directs every action, small and great, according to the will of God, performing the action at the same time with care and exactitude, and keeping his thoughts fixed upon the One who gave him the work to do. In this way he fulfills the saying, "I set the Lord always in my sight: for he is at my right hand, that I be not moved" and he also observes the precept, "Whether you eat or drink or whatsoever else you do, do all to the glory of God." ...We should perform every action as if under the eyes of the Lord and think every thought as if observed by him...fulfilling the words of the Lord: "I seek not my own will but the will of him that sent me, the Father."

St. Symeon the New Theologian

St. Symeon the New Theologian praised highly the struggle to contain our thoughts through *nepsis*:

...our whole soul should have at every moment a clear eye, able to watch and notice the thoughts entering our heart from the evil one and repel them. The heart must be always burning with faith, humility, and love. Do not fear the conflict, and do not flee from it: where there is no struggle, there is no virtue.

One of the reasons for the urgency involved in inner vigilance is that our enemy is always watchful: "Your adversary, the devil prowls around like a roaring lion seeking someone to devour," wrote St. Peter (I Peter 5:8). He is generally more vigilant than most Christians.

The monks of Mt. Athos have a habit of sleeping with their robes on at night. They do this as a symbol of their readiness to meet Christ if He were to come in the middle of the night. To be ready to meet Christ, of course, means more than just going to bed with your robe on. Yet such outward acts express the constant inner *nepsis* or watchfulness of the monks.

The Great Wall of China

The Great Wall of China was reputed to be impregnable, and it was, until one day a drunken guard left a gate unattended for a moment. At a pre-arranged signal hundreds of barbarians poured through the gate. Man himself is the gate keeper of his own heart. He has the ultimate right to choose who can gain entrance into his mind and heart. An enemy inside the fort is far more dangerous than an enemy outside the fort. Hence the constant need for vigilance.

St. Nicodemos of the Holy Mountain

Reinforcing the need for vigilance St. Nicodemos of the Holy Mountain counsels,

...every idea of evil and every form of passion enters the heart through the mediation and service of the senses. And if the senses are not guarded, then the evil passions are also not guarded. How can they be guarded and closed to such passions? Listen. The windows of the Temple of Solomon were covered with fine nets to prevent the entry of impure insects (cf. Ez. 41:6). This may serve as a reminder that he who does not want any impure passions of the senses to enter into his soul must drape his senses with [spiritual] nets. What are these nets?

It is the memory of death, for one; our account before Christ on the day of judgment; the memory of eternal suffering. Through these, man can put away the evil passions and sins, when they come before his eyes and his other senses. St. Neilos has confirmed that this is so: "Those who desire to keep their mind as a clean and pure temple, where the doors and windows are covered with fine nets to prevent the entry of any impure insects, must similarly cover their senses by meditating on the sobering realities of the future judgment which prevent the entry of any impure images to creep in."

St. Isaac the Syrian

St. Isaac the Syrian urges us not even to hold converse with the distracting thoughts of the evil one. He warns of the danger involved in such conversation:

Not to contradict or argue with the thoughts cunningly sown in us by the enemy, but to cut off all intercourse with them by prayer, is a sign of a mind that has found wisdom and power by grace. Its true understanding of the situation frees it from much (vain and superfluous) labor. By taking this short-cut, we cut out the devious circuits of a long ramble. For we do not at all times have the power to reduce to silence all opposing thoughts by argument and to conquer them. For the most part we receive wounds, and the healing of these injuries may take a long time. You are challenging foes with six thousand years experience behind them! Your conversation with them will provide them with the means of bringing about your downfall, for they are far superior to you in wisdom and knowledge. But even if you win, your mind will be defiled by their vile thoughts, and their foul stench will linger in your memory. By using the first method (i.e. by refusing discussion), you will be free from all these effects and from fear. There is no help apart from God.

Mother Theodora

Mother Theodora, one of the Desert Mothers, counsels:

. . . you should realize that as soon as you intend to live in peace, at once evil comes and weighs down your soul through accidie (sense of boredom), fainthearteredness, and evil thoughts. It also attacks your body through sickness, debility, weakening of the knees, and all the

members. It dissipates the strength of soul and body, so that one believes one is ill and no longer able to pray. But if we are vigilant, all these temptations fall away.

Other Church Fathers

Bishop Ignatius Brianchaninov states that there can be no prayer without *nepsis* or attention:

Prayer is robbed and ruined when during its performance the mind does not attend to the words of the prayer but is occupied with idle thoughts and fancies. Prayer is smirched and defiled when, during prayer, the mind is distracted and the attention turns to sinful thoughts and fantasies presented by the enemy. When sinful thoughts and fantasies appear to you, do not pay the slightest attention to them. The moment you see them with your mind, enclose your mind in the words of the (Jesus) prayer all the more earnestly, and implore God with the most fervent and attentive prayer to drive your murderers away from you.

Bishop Ignatius then proceeds to describe how the evil one tries to distract our thoughts from prayer:

For his invisible warfare or conflict with man, especially by means of sinful thoughts and imaginations, the fallen angel relies on the mutual affinity of the sins one with another. This conflict never ceases day or night, but it becomes specially intense and furious when we stand for prayer. Then, according to the expression of the holy Fathers, the devil gathers the most monstrous thoughts from everywhere and pours them on our soul. First, he reminds us of all who have wronged or offended us. He tries to present all the insults, wrongs and injuries inflicted on us in the most lurid colours. He points out the necessity for retaliation and resistance to them by demanding justice, common sense, the public good, self-preservation, self-defense. It is obvious that the enemy tries to shake the very foundation of prayer, namely forgiveness and meekness, so that the building erected on this foundation may collapse of its own accord. And this is just what happens, because a person who is full of resentment and who does not forgive his neighbour's sin is quite unable to obtain compunction or concentrate when he prays. Angry thoughts dissipate prayer; they blow it aside, just as a violent wind scatters seeds thrown by a sower on his field; so the field of the heart remains unsown, and all the ascetic's hard work comes to nothing. It is a well-known fact that forgiveness of wrongs and offenses, changing condemnation of our neighbours into kindness and mercy so that we excuse them and blame ourselves, provides the only solid basis for successful prayer.

St. Theophan The Recluse

St. Theophan the Recluse explains how we can control our thoughts through vigilance and prayer,

God is everywhere: see that your thoughts too are always with God. How can this be done? Thoughts jostle one another like swarming gnats, and emotions follow on the thoughts. In order to make their thought hold to one thing, the Fathers used to accustom themselves to the continual repetition of a short prayer, and from this habit of constant repetition this small prayer clung to the tongue in such a way that it repeated itself of its own accord. In this manner their thought clung to the prayer and, through the prayer, to the constant remembrance of God. Once this habit has been acquired, the prayer holds us in the remembrance of God, and the remembrance of God holds us in prayer; they mutually support each other. Here, then, is a way of walking before God.

The Process of Sin

The Church Fathers, who spent their lives studying how the mind works, have a deep understanding of the process of sin which they explain as follows,

1. The mind receives a suggestion or stimulation. If the mind is attentive, it will notice the provocation and will close the door on it. If not, then,

2. The soul will dialogue with the suggestion and give its assent to it (as Eve did with the serpent), whereupon it becomes sinful because it consents to the thought with some pleasure.

3. There is a union or coupling with the thought in which the mind surrenders itself to the suggestion and begins to dwell with it.

4. The mind is made captive by the thought as it readily consents to it time and again.

5. Finally we fall so completely under the power of the suggestion that we are no longer free to resist it. It becomes a passion. We become its slaves.

Tito Colliander describes the process as follows,

The impulse knocks like a salesman at the door. If one lets him in, he begins his sales talk about his wares, and it is hard to get rid of him even if one observes that his wares are not good. Thus follows consent and finally the purchase, often against one's own will.[1]

Thus, we actually invite the demons within us by not guarding the mind, by not posting a guard at the door of the mind. Hesychius of Jerusalem said that one can be free of sin by guarding the mind through prayer and alertness. When you have a treasure in your house, you stand guard at the door. This is why the Fathers of the *Philokalia* urge us to be vigilant.

"Seal your senses with stillness and sit in judgment upon the thoughts that attack your heart," said St. Thalassios.

To Be Completely Present to Where We Are

Nepsis means to be completely present to where we are just as a mother has an attentive ear to the least sound of her baby in the crib even as she talks on the phone or vacuums the rug. Love is attentive and watchful.

Bishop Kallistos Ware tells us that "watchfulness means, among other things, to be present where we are—at this specific point in space, at this particular moment in time.

All too often we are scattered and dispersed, we are living, not with alertness in the present, but with nostalgia in the past, or with misgiving and wishful thinking in the future... The *neptic* man, then, is gathered into the here and the now. He is the one who seizes the *kairos*, the decisive moment of opportunity."[2]

Tito Colliander describes such attentiveness:

The spider may be another example for you. In the middle of his web he sits and feels the smallest fly and kills it. Likewise prayer

---

[1] "The Way of Ascetics." Tito Colliander, St. Vladimir's Press. Crestwood, NY. 1960. p. 50.
[2] "The Orthodox Way." Kallistos Ware. SVS Press. Crestwood, NY. 1981.

watches in the middle of your heart: as soon as a trembling makes it known that an enemy is there, prayer kills it.

To leave off praying is the same thing as deserting one's post. The gate stands open for the ravaging hordes, and the treasures one has gathered are plundered. The plunderer does not need long to accomplish his work: anger, for example, can destroy everything in a single second.[*]

Two Examples of Vigilance

The following are two examples of vigilance as the practice of being completely present to what we are doing at the moment.

Once at the Holy Monastery of Iviron, when the priest officiating began to cense the brothers at their pews, he passed by one of them without censing him. After the dismissal of the Divine Liturgy the priest was asked to give an explanation. He said that when he reached the pew of that certain brother he saw it empty! They then called aside the brother and said to him:

"We beg you to keep watch over yourself because the priest is humble and whatever he saw he told us."

The brother said contritely:

"The priest is right because even though I was at my pew, my mind was on the property of the monastery (metochion)."

Following is another example. In the cemetery of the Skete of St. Anna, in a small room and charnel house many years ago the priest-monk Matthew lived a hermit's life praying unceasingly. One day Fr. Matthew heard a noise. He opened the door of the cemetery and saw many young handsome men who were bringing bones and arranging them there, and others who were taking bones and leaving. Fr. Matthew became ecstatic when one of them said to him:

"Why are you perplexed Fr. Matthew? We are angels of God and were given the commandment by the Holy Mother of God to do what you are seeing. We are transferring the bones of those who, possessing great virtue, brought their mind here constantly to Mt. Athos, wanting to complete the road of their life here, but did not manage to fulfill their desire. Since they had this strong desire we are therefore bringing their bones here so that they will be resurrected here at the Second Coming. The other bones, continued the angel, which you see

---

[*] "The Way of the Ascetics." Tito Colliander. SVS Press. Crestwood, NY. 1985.

us transferring from here to the world, belong to those who were here in body but their mind was in the world, remaining uncorrected despite the advice of the Fathers and wanting to have ties with parents and other lay people. That is why they will not be resurrected here on Mt. Athos on Judgment Day but in the world."

St. John the Solitary

The need for vigilance is emphasized by John the Solitary:

At the time when the master of the house does not expect it, the thief comes and breaks into his home. For this reason it is essential that our mind should be awake at all times—like a wakeful pilot in charge of a ship. You know very well that it is through labor, vigilance, toil, and all sorts of vexations that a ship is constructed and completed, but it can be wrecked in only a short moment. Similarly the likeness of a human person can be well depicted in a portrait only by means of careful skill and the proper mixture of colors and paints, yet it can be destroyed in just a brief moment: it does not take much to destroy it despite the labor that it took to make it. Destruction is much easier than construction, pulling down than building up.

Pseudo-Macarius

Pseudo-Macarius stresses the importance of *nepsis*,

This is the true foundation of prayer: keeping watch over your own thoughts and giving yourself to prayer in great tranquillity, in great peace, in such a way as not to disturb others... You will then have to wage war on your own thoughts and cut back their rampant growth...push ahead towards God, refrain from doing as your thoughts would have you do, but on the contrary lead them back from their dispersion, sifting the natural thoughts from those that are bad. The soul subjected to sin advances as if across a river choked with reeds and sedge... Anyone wishing to cross over must reach out with his hands and laboriously root out by force the obstacles in his way. Thus do thoughts from the enemy imprison the soul as in a straitjacket. It requires great zeal and great alertness to discern them.

Post a Guard

There are several sayings of the Fathers whose theme is: "Be the doorkeeper of your heart, so that the stranger does not enter; say 'Are you one of ours, or one of the enemy?' We are called to post a guard at the door of the heart."

St. Theophan the Recluse wrote,

After every thought has been banished from the soul by the memory of God's presence, stand at the door of the heart and watch carefully everything that enters or goes out from there.

St. Nicodemos of the Holy Mountain issues a clarion call to guard all the senses which he calls gateways to sin:

St. Isaac has noted, the enemy is standing and observing day and night directly against our eyes to detect which entrance of our senses will be opened for him to enter. Once he enters through one of our senses because of our lack of vigilance, then this devious shameless dog attacks us further with his own arrows. We must also struggle to protect our senses because it is not only through curious eyes that we fall into the sin of desire and commit fornication and the adultery of the heart, as the Lord noted. There is also the fornication and the adultery of the sense of hearing, the sense of smell, the sense of taste, the sense of touch, and all of the senses together. Therefore, St. Gregory the Theologian has written in his heroic counsel to the virgin: "Virgin, be truly a virgin in the ears, in the eyes and in the tongue! Every sense that wanders with ease, sins." St. Gregory of Nyssa also said: "The Lord has spoken, I believe, about all the senses, so that following His words we can include that the one who hears lustfully, the one who touches and the one who uses every inner power in us to serve pleasure has actually committed the sin in his heart.

Guard the Senses

The wise St. Syngletike said,

Even when we do not want it, the thieves will enter through the senses. For how is it possible for a house not to be darkened by the smoke entering from outside through the doors and windows that have been left opened?

Paul Evdokimov wrote, "Vigilance allows us to recognize evil before being tempted . . . The spiritual masters make use of an image that was familiar in the desert: Strike the serpent on the head before he enters the cell. If the serpent enters, the struggle will be much more laborious."*

St. Macarios tells of how Adam was tempted through the senses,

Adam was created pure by God to serve him... However, the devil approached him and spoke to him and it was from without through the hearing that he was first received. It was after this that the devil entered his heart and pervaded his entire being.

Evagrius of Pontus warns,

Be the door-keeper of your heart and do not let any thought come in without questioning it. Question each thought individually: "Are you on our side or the side of our foes?" And if it is one of ours, it will fill you with tranquillity.

We read in the *Philokalia,*

Vigilance is a firm control of the mind. Post it at the door of the heart, so that it sees marauding thoughts as they come, hears what they say, and knows what these robbers are doing, and what images are being projected...so as to seduce the mind by phantasy.

Abba Bessarion wrote, "The monk should be all eye." The purpose of vigilance is to rouse the spirit from sluggishness and make us wide awake, *neptikos.*

It is no wonder that Abba Poemen often said, "We do not need anything except a vigilant spirit."

St. Basil adds, "We must watch ourselves and always have our attention in an awakened state."

C.S. Lewis quotes a Puritan clergyman who said, "The true Christian's nostril is to be continually attentive to the inner cesspool."

A gentleman in India once got a tiger cub and tamed it so that it became a pet. One day when it had grown up, it tasted blood, and the old tiger-nature flashed out. It had to be killed. So with the old nature. It never dies, though it is subdued; and unless one is watchful and prayerful, it will gain the upper hand and destroy us.

---

* "Ages of the Spiritual Life." P. Evdokimov. SVS Press. Crestwood, NY. 1998. p. 175.

St. Andrew of Crete warns us on what happens when we cease to be vigilant:

The end draws near, my soul, the end draws near;
Yet you do not care or make ready.
The time grows short, rise up: the Judge is at the door.
The days of our life pass swiftly, as a dream, as a flower.
Why do we trouble ourselves over what is all in vain?
I am deprived of the bridal chamber, of the wedding and the supper;
For want of oil my lamp has gone out;
While I slept the door was closed;
The supper has been eaten;
I am bound hand and foot, and cast out.

Proseuche (Prayer) and Prosoche (Attention)

Thus, vigilance, *nepsis*, is achieved by guarding closely the senses, by the constant remembrance of death, and especially by the Jesus Prayer. In fact, the Church Fathers often quoted one sentence of Evagrius because it contained a suggestive alliteration of two Greek words *proseuche* (prayer) and *prosoche* (attention). Attentiveness and prayer belong together. No one can be truly attentive without the power that comes from prayer. To be successful, a person's efforts to be vigilant must be buttressed by God's power. In fact, it has been said that *prosoche* (attention) is the mother of *proseuche* (prayer). "Watch and pray," said Jesus, "that you enter not into temptation..." Watchfulness and prayer are inseparable in the unseen warfare with the unclean thoughts and demons.

Concentrate Unceasingly on God

A brother once asked a certain Elder:

"What activity should the heart be occupied with in order to be benefited?"

And the Elder replied:

"The perfect activity of the monk is to concentrate unceasingly on God."

The brother said:

"But the evil thoughts do not allow the intellect to call on God. How should it expel them?"

The Elder said:

"The intellect cannot completely achieve this on its own because it does not have such strength. When the thoughts attack, it is profitable to immediately flee towards God and He will disperse them. Because God is a 'consuming fire'."

The negative aspect of vigilance is to keep away all evil thoughts that come from the outside. This leads to the positive aspect of vigilance which is to be more attentive to God through prayer. Thus, attention becomes the mother of prayer. "The essential and indispensable part of prayer is attention, without attention there is no prayer," said St. Theophan the Recluse.

Do Not Pray for an End to Struggle

Vigilance is never easy. It requires constant struggle. The Fathers tell of a monk who prayed to God about the conflict brought about by the constant struggle to be vigilant. He wanted the struggle to come to an end. It did come to an end. He went to see his spiritual father and said to him, "I see myself in unbroken peace, without any conflict or struggle." The spiritual father said to him, "Go and pray to God that the warfare may return, because through conflict the soul comes to proficiency and victory. And when the struggle comes, do not pray for it to be taken away, but that the Lord may give patience in persecution."

The Slumber of Sloth

The enemy of vigilance is spiritual laxity or the slumber of sloth. Jesus experienced such physical and spiritual slumber with his disciples in the Garden of Gethsemane,

And he came to his disciples and found them sleeping, and he said to them, "So, could you not watch with me one hour? Watch and pray that you may not enter into temptation... Again for the second time he went away and prayed... And again he came and found them sleeping, for their eyes were heavy. So, leaving them again, he went away and prayed for the third time... Then he came to the disciples, and said to them, "Are you still sleeping and taking your rest?" (Matt. 26:40-45).

St. Paul considers the slumber of sloth as the enemy of vigilance,

For you are all sons of light and sons of the day; we are not of the night or darkness. So, then, let us not sleep, as others do, but let us keep awake and sober. For those who sleep, sleep at night... But since we belong to the day, let us be sober... (I Thess. 5:5-8).

The Bible sounds the alarm of vigilance because we have always suffered from what someone called "a sleeping sickness of the soul." "You know what hour it is," writes St. Paul, "how it is full time now for you to wake from sleep" (Rom. 13:11).

Fully Alive. Fully Awake

In the second century St. Irenaeus wrote, "The glory of God is a human being who is fully alive." Fully alive means fully awake, alert, attentive, vigilant. "Be watchful," says Jesus (Rev. 3:2).

We are called to be awake to the God who made us and loves us, awake to one another, and awake to the world around us. The prophets were awake to God. Paul was blinded awake on the Damascus road. When a certain person was asked, "Are you a god?" he replied, "No, I am not."

"Are you an angel, then?"

"No," he said.

"Then what are you?"

"I am one who is awake," he replied.

Archbishop Anthony Bloom said so well, "How many of us sleep our life through? We call it daydreaming or being imaginative. But in all truth it is slumber; reality becomes a dream, while dreams acquire cogency and our days themselves become nights and our lives sleep-walking."*

To understand how dangerous spiritual slumber is to the soul we need to listen to some of the troparia (hymns) of the Church:

Enlighten my eyes, O Christ God, lest I sleep to death; lest my enemies say: 'I prevailed over him'" (The Great Compline).

My soul, my soul—arise!
Why are you sleeping?

---

* "Meditations." Dimension Books. Denville, NJ. 1971. p. 97.

The end is at hand;
destruction hangs over you.
Come again to your senses
that you may be spared by Christ our God,
who is everywhere, filling all things.
— *The Canon of St. Andrew*

The following prayer from the Great Compline issues another call to wakefulness:

O Lord, Thou knowest well the alertness of mine invisible enemies and the weakness of mine own wretched body, for Thou Thyself hast fashioned me. Wherefore I entrust my soul to Thine hands: cover me with the wings of Thy bounty, lest I sleep to death; enlighten my spirit with the delight of Thy divine word; awaken me at the time of Thy glory, for Thou alone art a gracious God and the Lover of Mankind.

St. Maximos warns us of the enemy's stealing Christ from us through lack of vigilance:

So, brethren, let us not sleep, but keep watch about Our Lord and Saviour, to make sure with unceasing vigil that no one shall steal Him from the sepulchre of our hearts, lest we may have to say at some time: they came while we were sleeping and stole Him away. For we have enemies who will try to steal Christ from our hearts, would we lapse into sleep. So with unceasing watch let us keep Him within the sepulchre of our souls; there let Him rest; there let Him sleep; there when He wills, let Him rise again.

Another saint of the Church prayed,

I am overcome with the slumber of sloth, and the sleep of sin oppresses my heart. Make use, my soul, of the time for repentance; shake off the heavy sleep of sloth, and hasten to watch.

Nepsis (Vigilance) Begets Diakrisis (Discernment)

One of the many benefits of growing in watchfulness is the gift of discernment. Bishop Kallistos Ware explains how this happens:

Growing in watchfulness and self-knowledge, the traveller upon the Way begins to acquire the power of discrimination or discernment (in Greek, diakrisis.) This acts as a spiritual sense of taste. Just as the physical sense of taste, if healthy, tells a man at once whether food is moldy or wholesome, so the spiritual taste, if developed through ascetic effort and prayer, enables a man to distinguish between the varying thoughts and impulses within him. He learns the difference between the evil and the good, between the superfluous and the meaningful, between the fantasies inspired by the devil and the images marked upon his creative imagination by celestial archetypes. *

Proschomen! Let Us Be Attentive!

Practicing *nepsis*, watchfulness, is exceedingly important during the liturgy. Myriads of distracting thoughts plague us when we come to worship. Our minds drift to our afternoon plans, business deals etc. It is impossible to pray with such distractions. We need to refocus continually and return to the words we are praying. It is for this reason that we are commanded often to pay attention during the liturgy with the words, *"Let us attend! Let us be attentive!"* We are being awakened, brought back to the words we are praying.

I am reminded of a little five-year-old girl who had her own way of waking up her mother. When her mother had one of those days when she would forget everything, she would go up to her mother, knock on her head, and shout in her ear, "Wake up in there! Wake up in there!"

This is the function of the words, *"Wisdom. Be attentive"* during the liturgy. They are knocking on our head and shouting in our ears, "Wake up in there! God is about to share with you His words of wisdom and eternal life. Pay attention!" "Pay attention, come to me; listen, and you will live," says the Lord (Isaiah 55:3).

A Romanian Orthodox Christian told of going to church early one Sunday for the liturgy:

"This Sunday I went to church earlier than usual, and I watched the Candle Lady lighting the wicks of the votive lamps under each icon. It was like seeing each saint coming to life, waking to be part of the Holy Liturgy."

---

* "The Orthodox Way." Kallistos Ware. SVS Press. Crestwood, NY. 1981.

Since each of us is the image of God, there is a votive light in each heart. The words, "Wisdom! Be attentive!," are intended to light the wicks of those inner lamps, to make us fully awake for the Holy Liturgy. They are a call to *nepsis*, vigilance.

The key words of *nepsis* are, "Watch and pray." In the words of Philotheus,

At every hour and moment let us guard the heart with all diligence from thoughts that obscure the soul's mirror, for in that mirror Jesus Christ, the wisdom and power of God the Father, is...luminously reflected.

Arch-Enemy of the Soul: Logismoi

The fathers of the *Philokalia* emphasized the importance of *Nepsis* or vigilance because they believed that the arch-enemy of the soul is a certain kind of thought which they described with the word *logismos*. *Logismoi* are essentially a train of thoughts that befog and pollute the mind so that bit by bit it drifts away from reality into a world of fantasy. In the writings of the Desert Fathers, *logismoi* are thoughts caused by demons. Such thoughts are the seeds of the passions, those impulses that emerge from the subconscious and soon become obsessive. *Logismoi* are important because all battles are won or lost first in the internal dialogue of the mind. For example, virtue is natural to us, while vice is unnatural. Yet, vice is made to appear far more attractive than virtue because the *logismoi* step in, and, backed by demons, darken the mind, preventing it from seeing the beauty of virtue, while clothing vice with an artificial attractiveness.

How Logismoi Attack Us

Evagrius points out that through such *logismoi* the demons can attack us directly through the annoyances of other people and the tensions caused by living together in communities, cities, and villages. Or, says Evagrius, in the desert these same demons can attack hermits directly in hand-to-hand combat. Nor is it just the hermits alone who are attacked in such hand-to-hand combat. Try praying, for example. It may seem as if you are doing nothing, but in no time at all your mind will be running in circles. It will start off in three or four directions at the same time, ceaselessly following one train of thought after another. And even if one manages to concentrate fully in prayer for a few moments, new *logismoi* will come to tempt us with pride by telling us how spiritual we have become!

Overcoming Logismoi

The intellect (*egemonikon*) cannot protect itself from harmful thoughts. It needs the power of pure prayer. It needs fasting since an intemperate stomach begets an intemperate intellect. It needs the Eucharist which enlightens the intellect. As the pre-Communion prayer states, "The Body of God both deifies and nourishes me. It deifies my soul and wondrously nourishes my mind." It needs the Holy Spirit. Sts. Ignatius and Kallistos write, "It is not possible to raise the intellect without the Holy Spirit." Finally, the intellect (*egemonikon*) needs our cooperation in setting aside all worldly cares which serve to cloud and drown the intellect. In the words of the Cherubic Hymn, "We who mystically represent the Cherubim, as we sing the thrice-holy hymn to the life-giving Trinity, let us set aside all worldly cares that we may receive the King of all invisibly escorted by the angelic host." Thus fortified by prayer, fasting, the Eucharist, the Holy Spirit, and the setting aside of worldly cares, the intellect (*nous, egemonikon*) will be able to serve as a powerful gatekeeper, warding off the *logismoi*, which are the seeds of passions.

CHAPTER TEN

Asceticism

After a long struggle with the demons in the desert, Anthony looked up and saw as it were the roof opening and a beam of light coming down to him. The demons suddenly were gone and the pain in his body ceased at once and the building was restored to its former condition. Anthony, perceiving that help had come, breathed more freely and felt relieved of his pains. And he asked the vision: "Where were you? Why did you not appear at the beginning to stop my pains?" And a voice came to him: "Anthony, I was here, but I waited to see your struggle. And now, because you held out and did not surrender, I will ever be your helper and I will make you renowned everywhere" (Life 10).

Asceticism with humility is valuable, but asceticism without humility is extremely dangerous.
— Evagrius

Another Father says,
It is better to fail with humility than to succeed with pride.

CHAPTER TEN

Asceticism

There is a story about King Ebrahim, a wealthy man, who was at the same time very sincere and very concerned about religious matters. One night the king was roused from sleep by a fearful stumping on the roof above his bed. Alarmed, he shouted: "Who's there?" "A friend," came the reply from the roof. "I've lost my camel." Perturbed by such stupidity, Ebrahim screamed: "You fool! Are you looking for a camel on the roof?" "You fool!" the voice answered. "Are you looking for God in silk clothing, and lying on a golden bed?" These simple words, we are told, filled the king with terror; he rose from his sleep to become a remarkable saint.

Jesus never told us that we would find God "in silk clothing and lying on a golden bed." On the contrary, He told us specifically that we were to take up our cross and follow Him.

The Legacy of Jesus to the Disciples

Matthew the Poor, the saintly Coptic Orthodox monk, wrote about the legacy Jesus left His disciples:

The Apostles inherited the entire life of Christ, and were eyewitnesses and partakers of His works and acts. They inherited the lengthy fasts they saw Christ Himself perform, as Christ told them: "This kind cannot be driven out by anything but prayer and fasting" (Mk. 9:29). They inherited night-long prayers ("Watch and pray"). They inherited agony in prayer with frequent prostrations and sweat like drops of blood: "And being in agony He prayed more earnestly; and His sweat became like great drops of blood falling down upon the ground... And He said to His disciples, 'Why do you sleep? Rise and pray'" (Lk. 22:44-46). They inherited endurance and patience amid the insults of the hierarchy and the betrayal of comrades: "If they persecuted me they will persecute you" (Jn. 15:20). They inherited ministry in markets among the sick, the sinners, and the poor. They inherited agony, suffering, and crucifixion, the most precious and exquisite gift they inherited from Christ: "The cup that I drink you will drink" (Mk. 10:39).[*]

---
[*] "Communion of Love." Matthew the Poor. SVS Press, Crestwood, nY. 1984. p. 4

Thus, we see that Jesus set the example for what His disciples were to experience. It was a constant effort toward conforming the human will and mind to the will and mind of God. This is what the Fathers of the *Philokalia* call *askesis*, discipline or struggle.

What is Askesis

Fr. Stanley Harakas defines *askesis* as follows:

...evil is overcome by a complex set of activities known under the collective name of askesis. Askesis is struggle; it is the various methods used to fight the passions and evil habits, to overcome temptation. Askesis is exercise, practice and training. It is the exercise of will toward growth in the direction of Theosis. Askesis has wide application in the Orthodox Christian life. It has been used to refer to the study of Scripture, to the practice of piety, to the devout life in general, to spiritual discipline such as prayer and fasting, to austere asceticism, and as a technical term referring to the monastic life with special reference to the penitential practice, etc. Here we speak of it as the struggle against sin, evil and the passions. "When evil persists, askesis needs persistence" says Thallasios... The whole of Christianity is the life of askesis. The total life of the faithful is a path of ascetic practice in imitation of Christ, the Apostles and all the Saints, a path of painful askesis and repentance within the grace and love of God, so that we can enter into a spiritual life, a life which is governed by God and doxological at its center. The acceptance of agona (struggle) as a principle of life is essential to the overcoming of evil. Evil does not just disappear because we are baptized or converted, or even because we love God. More specifically, this holds true regarding specific temptations. There is no virtue without temptation; temptations exist to be struggled against. There is no "cheap grace." Evil, sin and temptation must be overcome by a synergy of grace and painful and difficult agona (struggle).*

Askesis may be defined also as pruning the tree that it may bear more fruit. "My Father is the vinedresser. Every branch... that bears no fruit, he takes away, and every branch that does bear fruit he prunes, that it may bear more fruit" (Jn. 15:1-2).

---

* "Toward Transfigured Life." Stanley Harakas. Light and Life Publishing Co. Mpls, MN. 1983.

Divesting Oneself of Spiritual Fat

Olivier Clement describes *askesis* as "an awakening from the sleep-walking of daily life. It enables the Word to clear the silt away in the depth of the soul, freeing the spring of living waters." Elsewhere he writes that "the purpose of *askesis* is to divest oneself of surplus weight, of spiritual fat."[*]

Askesis is not simply the practice of certain specific disciplines, it is an entire way of life, a lifestyle.

Once they asked Abba Silouan, "What asceticism do you practice, Father, to receive this wisdom?" And he answered, "I never left a thought in my heart that might anger God."

A proverb says, "If you don't wash out the stone and sand, how can you get to the gold?" *Askesis* is washing out the stone and sand to get to the gold.

Restoring the Original Beauty of the Image

Askesis is *Philokalia*, love for the beauty of God's darkened image in man which it strives to restore to its original beauty. *Askesis* is the struggle to renounce my ego which looks at the world as existing only to satisfy my needs and desires. *Askesis* is described by St. Paul as "pressing on toward the mark for the prize of the high calling of God in Christ Jesus" (Phil. 3:14).

The purpose of *askesis* according to Paul Evdokimov is "to break pride and to make humility the unshakable foundation of the human spirit." In the words of St. Ignatius of Antioch: "To allow oneself to be ground between the grindstones of humility in order to become a sweet and agreeable bread for the Lord."

Not Askesis Alone but with God's Grace

Growth toward theosis is realized by God's grace and by our training or *askesis*. Such training consists of such practices as fasting, vigils, prostrations, meditation, inner attention (*nepsis*), works of charity, prayer, etc. These practices may involve great effort and even pain at times, but in the words of St. Gregory the Sinaite, "No work, whether bodily or spiritual, which lacks pain or effort, ever produces fruit. For 'the kingdom of God suffers violence,' says the Lord 'and the violent take it by force.'" The "no pain, no gain" concept applies

---

[*] "The Roots of Christian Mysticism." New City Press, NY. 1995. p. 131.

to spiritual growth as well. We read in Hebrews 12:11, "For the moment all discipline seems painful rather than pleasant; later it yields the peaceful fruit of righteousness to those who have been trained by it."

St. Isaac the Syrian wrote:

There is no virtue which does not have continual struggle yoked to it.

The Pain Passes but the Beauty Remains

In old age, Pierre Auguste Renoir, the great French painter, suffered from arthritis, which twisted and cramped his hands. Henri Matisse, his artist friend, watched sadly while Renoir, grasping a brush with only his fingertips, continued to paint, even though each movement caused stabbing pain.

One day, Matisse asked Renoir why he persisted in painting at the expense of such torture.

Renoir replied, "The pain passes, but the beauty remains."

Whatever pain or discomfort is involved in *askesis* does indeed pass, but the beauty of holiness it produces remains.

The instruments used in training toward theosis are important as spiritual disciplines but are of no value in themselves. They do not help us gain any merit toward salvation which is a pure gift of God's grace. They are but means to an end.

The Narrow Gate

St. Nectarios of Aegina wrote, "The path of virtue is a path of effort and toil; Jesus said, 'Straight is the gate, and narrow is the way, which leads to life, and few there are that find it.'"

Emphasizing the importance of *askesis*, St. Ephraim the Syrian wrote, "*Askesis*, my child, is not a game; it requires perseverance and a great deal of discipline to achieve the redemption of the soul."

"Asceticism is the mother of sanctification," wrote St. Isaac the Syrian.

Through *askesis* we are called to die in order to live. We must become "dead indeed unto sin, but alive to God through Christ Jesus our Lord" (Rom. 6:11).

Since the mind and heart must first be cleansed of earthly cares, sins, evil thoughts, and habits before it can "see" God, there will always be need for *askesis* to purify the heart. "Blessed are the pure in heart, for they shall see God," said Jesus.

Paul Evdokimov writes,

The Gospel speaks of the unclean spirit who, finding a human soul "swept and decorated," settles there again with seven other spirits. Asceticism has purified the soul. It also keeps its role of vigilant sentinel.*

Without a vigilant mind, the demons that were expelled through *askesis* will eventually find their way back to the empty soul.

Realize Your Potential

We must bear in mind at this point that the ascetics of the *Philokalia* are those who are advanced in the spiritual life. They are the ones who are pushing 300 on the spiritual bench press. I may be pushing only 75. Their example, however, inspires me to press on to exceed my present limit of 75. We emphasize at this point the importance of consulting with your spiritual father so as not to overestimate or underestimate your true capacity. We need to remember that the main purpose of *askesis* is not negative but positive. Its primary purpose is to help us develop our God-given charisms that we may achieve theosis, God-likeness.

Who is an Ascetic?

The concept of *askesis* is quite broad. For example. St. Irenaeus considers fasting an ascetic practice. Eusebius of Caesarea considers suffering for the faith as *askesis*. St. Cyril of Jerusalem considers a person who perserveres in prayer an ascetic. St. Jerome defines as ascetic one who gives his possessions to the poor and lives a life of poverty. Cyril of Alexandria considers the person who lives a life of self-denial an ascetic. According to St. John Chrysostom one who practices the virtues of the gospel is an ascetic. The Church includes under the umbrella of asceticism those who minister to the poor, those who read the Bible regularly and those who receive the holy Eucharist faithfully.

---

* "Ages of Spiritual Life." P. Evdokimov. SVS Press. Crestwood, NY. 1998. p. 126.

Biblical Examples of Askesis

The Bible gives us many examples of asceticism. Jesus, for example, spent 40 days and 40 nights in the wilderness fasting and praying. John the Baptist lived a simple life in the wilderness, preparing the way for the Messiah. Moses gave up the luxury of the palace for the hardship of the desert. And what about the true ascetic heroes of Hebrews 11? Take time to read their exploits.

St. Paul on Askesis

The Apostle Paul was often "in toil and hardship, through many a sleepless night, in hunger and in thirst, often without food, in cold and exposure" (II Cor. 11:27-28). He describes the purpose of asceticism as follows:

Do you not know that in a race all the runners compete, but only one receives the prize? So run that you may obtain it. Every athlete exercises self-control in all things. They do it to receive a perishable wreath, but we an imperishable. Well, I do not run aimlessly, I do not box as one beating the air; but I pommel my body and subdue it, lest after preaching to others I myself should be disqualified" (I Cor. 9:24-27).

St. Paul speaks of asceticism again when he writes, *"And those who belong to Christ Jesus have crucified the flesh with its passions and desires"* (Gal. 5:24).

Elsewhere St. Paul writes,

For we are not contending against flesh and blood, but against the principalities, against the powers, against the world rulers of this present darkness, against the spiritual hosts of wickedness in the heavenly places... Stand therefore... Pray at all times in the Spirit, with all prayer and supplication (Eph. 6:12,14,18).

The "Weapons of Righteousness"

In II Cor. 6:4-10 St. Paul speaks of the "weapons of righteousness." We are to use these weapons, he says, as we "wage war not according to the flesh, for the weapons of our warfare are not fleshy but (have) the power of God to overthrow strongholds" (II Cor. 10:3-6). "Every day we fight within our own hearts," said St. Augustine referring to this inner warfare.

We are to use these God-given "weapons of righteousness" "to cleanse ourselves from all defilement of flesh and of spirit, perfecting holiness in the fear of God" (II Cor. 7:1). "Put on the armor of God that you may be able to stand against the wiles of the devil" (Eph. 6:11), writes St. Paul.

The Weapons of Righteousness Are to be Used

If our salvation has been accomplished totally by God, as some believe, and there is no need for *askesis* since there is nothing left for us to do, then why the need for the "weapons of righteousness"? Why the need for "perfecting holiness in the fear of God"? Why the need to "pommel my body and subdue it"? Why the need to "crucify the flesh with its passions and desires"? Why does St. Peter warn: "Be watchful. For your adversary the devil, as a roaring lion, goes about seeking someone to devour" (1 Peter 5:8).

The purpose of askesis and its many disciplines (prayer, fasting, etc.) is to bring us into God's presence so that He can make us righteous as He alone can. If I fast, for example, fasting does not make me one bit righteous before God. All it does is place me before God so that He may accomplish His work of righteousness in me. "Even if we reach the summit of virtue, we are saved only by God's mercy," said John Chrysostom.

A Christianity Without Asceticism

Although ascetic struggle has been a vital part of Christian spirituality for 2000 years, an anti-ascetic attitude became part of the Protestant ethos since the time of Martin Luther. This attitude has created an American hostility to the Orthodox idea of spiritual and ascetic struggle, which led Frank Schaeffer to write, "The American 'God' loves you and has a wonderful plan for your life, but he does not want you to have to struggle to realize it . . . It is the illusion of the crucifixion without nails, of salvation through self-realization, of worship as entertainment, not the faith of the Fathers believed in by all Orthodox Christians everywhere since the beginning."[*]

Dietrich Bonhoeffer called this kind of Christianity "cheap grace."

---

[*] "Letter to Aristotle." Frank Schaeffer. Regina Press. Salisburg, MA. 1995.

If all one has to do in order to be saved, according to evangelical Christianity, is to "accept Jesus into your heart by faith," why the need for struggle? As someone said, "The American idea of roughing it is cutting filet mignon with a dull knife."

Askesis Does Not Involve Judaic Law but the Holy Spirit

Whatever we do in the way of *askesis* (training, discipline), we do, not because we believe that such activity will win us the grace of God (which is a pure gift of God). Such spiritual activity (*askesis*) is our *response* to the grace of God. It is performed with the grace of God, in order to fill us with God's grace. *Askesis* is totally different from the "works" of the Judaic law. Fr. George Florovsky wrote, "St. Paul clearly distinguishes between the 'works' of the Judaic law and the 'works' of the Holy Spirit required of all Christians."

The works of the Holy Spirit are just that: not our works but works accomplished by the Holy Spirit in us. If we think we can do battle with the devil on our own, we cannot but fail. This was certainly the experience of St. Paul as he expressed it in Romans 7:18-19, "I can will what is good, but I cannot do it. For I do not do the good I want, but the evil I do not want is what I do."

The Fathers of the *Philokalia* understood from bitter experience that the demonic force of pride, especially pride in their own achievement, could wreak havoc on their souls. That is why they considered humility one of the greatest virtues.

It Takes a Miracle

Fr. Thomas Hopko tells of speaking to the student body at Vassar College on the topic "Heterosexual Monogamous Marriage." He spoke of God's passionate, erotic love for the world, and how, in the Orthodox tradition, Easter is the great nuptial celebration of Christ the Bridegroom coming to win his harlot bride. In fact, he said, the whole Bible is about God's mad love affair with us. He then went on to talk about husband-wife fidelity. When his talk was over, a student in the audience raised his hand and said, "Do you really believe all that?"

Fr. Hopko answered, "Though my name is Thomas, I try! I believe fidelity is a sign of love, obedience, humility, and submission to one another in bringing the kingdom into the world."

The student replied, "Well, if you ask me, it would take a miracle to pull that off!"

Fr. Hopko replied, "Well, at least one person understood my talk today!"

Chastity and fidelity in marriage are considered to be a form of *askesis*. Like all other expressions of *askesis*, they are indeed "miracles" of God, brought about certainly not by our efforts alone but by God's grace.

Athletes of God

The spiritual disciplines of *askesis* train the body, mind, and spirit for the things of God. "Train yourself in godliness," says St. Paul (I Tim. 4:7). In Paul's day many attended the Greek gymnasia where athletes trained in order to participate in the Olympic games. And Christians from the earliest centuries considered themselves to be the athletes of God (*athletai Theou*).

For Fr. Maximus of Mt. Athos, *askesis* is the exercise of the soul. Its purpose is to overcome one's passions so that the Holy Spirit may flow through the person, who is emptied of pride. Although the word "ascetic" has acquired a negative meaning in the West mostly because it has become equated with masochism, Fr. Maximus explains that the authentic ascetic is no more masochistic than the Olympic marathon runner who subjects himself to strenuous exercises in order to achieve his objective. Thus, the person who practices asceticism is an athlete of God, a gymnast of the soul.

Training and Trying

There is a great difference between *training* and *trying* when it comes to athletic contests. In the words of Richard J. Foster,

Now, it is important to distinguish "training" from "trying." I might try very hard to win a marathon race, but if I have not trained, I will not even finish, not to mention win. Without training, the resources simply are not in my muscles, they are not in the ingrained habit structures of my body. On the day of the race, no amount of trying will make up for the failure to train. It is the training that will enable me to participate effectively in the race. The same is true in the spiritual life. Training builds interior habits within us, "holy habits."

This is what Christian *askesis* is all about: not just trying but also training.

It Takes Practice

Christian *askesis* involves practice. In the words of Henry Drummond:

What makes a man a good athlete? Practice. What makes a man a good artist, a good sculptor, a good musician? Practice. What makes a man a good linguist, a good stenographer? Practice. What makes a good man? Practice. Nothing else. There is nothing capricious about religion...If a man does not exercise his soul, he acquires no muscle in his soul, no strength of character, no vigor of moral fibre, no beauty of spiritual growth. Love is not a thing of enthusiastic emotion. It is a rich, strong, manly, vigorous expression of the whole round Christian character—the Christ-like nature in its fullest development. And the constituents of this great character are only to be built up by ceaseless practice.

"Therefore endure hardness as a good soldier of Jesus Christ," writes St. Paul (2 Tim. 2:3).

Focused Living Through Askesis

No steam or gas drives anything until it is confined. No life ever grows holy until it is focused, dedicated, and disciplined through *askesis*.

Frances G. Wickes wrote, "Until a man has conquered in himself that which causes war, he contributes consciously or unconsciously, to warfare in the world." *Askesis* is the struggle to conquer in oneself that which causes warfare.

Askesis is necessary today in order to fight against the instinct of greed, of blind power and the flight into hedonism.

Someone said, "It takes time to be holy. It takes work. It takes struggle. It takes blood, sweat and tears. It takes self-denial, study, diligence, and travail, and all of these are now out of date." They may be out of date in the secular world but they were never out of date in the spiritual world of the *Philokalia*.

We need to emphasize that there is a very important social dimension to *askesis*. We consume more energy than ever before. We eat too much, drink too much, drive too much, air-condition too much. We are rapidly depleting most of the world's resources of energy and food. The ancient discipline of *askesis* takes on an added urgency in today's world.

Saying "No" to the World in Order to Say "Yes" to Christ

Following is a list of ten items you will probably never find on the training regimen of an athlete preparing to compete in the Olympics:

Late-night TV	Drugs
Skydiving	Sleeping in
Rich desserts	Fast foods
All-night parties	Smoking
Alcohol	Soft Drinks

The reason athletes say "no" to the above items is that they wish to say "yes" to winning. In the same way, the reason the Christian says "no" to sin through *askesis* is because he wishes to say "yes" to Christ.

The Golden Buddha

Years ago Siamese monks, realizing that their country would soon be attacked, covered their precious golden Buddha with an outer covering of clay in order to keep their treasure from being looted by the Burmese.

Many years later after all the monks had died, a workman noticed a shining crack in the clay. Chipping it away he discovered the statue of the golden Buddha.

Are we not all, like that clay Buddha, covered with a shell of clay created by sin? And yet underneath each of us is the golden Christ—the image of God in us—waiting to be chipped away through *askesis* to reveal the glory of God and lead us to theosis.

Secular Askesis

Americans do practice a form of *askesis*. Look at how many foods they don't eat. Look at how much they run, jog, swim, work out, play tennis, eat health foods, consume vitamins, etc. But why do they practice this type of *askesis*? They do it for good looks! For a longer life! For better health! Would that they would also practice the spiritual kind of *askesis* that the athletes of God in the *Philokalia* practiced. If they did, there would be fewer drug and alcohol treatment centers, less need for therapists and psychiatrists, fewer broken homes, and more sane and balanced living.

Every one of us has been given a garden to tend in our heart. Whether that garden produces weeds or flowers or fruits depends on how we tend it.

Askesis is a Means to an End

Askesis was never considered to be an end in itself.

St. Seraphim of Sarov, for example, explains:

Prayer, fasting and all other Christian practices, however good they may be in themselves, do not constitute the aim of our Christian life, although they serve as the indispensable means of attaining this end. The true aim of our Christian life consists in the acquisition of the Holy Spirit of God. As for fasts, and vigils, and prayer, and almsgiving, and every good deed done for Christ's sake, they are only means for acquiring the Holy Spirit of God.

Ascetic practices are undertaken to enable the body to be energized by the Holy Spirit. The true end of *askesis* is deification or union with God. It has been said that for the Christian heaven is not a goal but a destination. The goal is that "Christ be formed in you" (Gal. 4:19). Such is the goal of *askesis* which is but a means to the end of forming Christ in us.

> The troparion (hymn) of the virgin martyrs says,
> *It's You whom I desire;*
> *in seeking You, I struggle*
> *and I crucify myself with you,*
> *in order to live in You.*

The Way of Love

The desert monks understood that their rule of life was not an end in itself as the following story indicates, "A brother went to see an anchorite and as he was leaving said to him, 'Forgive me, abba, for having taken you away from your rule!' But the other answered him, 'My rule is to refresh you and send you away in peace.'"

The real aim of the monks' lives was not asceticism but God Himself, and the way to God was the way of love. For God is love. Though they practiced austerity themselves, when they received guests, they received them as if they were Christ, hiding their austerity, and welcoming them with great charity. Archimandrite Sophrony wrote, "Acquiring...love is the ultimate purpose of Christian asceticism."*

"Above all these put on love which binds everything together in perfect harmony" (Col. 3:14).

The ascetic ideal is to cultivate love for God in man's mind, heart, and soul. This is the first and great commandment: "You shall love the Lord your God with all your mind, heart, soul, and strength, and your neighbor as yourself."

The Church Fathers keep warning us that if ascetic discipline is devoid of love in the Lord, it turns into a source of depression and pride on account of self-righteousness. "No asceticism deprived of love comes near to God," said Paul Evdokimov.

Askesis Sets Us Free

The purpose of *askesis* is not to stifle us but to set us free. The *body* is enslaved by the *flesh*. Attached to so many things, the body lusts after many unattainable prizes that ultimately it becomes enslaved. *Askesis* helps liberate the body from its compulsions. If we overeat, *askesis* seeks to help us overcome that enslavement. If we continually crave power and approval, *askesis* seeks to help us grow beyond this craving. If we are enslaved by lust, *askesis* seeks to help us shatter its shackles. Far from being stultifying and burdensome, the true goal of *askesis* is to set us free in spirit that we may commit ourselves totally to Christ our God. Paul Evdokimov wrote, "The three monastic vows form a great charter of human liberty. Poverty sets man free from the domination of the carnal...chastity liberates man from the dominion of the materialism...obedience liberates from the idolatrous domination of the ego..."*

Someone said, "In asceticism there are many thorns, but, oh, what roses!"

Askesis is for All

St. Nikodemos of the Holy Mountain invites all, monks and laity alike, to the practice of *askesis*:

...come and eat the bread of knowledge and wisdom, and drink the wine which spiritually delights the heart...and become inebriated with the truly alert inebriation. Come all...together, lay people and monastics, all of you who seek to find the kingdom of God which is within you, as well as the treasure which is hidden in the field of your heart. And this is the sweet Christ.

Though the writings of the *Philokalia* are intended for monastics, there is much that can be gleaned for use by the laity but always with the counsel of a spiritual father.

The Need for a Spiritual Father

Askesis should be practiced soberly and wisely, not out of grief or pain but in joy and happiness. In so doing, we should always seek the advice of a prudent spiritual father so that we may not exceed the limits of our ability.

Fr. Henri Nouwen offered sound advice in this respect:

It is clear that the discipline of the heart calls for some direction. We are very susceptible to self-deception and we are not always able to detect our own fearful games. Therefore it is of great value to submit our prayer life from time to time to the supervision of a spiritual guide. A spiritual director in this strict sense is not a counselor, a therapist or an analyst, but a mature fellow Christian to whom we choose to be accountable for our spiritual life and from whom we can expect prayerful guidance in our constant struggle to discern God's active presence in our lives.

An Askesis for Lay People

Fr. Theodore Stylianopoulos explains that if *askesis* is defined as "spiritual discipline", "spiritual striving," or "spiritual training" we will always have need of it. Yet he warns that laypeople need not

---

* "We Shall See Him as He Is." Arch. Sophrony. Stravropegic Monastery of St. John the Baptist. Essex, England. 1987. p. 52.

identify with some of the radical ascetic practices of the monastics:

However, askesis should not be identified with the extreme external disciplines associated with the word "ascetic"—harsh fasts, long vigils, and strict self-denial regarding every earthly blessing. Rather the essence of askesis involves the struggle in our hearts between good and evil, God and Satan, the Kingdom and the world. Its goal is the new life in Christ. Its principles are the teachings of Christ. Its power is the grace of Christ experienced especially in the Eucharist and in personal prayer. Askesis is for all, not only monastics. Each Christian is called to be a spiritual athlete who with his whole mind, heart and actions contends, within himself, family, and community, for the supreme priority of the Kingdom, believing that all the other necessary things will be given to us as well by God.*

There are not two separate spiritualities, one for the monks and another for the lay people. There is only one spirituality for all. St. John Chrysostom wrote,

When Christ orders us to follow the narrow path, he addresses himself to all. The monastics and the lay persons must attain the same heights. Those who live in the world, even though married, ought to resemble the monks in everything else. You are entirely mistaken if you think that there are some things required of ordinary people, and others of monks . . . they will have the same account to render.

Askesis in Today's World

There are some ascetic practices that can be best practiced in a monastery. There are others that must be practiced at home. The monk who keeps vigil in church praying in a night service, writes A.N. Tsirintanes, must understand the mother who is kept awake all night by her crying baby, which baby might yet one day become a St. Basil. Both the monk and the mother are performing commendable tasks of *askesis.*

Speaking of the need for a new form of askesis, Paul Evdokimov writes,

Today mortification would be liberation from every kind of addiction—speed, noise, alcohol, and all kinds of stimulants. Asceticism would be necessary rest, the discipline of regular periods of calm and silence, when one could regain the ability to stop for

---

* "A Year of the Lord: Liturgical Bible Studies," Vol. 3. T. Stylianopoulos. 1983. Department of Religious Education, Brookline, MA. p. 98.

prayer and contemplation, even in the heart of all the noise of the world, and above all then to listen to the presence of others. Fasting, instead of doing violence to the flesh, could be our renunciation of the superfluous, our sharing with the poor and a joyful balance in all things. Asceticism will rid itself of a penitential mentality and will become a preventive therapy.*

Baptism Prepares Us for Askesis

St. John Chrysostom points out that "we are baptized in order to struggle" referring to *askesis*. The body is anointed with oil and chrism in holy baptism to prepare it to wrestle with the enemy. Another ritual in baptism that relates to *askesis* is the rite of tonsure, the cutting of a lock of the infant's hair. The same rite is used for the consecration of a monk. The words of the prayer used are identical: "O Lord our God...bless this thy servant who has come to offer you the first fruits of the cutting of his hair." The meaning of this practice is quite clear: it signifies the total offering of one's life, that each one of us is called to a life of total consecration to God even outside the monastery or convent. We are called, in the words of Paul Evdokimov, "to a life of interiorized monasticism which is being totally surrendered to the demands of the gospel."

Thus, we are baptized to emerge victorious in our struggle against sin. The baptismal anointing shows that we have declared war on everything that is against God, especially on the devil and his angels. When we are baptized and receive the Holy Spirit, the devil declares war on us, but through baptism, the sacraments, and prayer we are more than well equipped to resist with all the "armor of God."

The Cost of Discipleship

Askesis may well be described as "the cost of discipleship," an expression used by Bonhoeffer to distinguish between what he called "cheap grace" and "costly grace." Cheap grace, he thundered, is the Church's "deadly enemy." It is the fallacy that, since Christ has paid up for us in advance, we can get everything for nothing. "Cheap grace is grace without discipleship, grace without the cross, grace without Jesus Christ, living and incarnate." Costly grace "is *costly* because it calls us to follow, and it is *grace* because it calls us to follow *Jesus*

---

* "Ages of Spiritual Life." P. Evdokimov. SVS Press. Crestwood, NY. 1998. pp. 64-65.

Christ." It is costly because it costs you your life.

The Icon of St. John of the Ladder

An icon that captures the need for ascetic discipline in our walk with Jesus is the traditional one for the Sunday of St. John of the Ladder. It portrays monks climbing a ladder toward Christ who stands at the top of the ladder. Some monks are shown falling off the ladder into the hands of waiting demons. This icon expresses the need for constant vigilance and discipline in the spiritual life. Not all make it to the top. God's word is replete with admonitions to vigilance and *ascesis*, i.e., "Enter by the narrow gate...For the gate is narrow and the way is hard, that leads to life, and those who find it are few" (Matt. 7:13-14). "Work at your salvation in fear and trembling" (Phil. 2:12). "This kind can be driven out only by prayer and fasting" (Mark 9:29). "...I pommel my body and subdue it, lest after preaching to others I myself should be disfigured" (I Cor. 9:27).

Becoming a Christian does not remove struggle from life; it often adds struggle. Some of the most committed Christians—the saints—lived some of the most difficult lives. "When Christ calls a person, He bids him come and die," wrote Dietrich Bonhoeffer.

St. Ephrem's Prayer

The whole concept of *askesis* in the Orthodox Church is summarized in the beautiful prayer of St. Ephrem which is recited in the Lenten services:

O Lord and Master of my life, grant me not a spirit of slothfulness, of discouragement, of lust of power, of vain babbling.

But vouchsafe unto Thy servant the spirit of continence, of meekness, of patience and love.

Yea, Lord and King, grant that I may perceive my own transgressions and judge not my brother.

Askesis As Cooperation

All of the above-mentioned means towards theosis—prayer, the sacraments, repentance—require our cooperation. This cooperation is expressed in Orthodox theology by the word *askesis*, which may be defined as a constant, persistent striving toward the goal of theosis.

The aim of *askesis* or struggle is never to gain merit, or payment or reward from God. It represents the struggle that is involved in renouncing our sinful will in order to yield ourselves totally to God in self-surrender as we journey toward theosis or union with Him.

Askesis and Crucifixion

Askesis might be viewed in the light of the crucifixion. Christ did not die instead of us, so that we would not have to die. He died for us, so that we could die with Him, and in dying with Him, have life. His is the only death that leads to life. Our death, our dying to sin, apart from His, does not lead to life. But in Baptism, Jesus draws us into His own dying (Rom. 6:3). This dying with Christ in order to rise with Him is what we Orthodox mean by *askesis*.

Through *askesis* we are called to die to sin and self so that we may live the life of God. We must become "dead indeed unto sin, but alive unto God through Jesus Christ our Lord" (Rom. 6:11). Such *askesis* is not limited to the practice of certain specific rituals such as fasting, vigils, prayer, etc., it is rather a whole way of life. To deny ourselves in this way is part of the *askesis*, the training for theosis. Such *askesis* serves to conform us to the image of God as we grow toward theosis.

CHAPTER ELEVEN

Theosis

Opening a Chinese fortune cookie one day, I read these words, "You are destined for greatness." That is exactly what the Orthodox teaching of theosis teaches us. It says, "You are destined for the greatest greatness there is: union with God or theosis."

CHAPTER ELEVEN

Theosis

What is the goal of Orthodox spirituality? Very simply, it is the attainment of union with God and consequently theosis or deification.

According to its compiler, St. Nicodemos of Mount Athos, the *Philokalia* is the "instrument itself of deification." Thus, the *Philokalia*, the single most important collection of Orthodox spiritual texts is, in effect, perhaps the best guidebook, next to the Bible, to the means of theosis. Its purpose is precisely to help us fulfill our calling to theosis or union with God.

What is Theosis?

What is theosis?

One Orthodox Christian wrote after reading, "Partakers of Divine Nature" by Archim. Christoforos Stavropoulos, translated by Fr. Stanley Harakas (Light and Life Publ. Co. Mpls, MN):

When I first encountered this 95-page book, I was unfamiliar with the doctrine of theosis, or the divinization of human beings. I was completely awed to realize that God's intention for each of us was to become gods, the likenesses of God, by sharing with and uniting in His nature. It appeared that theosis stood at the center of all Orthodox Christian teachings, and yet, I had never heard of it in my very traditional upbringing.

Theosis is Foundational

Yet, theosis is foundational for Orthodox Christians. It is our purpose and goal in life.

When an Orthodox priest was asked once what he thought was the foundational teaching of the Orthodox Church, he replied, "Theosis." And he was right. For Orthodoxy our salvation and redemption mean our deification.

Union with God

Union with God—theosis—is not a minor topic of faith or doctrine for Orthodox theology. It is, rather, the basis of all faith and doctrine. It is the ultimate aim of God for sending His only Son into the world to become man. As St. Paul writes, "For He (God) has made known to us in all wisdom and insight the mystery of His will, according to His purpose which He set forth in Christ as a plan for the fullness of time, to unite all things in Christ, things in heaven and things on earth" (Eph. 1:9-10). In other words, the mystery of union between humanity, i.e., all of us and Christ is the ultimate aim of the incarnation, the crucifixion, the resurrection—nay, of creation as a whole. Thus, union with God is the foundation of the Church and the mystery of the Gospel. It was this *Theia Enosis* (union with God) that Christ petitioned the Father to grant in our behalf when He prayed in John 17:21, "...that they also may be (one) in us."

From Dust to Theosis

Brother Aiden of Mount Athos has written, "Man is made both out of the soil (of the earth) and the breath of God; if man allows the divine breath (the Holy Spirit) to direct him, he will be raised up into glory, his body included; if on the other hand he follows the material part of his nature (his passions), he will hear the terrible words, 'You are dust, and to dust you shall return.'"

Thus, if we allow the dust in us to be animated by the breath of the Holy Spirit, then by God's grace we can rise from dust to image of God; from dust to likeness of God; from dust to sons and daughters of God; from dust to heirs of God's eternal kingdom; from dust to partakers of divine nature; from dust to theosis, becoming gods by grace as Jesus is God by nature.

Man: "Anthropos"

The Greek word for man *anthropos* is connected with the verb *anarthein*, meaning "to look up." Unlike most of the other animals, humans stand upright, with their eyes toward heaven and their gaze toward the stars. In Latin, on the other hand, the words for man and human, *homo* and *humanus* are linked to the noun *humus*, which means earth. The human being, then, though human and related to the earth is created to look up to heaven. Created in God's own image and capable of union with God, man is indeed, according to St. Gregory the Theologian, a *zoon theoumenon*, an animal that is called by God to be deified.

"We Shall Be Like Him"

"We know that, when He shall appear, we shall be like Him, for we shall see Him as He is" (I John 3:2). "We shall be like Him." We shall be gods by grace as He is God by nature. Like Him (Jesus) we shall be Christified, deified, engodded. It seems almost too good to be true. It is enough to make us stand up and leap for joy. Yet, this is our glorious destiny! This is what awaits us when the Lord comes again. "We shall be like Him; for we shall see Him as He is."

Of course, our becoming "partakers of divine nature" is not a natural possibility; it is, rather, a response to God's great gift of love in what He did for us in the Incarnation. He became man that we might become sons and daughters of God through the Spirit and thus share in the life of the Trinity.

The Purpose of Being is to Become

When asked what he thought the business of the Church was, one person said, "It is to show people what they can become by the grace of God." The one thing that holds us back from becoming what God created us to be is sin. That is why the Church calls on us constantly to repent: because it is sin that holds us back from greatness, from achieving our great potential of theosis.

Theosis: Our Potential

Orthodox theology calls the potential for which God created us: THEOSIS. Don't be frightened by this word. It's really a very simple concept, namely, the core of the good news of Orthodox Christianity is that we are called to share in the very life of God. Salvation in Orthodox understanding is much more positive than it is negative. It means not only justification and forgiveness of sins; it means also—and even more so—the renewing and restoration of God's image in us, the lifting up of fallen humanity through Christ into the very life of God. Christ forgives us and frees us from sin and death that we may proceed to fulfill our potential, which is to become like God in Christ and to share in His life.

Christ came to save us *from* sin *for* participation in the life of God. In other words, we are saved *from* sin *for* theosis, which is our great potential.

Jesus came to earth to tell us:

You give me your time, and I will give you my eternity. You give me you weary body, and I will give you my rest. You give me your sins, and I will give you my forgiveness. You give me your broken heart, and I will give you my healing. You give me your emptiness, and I will give you my fullness. You give me your humanity, and I will give you my divinity.

Theosis: Positive Aspect of Salvation

Theosis is the positive aspect of salvation. To describe theosis we may use the following words:

- transfiguration of man,
- putting on Christ,
- the restoration of the image of God in us,
- restoration of communion with God,
- participation in the life of God,
- incorruption,
- receiving the Holy Spirit,
- becoming temples of the Holy Spirit,
- ascending to the throne of God,
- participating in the kingdom of God,
- being by grace what God is by nature.

Theosis is...

To describe further what our potential—theosis—is, we may say the following:

Jesus came to lift the fallen all the way from the gutter of sin to the throne of God in theosis.

Theosis is what God wants for us who are created in His own image: to become like Him in whose image we are made.

Theosis is a personal sharing in the life of God through faith, prayer and the sacraments.

Theosis means sharing God's life, and since God's essence is love, theosis means being perfected in love.

Theosis is the rich potential God has placed in each baptized person.

Theosis is the name for the process of salvation, initiated in baptism, by which we are Christified, i.e., united to Christ and changed into His likeness.

Theosis is the transfiguration of our lifestyle, implying concern for our neighbor, mutual sharing, love, stewardship of ourselves, of our possessions and of the earth.

Fr. George Florovsky wrote, "Theosis means no more than an intimate communion of human persons with the living God. To be with God means to dwell in Him and to share His perfection."

Saved for Theosis

Christ the Savior came to redeem us from sin that we might proceed to acquire the gift of theosis which He offers us by grace. Salvation does not end with the forgiveness of sins; it begins there. It is at baptism that our journey to God, to theosis, begins. Salvation is not only a matter of "Are you saved?" It is also a matter of "Are you being deified? Are you growing in Christ?" We are saved *from* sin *for* theosis. "Original sin," said Fr. George Florovsky, " was not just an erroneous choice...but rather a refusal to ascend toward God."

Salvation is an ongoing process that leads from initial salvation in baptism, through sanctification, and on to "deification by grace."

From Egypt to the Promised Land

Vladimir Lossky wrote, "What does it matter being saved from death, from Hell, if it is not to lose oneself in God." St. John Chrysostom said, "It is not enough to leave Egypt (sin and death), one must also enter the Promised Land (theosis). Between Egypt and the Promised Land lies a desert." Hence the need for ascesis (struggle, discipline, war against the passions) in our journey through the desolate desert of sin and death toward theosis (the promised land).

Theosis in Everyday Life

Theosis is a beautiful word but what does it say to those who are trying to cope with a terrible illness, or struggling to make a go of a sour marriage, or to those who are burdened with anxieties and cares? Theosis has everything to say to struggling humanity. It tells us that we have the capacity through the presence of God within us to transcend and overcome any and every difficulty in life, including the greatest of all: death. Theosis tells us that we are not paupers or beggars but sons and daughters of God, sharing His glory, partaking of His Nature, destined to inherit His eternal kingdom. Theosis tells us that we are more than conquerors through Him Who loved us. Theosis tells us to "hang in there" no matter how hard the struggle or the temptation because God has great things in store for us. As St. Paul says, " I consider that the sufferings of this present time are not worth comparing with the glory that is to be revealed to us" (Rom. 8:18).

A Basic Inner Drive Toward Theosis

God has created all human beings with a basic drive toward union with Him. All human beings are desperately searching for happiness, but many do not know who it is who alone can ever satisfy this yearning. If we suppress this basic image and these drives given us by God for becoming sharers in his own divine trinitarian life, then our hearts will always remain restless until we rest in God Himself.

Living Examples of Theosis: The Saints

Theosis is not just a dogma, or a teaching of the Church. It becomes a living reality in the Theotokos and the saints of the church. Theosis takes on flesh and blood and becomes real in the saints who have been justified and sanctified and are thereby sons and daughters of the resurrection. The saints are "gods by participation" reflecting the light and love of Christ in their lives. The lives of the saints and their icons shine with the presence of God and serve to remind us of our high calling: to become gods by grace, "having been delivered from the bondage of corruption and death into the glorious liberty of the children of God" (Rom. 8:21).

The Rich Potential of Theosis

When we were baptized, God placed in us the rich potential of theosis, of sharing in the very life of God through faith, prayer and the sacraments. Again, let it be said that theosis—that seemingly difficult word of Orthodox theology—is really a very simple word. It means *becoming, becoming* more and more like God in Christ as we go through life; *becoming* all that God wants us to become by His grace, growing to the fullest potential that God intends for us; *becoming* partakers of God's nature, gods by grace as Jesus is God by nature.

Our true greatness lies in what God has called us to become: gods by grace: "Beloved, we are God's children now; it does not yet appear what we shall be, but we know that when He appears we shall be like Him, for we shall see Him as He is" (I John 3:2).

The Bible and Theosis

The Bible has much to say about theosis. The most quoted verse for theosis is one which seems rather isolated to some, i.e., II Peter 1:4, *...become partakers of divine nature*, or as the NEB translation says *to share in the very being of God*. Although II Peter is a very explicit statement about theosis, there are many other verses in the Bible that refer to salvation as *participation* or *sharing* or *fellowship* with God, or *indwelling* in the words of the Gospel of John.

St. Paul says that we are made to be *filled with all the fullness of God* (Eph. 3:19): what is "being filled with all the fullness of God" but theosis?

The Apostle John writes that God's Son and the Spirit appeared on earth to bring God's people and the world into the fullness of God's being and the life of the Kingdom: *And the word became flesh and dwelt among us, full of grace and truth, and we beheld His glory, glory as of the only-begotten Son from the Father...and of His fullness have we all received, grace upon grace...*(John 1:14-16).

In John 17:22-23 Jesus prays the prayer of theosis: *The glory that Thou hast given me I have given to them that they may be one as we are one: I in them and Thou in Me, that they may be perfectly one.* Is not theosis the perfect fulfillment of this prayer of Jesus!

For you know the grace of our Lord Jesus Christ, that though He was rich, yet for your sake He became poor, so that by His poverty you might become rich (II Cor. 2:16).

There is therefore now no condemnation to those who are in Christ Jesus... But you are not in the flesh, you are in the Spirit, if the

Spirit of God really dwells in you. Anyone who does not have the Spirit of Christ does not belong to Him. But if Christ is in you, although your bodies are dead because of your sin, your spirits are alive because of righteousness. If the Spirit of Him Who raised Jesus from the dead dwells in you, He who raised Christ Jesus from the dead dwells in you, He who raised Christ Jesus from the dead will give life to your mortal bodies also through His Spirit which dwells in you (Rom. 8:1, 9:11).

Theosis, participation in the life of God, is further evidenced in verses such as the following which speak of God in us: *We will come and make our home with him* (John 14:23*). It is no longer I who live, but Christ who lives in me* (Gal. 2:20). Paul's desire is that *Christ be formed in you* (Gal. 4:19).

St. Paul writes, "Do you not know that you are the temple of God?" (I Cor. 3:16). In other words, you already partake of divinity. You are already holy. God the Holy Spirit already dwells in you. Theosis begins when we are baptized and chrismated.

When the Apostle John says that *it does not yet appear what we shall be* He is referring to the future theosis of those who were now made children of God (I John 3:2).

Psalm 82:6 which is quoted by Jesus in John 10:34 is another strong reference to theosis: *I say, you are gods.* We see in this verse that even in the Old Testament which is the guardian of monotheism, the word "gods," which Jesus quotes, was applied to people. It speaks of the God-given potential of theosis.

Theosis and the Church Fathers

The Church Fathers have much to say about theosis. St. Ignatius of Antioch writes to his correspondents that they are "God bearers" (*theophoroi*) and "full of God" (*Theou gemete*). Clement of Alexandria writes, "The Word of God became man in order that you may learn from man how man may become God."

St. Basil writes, "Man is a creature who has received the command to become god." St. Maximus interprets this to mean that we are to "reunite through love the created nature (human) with the uncreated nature (divine grace)."

St. Symeon the New Theologian writes, "We become gods by disposition and grace, heirs of God and joint heirs with Christ, and together with this we receive the mind of Christ; and through it all we see God and Christ Himself, living in us according to His divinity, moving in a conscious way within us."

"He was made a sharer in our mortality," said Augustine, "He made us sharers in His deity."

St. Gregory, Patriarch of Constantinople writes in one of his *Theological Orations*: "On that day when God will be all in all, we will no longer be captive to our sinful passions, but will be entirely like God, ready to receive into our hearts the whole God and God alone. This is the perfection to which we press on."

The Doxastikon troparion (hymn) of the Praises of the Feast of the Annunciation says,

> *Adam of old was deceived:*
> *wanting to be God he failed to be God.*
> *God became man,*
> *so that He may make Adam god.*

St. Gregory of Nyssa writes, "Man's life is a strenuous and endless ascent toward God, that is, deification (theosis)."

St. Gregory the Theologian writes in his Easter Oration:

Yesterday I was crucified with Him; today I am glorified with Him; yesterday I died with Him, today I am quickened with him; yesterday I was buried with Him; today I rise with Him... We have become like Christ, for Christ became like us. We have become gods through Him, for He became man for us.

St. Symeon the New Theologian writes,

God the Word borrowed flesh from us, which he did not have by nature. He became man, which he was not. To those who believe in Him, He gives His own divinity to share, which neither angel nor man had ever acquired. And men became gods, which they were not, through adoption and grace.

"Man by the grace of God can become that which God is..." writes Maximus the Confessor.

St. Gregory of Nysssa says, "We hide within us something which causes us to resemble God, to participate in God; it is indispensable to possess in our being something which conforms us to participation in him."

St. Irenaeus relates the Incarnation to Theosis, "On account of His immense love for us, the Word of God, our Lord Jesus Christ, made Himself what we are, in order that we might become what He is Himself."

St. Maximus the Confessor tells us that the purpose of our creation is theosis,

God has created us in order that we may become partakers of the divine nature, in order that we might enter into eternity, and that we might appear like unto Him, being deified by that grace out of which all things that exist have come.

St. Peter Chrysologus sees the awesomeness of God in theosis,

What is more awesome than that God gives Himself to earth or that He places you in heaven? That He Himself enters a union with the flesh, or that He causes you to share in Divinity? That He Himself accepts death, or that He recovers you from death? It is indeed more awesome that earth is transformed into heaven, that man is deified, and that those whose lot has been slavery achieve dominion.

Man Does Not Become a God in Essence

We live in a day when popular psychology and the cults are propagating the deity of man by teaching people to say, "I am everywhere. I am omniscient. I am God." People pay expensively to enroll in seminars which tell them, "You are a supreme being. There is no death; man is God; knowledge of self is salvation and power." A famous actress and her spiritual advisor, for example, stand on Malibu Beach and, with their arms flung open to the cosmos, shout, "I am god! I am god! I am god!"

Obviously, this is not what we mean by theosis. In Orthodox theology, this is heresy of the very first order. Lucifer tried to become God and was thrown out of heaven because of it (Isaiah 14:12-15).

In theosis man does not *possess* God nor does he *become* God in essence. Rather, he *participates* in that which is given to him, thanking God for His ineffable grace.

Theosis in no way means that human beings *become God* in a

pantheistic sense. It means, rather, that believers enter into a personal relationship of communion with God through baptism and participate fully in God's life through prayer, the sacraments, and the Orthodox Christian way of life..

Our Goal in Life: Theosis

Zen Buddhism says, "In the beginning there was nothing. The purpose of life is to achieve union with nothingness." Orthodox Christianity says, "In the beginning there was God. The purpose of life is to achieve union with God not in His essence but through His energies."

Solzhenitsyn said once regarding our goal in life, "The meaning of earthly existence lies, not as we have grown used to thinking, in prospering, but in the development of the soul." I would add, "In the development of the soul toward theosis, toward becoming like God in Christ, toward sharing in His glory." This and none other is our great goal in life as we see in the story of creation when God said, "Let us make man in our image and likeness" (Gen. 1:26). A thing is perfect (*teleion*) if it realizes the purpose (*telos*) for which it was made. Man is perfect if he realizes the goal for which he was made: theosis. "Being an acorn is to have a taste for being an oak tree," wrote Thomas Merton.

A Mirror and an Icon

Christ holds up before us not only a mirror to help us see ourselves as we truly are (sinners); He also holds up before us an icon (Himself) to show us what we can become by God's grace, sons and daughters of God, partakers of divine nature.

The aim of the Christian life, which St. Seraphim of Sarov described as the acquisition of the Holy Spirit, can be defined equally well in terms of theosis, becoming like God, sharing His divine nature, since the purpose of the Holy Spirit in us is to deify us, to make us Temples of God's presence.

We need to remember at all times that the divine and the demonic are close; only a very thin line separates them. We who are capable of divinity are also capable of the demonic. If we do not strive for theosis, the alternative is enslavement to sin.

How Is Theosis Attained?

Theosis is a process that begins at baptism when the newly-baptized "puts on Christ." When this happens we are clothed with divinity. We become gods by grace. We become persons with a brand new potential: theosis. The seed of God is sown within us. As Meister Eckhart wrote, "The seed of God is in us. Given an intelligent and hard-working farmer, it will thrive and grow up to God, whose seed it is; and accordingly its fruits will be God-nature. Pear seeds grow into pear trees, nut seeds into nut trees, and God seed into God."

Unclaimed Treasure

Many of those who are baptized have in them the seed of theosis but have never made an authentic act of personal faith. Christ expects us to trust Him totally and "to commit ourselves and one another and our whole life" to Him as God as we pray repeatedly in our worship services. Without such faith the seed will not grow.

St. Gregory of Sinai wrote, "The gift which we have received from Jesus Christ in holy baptism...is...buried as a treasure in the ground..." It is as if we have a treasure within a sealed chest which we leave unopened and unclaimed. Thus, we do not enter into possession of the treasure (theosis) that actually belongs to us.

When at baptism we are deified by "putting on Christ," we are infused with the potential for love, communion with God, and theosis.

After being clothed with Christ through baptism, we are immediately chrismated with the Sacrament of Holy Chrismation through which we are sealed with the gift of the Holy Spirit Who comes to make His home in us. Thus, at Chrismation we are deified through the presence of the Holy Spirit.

The Eucharist

In addition to Baptism and Chrismation, we are made "partakers of divine nature" through the Eucharist which unites us with God. St. Gregory of Nyssa wrote, "He (Christ) sows Himself in the bodies of the faithful by means of his own Body which is composed of bread and wine. He thus is commingled with us, so that by our union with the immortal, we might share in immortality."

The Eucharist truly makes us "partakers of divine nature" when we receive "with the fear of God, with faith, and with love" the presence of Christ as He comes to us veiled under the bread and the wine. It is truly a life-creating (*zoopoion*) sacrament, imparting to us the very life of God through Jesus who is the living Bread (*artos zoes*). In receiving the deified flesh of our Savior, we too are deified as we receive the gifts and grace of theosis. Fr. Christopher Stavropoulos writes, "Through the Holy Eucharist, we are made divine...the person who communes...is invisibly fed and concurrently receives the seed of immortality and the resurrection from the dead."

Prayer

In addition to Baptism, Chrismation and the Eucharist, the next way by which we are made "partakers of divine nature" and achieve theosis is through prayer.

Theosis cannot happen without prayer. The Church Fathers say about prayer: "The power of prayer fulfills (completes) the sacrament of our union with God... Prayer uplifts and unites human beings with God" (St. Gregory Palamas). "The effect of prayer is union with God" (St. Gregory of Nyssa). "Sacred prayer, and it alone...joins God with man, and makes the two one spirit."

Other Means of Theosis

Other means of theosis are purity of heart which is achieved through daily repentance. "Blessed are the pure in heart for they shall see God," said Jesus.

The name of Jesus is also a means to theosis. Addressed to Jesus, the Jesus Prayer is a means of realizing within ourselves the mystery of theosis. Fr. Sergei Bulgakov wrote, "The name of Jesus, present in the human heart, confers upon it the power of deification."

Keeping the commandments is another way that leads to theosis. Other means toward theosis are faith, fasting, the tears of repentance, *hysechia* or stillness, *nepsis*, or watchfulness, almsgiving, *ascesis* or struggle against the passions, and above all love, for "love makes a man god" in the words of the Fathers of the *Philokalia*. The ability to love divinely is a gift of the Holy Spirit.

St. Isaac the Syrian wrote, "When we have reached love, we have reached God and our way is ended. We have passed over to the island that lies beyond the world where is the Father with the Son and the Holy Spirit."

The Lord did not distribute talents equally, but He has distributed equally to all the same great potential of theosis.

Bishop Ware's Five Points on Theosis

Bishop Ware helps us better understand theosis by making the following five points:

Firstly, theosis is not reserved for a select few special saints. It is something in which all baptized and chrismated Christians are called to share. If we love God, keep His commandments, rise as often as we fall (through repentance), we are already in the process of being deified.

Secondly, being deified does not mean that we cease to be conscious of sin. Theosis not only presupposes a continual act of repentance, but also sensitizes us to sin so that we are in a constant state of penitence. That is why we continue to pray the Jesus Prayer to the very end of our lives: "Lord Jesus, Son of God, have mercy on me, the sinner."

Thirdly, there is nothing extraordinary about the methods we follow to achieve theosis. We continue to participate in the liturgy every week, receive the sacraments regularly, pray, read God's word and obey God's commandments.

Fourthly, there is nothing solitary about theosis. It presupposes love of God and love of neighbor. "There is nothing selfish about deification," writes Bishop Ware, "for only if he loves his neighbor can a man be deified." "From our neighbor is life and from our neighbor is death," said St. Anthony.

Fifthly, as an expression of love of God and love of man, theosis is very practical. It includes not only silence and prayer but also caring for the sick in the hospital of Caesarea as did St. Basil, and helping the poor of Alexandria as did St. John the Almsgiver, etc.[*]

---

[*] "The Orthodox Church." T. Ware. Penguin Books. Baltimore, MD. 1963. pp. 246-247.

Life is Worth Living

Life is worth living for many reasons. It is worth living because Christ loves you. It is worth living because Christ died for you and rose again to give you life. It is worth living because with Christ, life is both eternal and abundant. But life is worth living, above all, because in Christ your destiny is theosis, becoming Christ-like, god by grace. Therefore choose Christ and live. With Christ, life can be lived meaningfully, divinely, royally, victoriously, and eternally.

CHAPTER TWELVE

The Passions: What are they? How can we overcome them?

The Fathers of the Philokalia offer the following weapons with which to fight the passions:
1. Prayer, especially the Jesus Prayer
2. The remembrance of the name of Jesus.
3. The remembrance of the Lord's passion.
4. The remembrance of death. "He who has acquired the remembrance of death will never be able to sin."
5. The remembrance of the Last Judgment, especially eternal suffering.
6. Nepsis, watchfulness, vigilance.
7. By not feeding the passions, thus, starving them.
8. By waging war against them through ascesis.
9. By putting on the armor of God through the reading of God's word and the writings of the Church Fathers.
10. Through the sacraments, especially Confession and the Eucharist.

CHAPTER TWELVE

The Passions: What are They? How Can We Overcome Them?

Victor Hugo has a story that describes the terror of sailors on a ship on a storm at sea. As the waves lash the frail vessel the sailors feel a shudder and a thud. They look at each other and know: the cannon in the hold of the ship has broken loose from its moorings. Each lurch of the ship in the storm sends the cannon crashing into the wooden hull of the vessel.

Hugo describes the plight of the sailors who disappear into the dark hold, their faces drained of color. They crouch and dodge as the monster threatens to pin them to the wall. Finally they managed to chain the cannon back in place, and the ship was saved.

This is a parable of our own lives. There is something wrong down inside us. A monster threatens to destroy us. That monster consists of the passions which are described in detail by the Fathers of the *Philokalia*.

A Map of the Christian Soul

John B. Dunlop describes exactly how the Fathers encountered and studied the passions which, like the loose cannon on the ship, threaten to destroy us:

In early Christian symbolism the desert was the dwelling place of Satan who, despite all his apparent interest in human affairs, actually preferred to be alone. The exodus of the early monks to the desert was a direct challenge to Satan. St. Anthony, the spiritual father of all monks, went directly to dwell in the tombs and challenge Satan in his own kingdom of death. It was in the desert that these incredible men began to fill in the details of the "map" which had been bequeathed to them by the writings of the apostles and preserved by the death of the martyrs. The passions and temptations which must inevitably beset any Christian were unearthed and described with almost scientific precision. Pride, vainglory, sensual lust—each passion was isolated and catalogued. This "map" of the Christian soul was then passed on from one generation of ascetics to another, each generation profiting from the discoveries of the previous ones. Not only were the passions and temptations which afflict the soul unearthed, however, but a "system" was developed to combat them. This system was later to become known as "hesychesm" or "prayer of the heart."*

What are the Passions?

St. Gregory of Nyssa describes the passions as qualities we inherit from our animal nature:

The animals came into this world before we did and we have inherited some of their qualities. This is the spring from which our emotions are derived. Those qualities which secure self-preservation in animals have been transferred into human life and become passions... Human nature...has a double likeness. In the drive of the passions it reproduces the signs of the animal creation, but in the soul it has the features of the divine beauty.

A Zoo Within

There is a zoo of passions within us. Carl Sandburg thought he had a whole menagerie under his ribs. He felt in his nature the stirring of many animals. Even though we have received a new nature in baptism, the old nature still lurks within, waiting to drag us down. Often we classify some of our fleshly actions by relating them to animals that live by instinct. We say, for example, "He eats like a pig"—"He's as brave as a lion"—or "as stubborn as a mule"—or "as proud as a peacock." A man who pursues women is called a "wolf." A treacherous person is called "a snake in the grass." A grouchy person is called an "old bear." A coward is called "chicken." A dull person is called an "ox." The resemblance is certainly there, yet sometimes, we suspect, it is a bit unfair to the animals.

No matter how refined we may be, the flesh with all its primitive qualities can crop up anytime. The old nature never dies completely. That is why St. Paul wrote in I Cor. 10:12, "Wherefore, let him who thinks he can stand, take heed lest he fall."

Jung and Freud Expose the Passions

Carl Jung, the psychoanalyst, warned us that the evils of fallen

---

* "Staretz Amvrosy." John B. Dunlap. Notable and Academic Books. Belmont, MA. 1988.

man are still crouching in all of us. They remain alive and ugly in the dark recesses of the heart under the thin veneer of civilization. Only Christianity, he said, is keeping them in check. Freud burst open the dam holding back the flow of the unconscious. He, too, exposed the irrational forces, the passions, that can drag us down into the mud.

St. Paul was quite clear about the passions. He wrote, "I tell you, the deeds of the flesh are quite obvious, such as sexual vice, impurity, sensuality, idolatry, dissension...party-spirit...drinking bouts, and the like."

St. Isaac of Nineveh described the passions as follows:

...these are: love of riches; the gathering of possessions; fattening up the body, giving rise to the tendency toward carnal desire; love of honour, which is the source of envy; the exercise of position of power; pride and the trappings of authority; outward elegance; glory among men, which is the cause of resentment; fear for the body.

The Charioteer with Two Horses

Plato described the soul as the charioteer whose task it is to drive in double harness two horses, one of whom is "of noble breed," and the other of whom is "of evil breed." The noble horse is reason and the untamed horse is passion. The horse of evil nature weighs down the chariot and pulls it to the earth. It is a picture of warfare and tension.

That wild horse is inside each one of us. It needs to be tamed before it destroys us. The Apostle James wrote, "What is the cause of the fighting and quarreling that goes on among you? Is it not to be found in the passions which struggle for mastery in your bodies?" (James 4:1).

St. Gregory of Nyssa speaks of the Egyptian army in pursuit of the children of Israel as an image of the passions which enslave the soul of man:

For who does not know that the Egyptian army—those horses, chariots and their drivers, archers, slingers, heavily armed soldiers, and the rest of the crowd in the enemies' line of battle—are the various passions of the soul by which man is enslaved?

St. Paul talks of having "fought with beasts at Ephesus" (I Cor. 15:32). Whether he is referring to a literal fight against animals in an arena, or a fight against beastly opponents, the message he is conveying is that the real struggle is always an inner one, and the arena where the struggle with the beast takes place is the mind and heart.

Thoughts: The Seeds of Passions

To overcome passions, one must struggle with thoughts (*logismoi*), because it is thoughts that arouse the passions. Thoughts are the seeds of the passions, those impulses that emerge from the subconscious and soon become obsessive. To combat such thoughts one needs to practice watchfulness (*nepsis*) and prayer. Evagrius isolates and describes eight basic types of thoughts (*logismoi*) which he describes as thoughts of gluttony, fornication, love of money, depression (*lype*), anger, listlessness (*akedia*), and pride. The greatest of these is pride. "Whoever has pride," said Maximus, "has all the passions." This list was taken over later and adapted by Cassian to produce the familiar seven deadly sins.

Categorizing and naming the swarm of passions that afflict the psyche was important to the Fathers of the *Philokalia*, since it was a precious tool of discernment. It enabled them to track the subtle workings of the passions; it also helped them decipher the hidden ways the demons used the passions to ambush them.

Pride: The Root Cause

Describing pride which is the root cause of all the passions, St. John Climacus wrote,

Pride is a denial of God, an invention of the devil, contempt for men. It is the mother of condemnation, the offspring of praise, a sign of barrenness. It is a flight from God's help, the harbinger of madness, the author of downfall. It is the cause of diabolical possession, the source of anger, the gateway of hypocrisy. It is the fortress of demons, the custodian of sins, the source of hardheartedness. It is the denial of compassion, a bitter Pharisee, a cruel judge. It is the foe of God. It is the root of blasphemy.

The Ancients Deified Their Passions

The ancients deified their passions. They worshipped the animals within themselves. They bowed down before the passions of their own natures, which they could not control or understand. Bacchus was the deification of appetite. Aphrodite was the deification of the passion of lust. Jupiter the deification of war.

Man today may have outgrown the images of Bacchus, but he is still controlled by appetite. He has destroyed the temples of Venus, but he is still dominated by his lustful passions which threaten to destroy him.

The Passions Enslave

Brother Aidan of Mount Athos tells how the passions make us slaves to our lower nature:

The tragedy of the fall is that man allowed this divinely appointed movement to be reversed: instead of conducting the orchestra of the cosmos, fallen man allowed the lower cosmos to conduct him. Creation's natural skopos (purpose) was thus destroyed. This is why the Fathers have used the word passion to describe sins which dominate us; we literally suffer from, become passive slaves to, our lower nature. We cease to act, and become acted upon. We foolishly abdicate our power to rule, and submit to being ruled, and ruled by hard taskmasters.

St. Augustine described the chaotic slavery of the passions in graphic terms:

The passions rage like tyrants, and throw into confusion the whole soul and life of men with storms from every quarter, fear on one side, desire on the other, on another anxiety, or false empty joy, here pain for the thing which was loved and lost, there eagerness to win what was not possessed, there grief for an injury received, here burning desire to avenge it. Wherever he turns, avarice can confine him, self-indulgence dissipate him, ambition master him, pride puff him up, envy torture him, sloth drug him, obstinacy rouse him, oppression afflict him, and the countless other feelings which crowd and exploit the power of passion.

Who is Walking the Dog?

It is like a diminutive woman who takes her enormous Great Dane for a walk. The dog drags her along from tree to tree. She thinks she is walking the dog. In reality the dog is walking her. The same condition exists in us when the passions take over in our lives. They blind us as they lead us about, without our realizing that we are no longer free: we are being acted upon.

The Passions Blind

The passions do, indeed, blind those whom they possess. Yevgeny Yeftushenenko expressed this when he wrote, "Those who are conceived in a cage yearn for a cage." In other words, a person who is thoroughly enslaved yearns to go back to the cage if he is ever released from it. The cage, representing slavery, becomes the only reality there is for him.

This same idea of how the passions blind us is seen in the drunk who was arrested for disorderly conduct in New York City. He was singing, "I'm sitting on top of the world," even while he was being taken to jail. He was not sitting on top of the world. The world was sitting on top of him. But he was too blinded by his passion to realize it.

The Passion of Pornography

Let me share with you the example of a person who was enslaved by the passion of pornography. We will call him Joe. Joe was a sincere Christian who lived a tortured life. He was active in his church. He had a lovely young wife, and they had two fine children. He was successful at his job and well-liked by neighbors and friends. But Joe was hooked on pornography. He hid the magazines in his home and office. He sometimes sneaked out a quick stop at a porn shop. Whenever he was out of town on business, he would indulge his weakness. He tried to quit. He prayed. He made anguished promises to God. He set deadlines. He made solemn vows. Yet he would soon find himself using the magazines again. He couldn't control it. The situation seemed hopeless.

As much as he hated the label, Joe knew he was an addict. The pleasure he derived from pornography had taken over his life. The fantasy world he found within its pages was more important to him than the real world of family, work, and home. He knew he was wrong and in danger, but he could not stop.

The passion of pornography was in charge of Joe's life. He was no longer in control. So strong was the pull of the addiction that he could not resist it.

Other such passions or addictions are overeating, gambling, drug use, lust, smoking, alcohol, shoplifting, compulsive spending, etc.

This is the animal state to which the passions relegate us as described by St. John Damascene: "The irrational creatures are not free; they do not lead but rather are led by nature."

The Passion of Gambling

I heard of one Christian who became addicted to gambling in the form of the state lottery. The thought of winning several million dollars overtook her. At first she purchased only one ticket per week when she bought the family groceries. Then it was five tickets, then ten. She told herself she wouldn't miss the money. She convinced herself that her husband would be glad he would never have to work again. She was sure she could pick the winning numbers, and she even asked God to help her. She promised to give a large gift to church if she won. She began to sneak extra money. She had nearly emptied the family savings account before her husband realized what was happening and took her to someone who could help her regain control of her life.

Scratch the surface of any church congregation and you will find people struggling with all sorts of passions. In one congregation alone, it was discovered that there were several husbands who turned over their weekly paychecks to their pastor so that he could deliver them to their wives. Otherwise, they knew they would gamble them away.

Fr. George Florovsky described this condition of blindness and slavery induced by the passions when he wrote,

Passions are the place, the seat of evil in the human person. The impassioned man...does not act on his own but is rather acted upon... he loses his personality, his personal identity. He becomes chaotic, with multiple faces, or rather—masks. The "man of passions" is not at all free, although he can give an impression of activity and energy. He is nothing more than a "ball" of impersonal influences.

The Passion of Lust

A Christian who was possessed by the passion of lust described the hell he experienced:

I learned quickly that lust, like physical sex, points in only one direction. You cannot go back to a lower level and stay satisfied. Always you want more. I've experienced enough of the unquenchable nature of sex to frighten me for good. Lust does not satisfy; it stirs up. I no longer wonder how deviants can get into child molesting, masochism, and other abnormalities. Although such acts are incomprehensible to me, I remember well that where I ended up was also incomprehensible to me when I started...It cumulatively caused me to devalue my wife as a sexual being...Lust, I discovered, is the craving for salt by a man who is dying of thirst.

This is the kind of horrible enslavement that St. John Chrysostom described:

Indeed, to be a slave to one's belly, and to be possessed by the desire for temporal things, and to be angry, to bite, to trample is the part, not of men, but of wild beasts. Yet, the wild beasts, each one of them, has, so to speak, a single passion, and that according to its nature. But the man who has cast aside the rule of reason, and who has broken off from the way of life according to God, gives himself up to every passion. No longer does he become merely a wild beast, but some multiform and fickle monster—who can plead no excuse because of his nature. For, all his wickedness proceeds from his will and his intellect.

The same St. John Chrysostom points to where we can find help in overcoming the passion of lust:

Even if lust makes imperious demands, if you occupy its territory with the fear of God, you have stayed its frenzy.

Homosexuality as a Passion

Fr. Stanley Harakas speaks of homosexuality as a passion:

In the language of the Church, this is a "passion." It is a wrongful orientation of our desires. Passions are of many kinds, directed toward many objects, such a self (pride), money (greed), food (gluttony), extramarital sex partners (lust), others' property (theft), etc. When such passions exist, no matter how strongly felt, the Church counsels agona, that is, spiritual and moral struggle against them. In our commonly shared struggle against sin in whatever form, the Orthodox Church sees all persons working to fight temptation and overcome the passions. Toward this end the Church offers a panoply of spiritual weapons to overcome temptation and to struggle victoriously against the passions. These spiritual weapons including prayer, worship, fasting, the Sacrament of Holy Confession, reading of Scripture and of patristic and spiritual writings, Christian fellowship, as well as pastoral and psychiatric counseling which should be used by all including those who suffer from homosexual tendencies.*

How to Overcome the Passions

Is there hope for those who are enslaved by the passions of the flesh? There most certainly is! Having fought the passions personally the Fathers of the *Philokalia* have charted a way of victory for us. Echoing the words of the Apostle Paul, "And those who belong to Christ Jesus have crucified the flesh with its passions and desires" (Gal. 5:24), they demonstrate exactly how "the passions and desires" of the flesh can be crucified.

Victory Over Self

St. Nicodemos of the Holy Mountain considers the greatest victory to be the victory over self:

Once, when King Alexander was praised for having conquered the whole ecumene (world), he responded with the prudent remark: "All of my victories will prove to be vain, if I do not succeed to conquer myself." Many who have subdued their enemies, cities, and countries have later been subdued miserably by their own improper passions and have shamefully become slaves of their own passions. A certain Father was very correct when he said that "the first victory is the victory of self." St. Isidore Pelousiotes also said: "The true victor is not he who subdues the foreign barbarians, but he who wages spiritual warfare against the evil passions. Many who have conquered barbarians have in turn been shamefully subdued by their own passions."

---

* "Contemporary Moral Issues." S. Harakas. Light and Life Publ. Co. Mpls, MN. 1982. p. 94

Nepsis or Watchfulness

The Fathers of the *Philokalia* offer many weapons against the passions. Here are some:

Nepsis or watchfulness. St. Nicodemos of the Holy Mountain advises:

St. Isidore Pelousiotes ... has taught us how to guard the senses from evil passions. He said that the mind of man must stand firm like a king and emperor with awesome thoughts which are armed like soldiers to guard the entries of the senses and to prevent the enemies from entering. For, if they do not enter, the war and the victory will be easy. But if, on the contrary, they do enter then the war becomes difficult and the victory uncertain. This is why you too, brother, can, through these means, guard and close the windows of your senses, so that all the evil passions that are commonly referred to as bodily and external can be readily overcome.

Covering the Windows with Fine Nets

St. Neilos advises:

Those who desire to keep their mind as a clean and pure temple, where the doors and windows are covered with fine nets to prevent the entry of any impure insects, must similarly cover their senses by meditating on the sobering realities of the future judgment which prevent the entry of any impure images to creep in.

Another net or screen that can be used to filter out evil thoughts is the net of the Jesus Prayer which uses the power of the Name of Jesus to keep demonic spirits from entering the soul.

Starve Them!

Another way to wage war against the passions is to starve them. St. Nicodemos explains how this can be accomplished:

St. Poimen used to say: "When a serpent is shut within a vessel and does not receive any food, it will gradually die. So also with the inner passions of our heart, if they are isolated and do not receive the evil nourishment they need from the outside through the senses of the body, they in time are weakened and eventually die. Again the passions can be likened to certain tiny creatures found in the mud at the bottom of a lake. As long as they do not have anything to eat they are content to lie there in peace. But as soon as food is put into the water, you can see them immediately moving and rising up from the depth to get the food. In the same manner the passions remain peacefully within the heart as long as they do not receive from the outside through the senses any nourishment and pleasure. But as soon as such a pleasure enters, especially through the eyes, these passions move directly toward the desirable nourishment."

Cutting Off the Food Supplies

St. Nicodemos continues with more plans for subduing the enemy:

When a certain king plans to subdue easily an enemy city that is fortified by strong walls, he cuts off the food supplies to those people in the city and thus causes them such hardship that they in time decide to surrender themselves. The mind uses the same strategy in subduing the senses. Little by little the mind deprives every sensory faculty of its customary bodily and pleasurable passions. It no longer permits them to indulge themselves and thus easily and in a short period of time brings them under control. All the time that this method is being utilized to control the passions, the mind does not stand idle. Not at all. By receiving a certain ease and freedom from bodily concerns, the mind turns to its own natural and spiritual nourishment which is the reading of Sacred Scripture, the acquirement of virtues, the doing of the commandments of the Lord, the practice of prayer, the understanding of the purposes of the physical and spiritual creations, and all the other spiritual and divine thoughts and deeds which are to be found in the writings of the holy Fathers, especially those who are called the neptic Fathers in the anthologies of Philokalia and Evergetinos, and St. John Climacus and St. Symeon the New Theologian and others.

St. Maximus the Confessor confirms the way of fasting, askesis, and vigil described by St. Nicodemos. He writes,

Some remedies arrest the movement of passions and do not allow them to grow; and others weaken them and make them wither. Thus fasting, labour and vigil prevent the growth of lust; and solitude, contemplation, prayer and love of God weaken it and lead to its disappearance.

Prayer

Another way to wage war against the passions is through prayer. St. Theophan the Recluse wrote,

What do we do when attacked by some criminal? We strike out at him and shout for help. Our cries are answered by the police, who then rescue us from danger. We must do the same in inner warfare with the passions. Filled with anger against them, call for assistance: Help me, O Lord! Jesus Christ, Son of God, save me! O God, make speed to save me! O Lord, make haste to help me! Having thus called on the Lord, do not allow your attention to wander from Him, do not let it turn to what is happening within you, but go on standing before the Lord and imploring His help. This will make the enemy run away as though pursued by flames.

St. Isaac the Syrian wrote,

Just as the sun's rays are sometimes hidden from the earth by thick clouds, so for a while a person may be deprived of spiritual comfort and of grace's brightness; this is caused by the cloud of the passions. Then, all of a sudden, without that person being aware, it is all given back. Just as the surface of the earth rejoices at the rays of the sun when they break through the clouds, so the words of prayer are able to break through to drive the thick cloud of the passions away from the soul.

The Passion of Smoking

The story is told of how Father Silouan used prayer to discourage the passion of smoking:

In 1905 Father Silouan spent several months in Russia, often visiting monasteries. On one of his train journeys he sat opposite a shopkeeper, who in a friendly gesture opened his silver cigarette-case and offered him a cigarette. Father Silouan thanked him but refused to take one. The shopkeeper began talking, asking, "Are you refusing, Father, because you think it is a sin? But smoking is often a help in life. It relaxes you, and makes a few minutes' break. Smoking helps one to get on with one's life work or have a friendly chat, and in general..." And so on, trying to persuade Father Silouan to have a cigarette. In the end Father Silouan made up his mind to say to him, "Before you light up a cigarette, pray and repeat one "Our Father..."

To this the shopkeeper replied, "Praying before having a smoke somehow doesn't work." To this Silouan observed, "So better not start anything which cannot be preceded by untroubled prayer."*

Using the Bible and Righteous Indignation

In addition to watchfulness, starvation, and prayer, a fourth weapon against the passions is the Bible and anger. Evagrius provides an armory of scriptural texts in his *Antirrhetikos* to be used against various thoughts, just as Jesus did when tempted by the devil in the wilderness. He recommends also that, before praying against the thoughts, we should address them angrily, because anger dispels evil thoughts.

Askesis

Another powerful weapon that can be used against the passions is *askesis* or struggle. Bonhoeffer wrote, "If there is no element of asceticism in our lives, if we give free rein to the desires of the flesh... we shall find it hard to train in the service of Christ."

St. Theodoros the Great Ascetic said that when we "crucify the flesh with its passions and desires" (Gal. 5:24), thus mortifying the passions through *askesis*, we are, in effect, taking up the cross to follow Christ (Matt. 16:24).

Flee to the Source of Help

Yet another weapon against the passions is to run from the source of temptation as we flee to our source of help: God. St. John the Dwarf once told the following story to illustrate this point:

In one town, there lived a beautiful woman, a harlot who had many lovers. A prince suggested to this woman that he would take her to wife if she would promise to live honourably and faithfully in wedlock. She promised, and the prince took her to his court and married her. Discovering this, her former lovers plotted to bring her back to her old ways with them. They did not dare to confront the prince, but gathered behind the palace and began whistling. The woman heard the whistling and recognised it. She quickly blocked her ears and hid herself in an inner room of the palace, locking the door behind her, and was thus preserved from the new temptation. St. John explained

---

* "St. Silouan the Athonite." Archim. Sophrony. Monastery of St. John the Baptist. Essex, England. 1991. p. 70.

this story thus: the harlot is the soul, her lovers are the passions, the prince is Christ, the inner room is the heavenly court and the lovers who whistle and entice her are the demons. If the soul is constantly turned from its passions and flees God-ward, the passions and demons will take flight and flee from it.

Self-Love

Lastly, the Fathers of the *Philokalia* issue a warning against the danger of self-love in combating the passions. St. Maximus the Confessor writes,

Beware of the mother of evil—self-love, which is an irrational love for the body. For it is from this that are born, with seeming justification, the three first and fundamental passionate and irresistible thoughts, namely—those of gluttony, cupidity and vainglory, using as pretext the natural bodily needs, and thereupon giving birth to the whole tribe of passions. This is why it is so necessary, as has been said, to beware of self-love and to fight it with great watchfulness. For its destruction means the destruction of all its offspring.

St. Maximus continues on the danger of self-love:

It is clear that he who has self-love has all the passions... When you overcome one of the most vile passions, such as gluttony, or fornication, or anger, or greed of gain, you become assailed immediately by a vainglorious thought; and when you overcome it, a thought of pride takes its place... Vanity is eliminated by acting secretly, and pride by ascribing to God all that is well done.

Transfiguring the Passions

Some world religions, i.e., Buddhism and Hinduism are dedicated to the elimination of desire and passion. Buddha saw desire as the source of all evil, suffering, and conflict. He advised, "You must free your soul of desire. Cut it out from the roots. Remove every want from your heart. Then, in an utterly passionless existence you will find peace of mind, and after much practice come at last to Nirvana, a state of nothingness."

It's a good trick if you can do it: get rid of your headache by cutting off your head. Reduce the conflicts of personality by destroying the powers that make you a person.

According to the Fathers of the *Philokalia* the passions are not to be destroyed but re-directed toward God. "The soul is made perfect when its powers of passion have been completely directed towards God," wrote St. Maximus the Confessor.

St. John Climacus wrote of the transfiguration of the passions:

I have seen impure souls who threw themselves headlong into physical eros to a frenzied degree. It was their very experience of that eros that led them to interior conversion. They concentrated their eros (love) on the Lord. Rising above fear they tried to love God with an insatiable desire. That is why, when Christ spoke of the woman who had been a sinner, he did not say that she had been afraid, but that she had loved much and had easily been able to surmount love by love.

In the words of St. Maximos, "Every passion is curable through abstinence and love." Thus the passions are not to be destroyed. Rather, their powerful energy is to be re-directed toward God. Uncontrolled anger is to be re-directed into righteous indignation; sexual lust transformed into an *eros* love directed toward God, whom we are to love with both an *agape* and an *eros* love. Thus the passions are to be purified, not eradicated; transfigured, not eliminated.

By God's grace the passions can be turned into virtues: pride can become humility; lust can become *agape*, the sacrificial love that God has for us; anger can become righteous indignation against evil; greed can become generosity ("The half of my goods I give to the poor."); unfaithfulness can become steadfastness; envy can become "rejoicing with those who rejoice;" sloth can become diligence; sensuality can become spirituality—all of this can be accomplished by God's grace and our cooperation with His grace through askesis, prayer, and vigilance.

"Blessed are Pure in Heart for They Shall See God"

There can be no vision of God without purity of heart. "Blessed are the pure in heart: for they shall see God" (Matt. 5:8), said Jesus. Unless we transfigure the passions into virtues by God's grace, we shall be living in darkness, totally blinded by sin.

Pascal said once, "Since your reason inclines you to believe and yet you cannot believe, your inability to believe comes from your passions. Try, then, not to convince yourself by multiplying the proofs of the existence of God, but by diminishing your passions."

Francois Mauriac fully understood this truth when he said that the only reason to seek purity is the one mentioned by Jesus: only the pure in heart can see God. Purity, says Mauriac, is the condition for a higher love—for a possession superior to all possessions: God Himself. Sins are not a list of petty irritations drawn up by a jealous God. They are, rather, a description of impediments to spiritual growth. They stand in the way of our seeing God and becoming Christlike.

Come Up From the Cellar

It is not necessary for anyone to live constantly in the cellar of his dwelling. The cellar is important but it is not the whole house. If we dwell in that part of us which is like the animals, we may lose that higher part of ourselves, the image of God. Just as the mole once had eyes to see but lost them because he chose to live in darkness, so too we can lose the high faculties God has given us if we choose to live in the cellar of our passions.

It is possible for every basement dweller to go into the higher part of his existence by moving away from the passions and going higher by climbing the stairs. St. John Climacus names some of the stairs we need to climb in his book *Ladder of Divine Ascent*. They are: repentance, remembrance of death, blessed mourning which leads to joy, meekness, poverty, bodily vigil, humility, holy solitude, prayer, love, etc.

A Crown Awaits You

We need to listen to these words of encouragement by St. Nicodemos of the Holy Mountain,

Christ Himself is the one who will crown you every time you are victorious in the battle against the evil passions of the senses and you do not succumb to them. St. Basil said: "Suffering brings glory, and tribulation brings crowns." But you have been beaten once or twice (I hope not!). Be not completely overcome. Stand firm and courageous, calling upon God for help. If you do so, the grace of God will come directly to your help and He will not leave you to be completely overcome by the enemy.

Are the Passions Sinful?

St. Gregory of Nyssa said, "What is the origin of the passions? We have no right to blame our human nature for their origin, because it was formed in God's likeness."

Many of the Church Fathers teach that the passions are impulses planted in our nature by God. They are neutral in character and may be used for either good or bad. Abba Isaias (d.c.491) believed that anger can be used in a positive way against evil; jealousy can be sublimated into zeal for righteousness; even pride can be used in a positive way if it is used to affirm our value in God's eyes, especially when we are attacked by feelings of self-hatred and despair. St. Gregory Palamas refers to "divine and blessed passions," maintaining that our aim should be not their eradication but their transfiguration, re-channeling the energies of the passions into virtues.

Sin is an Aberration

The Desert Fathers believed that we are part of the creation that God called good, especially in that we were made in the image of God. As such, sin is an aberration; it is not natural to us at all. That is why Gregory of Nyssa, for example, spoke often of "returning to the grace of that image which was established in you from the beginning." He even considered it as our lifelong task to discover what part of the divine image God has chosen to reveal in and through us.

Thus the passions are not sins but sinful conditions or diseases that can develop into sins if we do not discipline them. St. Dorotheos observes that it is possible for someone to have passions but never to express them in concrete sinful acts.

When Do the Passions Become Sinful?

A temptation, for example, is neither a passion nor a sin. It is only when we accept the sinful thought, welcome it into our mind and heart, brood over it, feed it, and encourage it that it becomes a passion. It is when it becomes a passion that we become responsible for it. Passions do not start with any power over us; it is only as we yield to them more and more that they begin to enslave us. Abba Poemen says that "passions work in four stages—first, in the heart; secondly, in the face; thirdly, in words; and fourthly in evil deeds." At each of the four stages of growth we are free to prevent the passion or to allow it to grow to the next stage.

Drawing from the Eastern Fathers of the *Philokalia* (from the fourth to the fifteenth centuries), Fr. George Timko wrote,

The Fathers always stress that the chief delusion of man is that he thinks his body is making him sin. He blames his body all the time. If lust awakens in him, he says, "That is a God-given thing in my human nature." He thinks that lust originates with his sexual hormones and not with his mind. But the body is a neutral instrument, say the Fathers; don't blame it. If you want to discover the source of sin, you had better start looking at your mind. According to Mark the Ascetic, "Having sinned, blame your mind and not your body. For if the mind had not run on ahead into sin, the body would not have followed."*

The Cure of Passions: Apatheia or Dispassion

The fruit of the struggle against the passions is a positive state of grace that the Fathers of the *Philokalia* call *apatheia*. Although the word is borrowed from Stoic philosophy, it has nothing to do with stoic apathy. It is a positive state of self-control, or rather, Christ-control or Spirit-control. It is the stilling of all passionate thoughts through askesis, purity of heart, and the gift of tears. It is being anchored and rooted in God, in the peace that passes all understanding.

There is nothing of Stoic "apathy" here. It is a state of total dependence on God's grace, impossible to obtain on our own. Another name for the state of *apatheia* is dispassion. St. John Climacus describes this state when he writes, "The dispassionate man no longer lives himself, but it is Christ who lives in him." It is a sharing in the fullness of life that Jesus came to bring us (John 10:10). It is the restoration of the soul to its true nature. It is an entering into the true freedom of the sons and daughters of God. St. John Climacus describes dispassion when he writes,

A man is truly dispassionate...when he has cleansed his flesh of all corruption; when he has lifted his mind above everything created, and has made it master of all the senses; when he keeps his soul continually in the presence of the Lord.

---

* "Speaking of Silence." Edited by Susan Walker. Paulist Press, NY. 1987. p. 179.

Blessed dispassion raises the poor mind from earth to heaven, raises the beggar from the dunghill of passion. And love, all praise to it, makes him sit with princes, that is with the holy angels, and with the princes of God's people.

Olivier Clement describes the state of *apatheia* when he writes, "...a person in whom all the strength of the passions has been crucified and transfigured radiates the peace of paradise...For such a person the beauty of the body no longer arouses lust, but rather praise (to God)."

St. Isaac of Syria wrote, "Dispassion (*apatheia*) does not mean that a man feels no passions, but that he does not accept any of them."

Apatheia: The Path to Freedom

Fr. George Florovsky defines dispassion as the restoration of the personality through the Holy Spirit:

...a state of spiritual activity, which is acquired only after struggles and ordeals.... Each person's "I" is finally regained, freeing oneself from fatal bondage. But one can regain oneself only in God. True "impassability" is achieved only in an encounter with the Living God. The path which leads there is the path of obedience, even of servitude to God, but this servitude engenders true freedom.... In God the personality is restored and reintegrated in the Holy Spirit....

Apatheia is the state in which man is in charge of himself once again. He is not controlled by his passions but exerts control over them by God's grace.

Apatheia does not mean the suppression of any of the soul's powers, but their healthy functioning, so that we *desire* virtue and redirect the energy of the passions toward loving that which is holy and good.

The Supremacy of Love in Apatheia

A monk of the Eastern Church describes *apatheia* as "the state of a soul in which love towards God and men is so ruling and burning as to leave no room for (self-centered) human passions." Indeed, Evagrius, who introduced the word *apatheia* into monastic literature, said, "*Apatheia* has a daughter named *agape* (love)." St. Maximus the Confessor said, " If we genuinely love God, we cast out the passions by this very love." For it is love that gathers together all of man's powers under the direction of the Holy Spirit. The fruit of passionlessness, then, is love, and this is the doorway through which we must pass in order to know God.

The Gifts of Dispassion

St. Symeon the New Theologian says that to those who have reached the highest state of *apatheia* God grants the following gifts:

In death they are already honored with immortality. In darkness they walk as if it were day, in a light that does not set. In this body of mire they breathe as if they were in a paradise of exquisite delight, since they possess within them the Tree of Life, without forgetting the very bread of angels, the heavenly bread on which all heaven's immaterial beings nourish themselves in order to receive imperishable life. While involved in the world and its affairs, they proclaim in truth with St. Paul, "For us, our city is in heaven," where charity resides. Reunited with her lovers and surrounding them with an exuberant light, charity makes of them dispassionate ones, indeed, true angels.

Apatheia as Purity of Heart

Bishop Kallistos Ware describes apatheia as "purity of heart":

Purification of the passions leads eventually, by God's grace, to what Evagrius terms apatheia or dispassion. By this he means, not a negative condition of indifference or insensitivity in which we no longer feel temptation, but a positive state of reintegration and spiritual freedom in which we no longer yield to temptation. Perhaps apatheia can best be translated "purity of heart.! It signifies advancing from instability to stability, from duplicity to simplicity or singleness of heart, from the immaturity of fear and suspicion to the maturity of innocence and trust. For Evagrius dispassion and love are integrally connected, as the two sides of a coin. If you lust, you cannot love. Dispassion means that we are no longer dominated by selfishness and uncontrolled desire, and so we become capable of true love.*

The Story of One Man's Victory

To translate *apatheia* or dispassion into terms we moderns can understand, let us look at what happened to a person who was enslaved by the passion of lust. We shall try to describe the state of

---

* "The Orthodox Way." Kallistos Ware. St. Vladimir's Seminary Press. Crestwood, NY. 1979. p. 156.

dispassion he experienced after winning a fierce battle with lust through *askesis* (discipline) and prayer. We shall call his name John.

John now forces himself to look women in the eye instead of everywhere else. He stares straight ahead after a glimpse of a sexy billboard, and he flips past the suggestive pictures in magazines. He has cleaned out of his house everything that aroused him wrongly. He has rejected paid TV channels that featured sex films, and he controls the knob the rest of the time. He is careful about how he hugs friends of the opposite sex and refuses to touch a woman when others are not present.

The results are dramatic. Far from burning up with sexual desire, going mentally crazy, or having wild fantasies, John's longings and thoughts have come under control. His worship of Jesus has become more meaningful than ever. With discipline and an idol-free heart has come a sense of release from bondage. The gravitational pull to porno has disappeared. The war within still exists, but it does not overwhelm him any more. In Christ he has found adequate resources with which to resist.

Examples of Dispassion: The Saints

The saints of the Church are shining examples of such dispassion. They are the ones who have conquered the passions and in whom the transforming work of grace is fully evident.

Luther Burbank discovered in the realm of plant nature that every weed is a potential flower, and that the very qualities that make it a weed could make it a flower. Great sinners and great saints contain much the same stuff. The same instincts that made Napoleon could have made a Paul. Would you have chosen Matthew, a dishonest tax collector as your disciple: Or James and John, " the sons of thunder"? But Jesus knew that every weed is a potential flower, especially in the hands of God. So He chose Matthew. And so He chose even you and me.

"And those who belong to Christ have crucified the flesh with its passions and desires" (Gal. 5:24). But, as St. Symeon the New Theologian declares, Christian ascesis is a *zoopoios nekrosis*, a life-giving mortification or death of the passions and desires. From it flows the tranquil state of *apatheia* or dispassion, a foretaste of heaven, God's reward for those who have "fought the good fight."

The Church As a Spiritual Hospital

Fr. John Romanides teaches that the patristic tradition looks upon the Church as a spiritual hospital. The Fathers, he says, do not classify people as moral or immoral, good and bad on the basis of moral laws. They classify them as (1) sick in soul; (2) those being healed, and (3) those who are healed. All who are not in a state of illumination (photizomenoi) are sick in soul. According to the definition of the Sixth Ecumenical Council, sin is a sickness of the spirit. It is not only good will, good resolve, and moral practice which make an Orthodox, but also purification (katharsis), illumination, and deification. As a spiritual hospital, the purpose of the Church is to deliver us from the passions and lead us to good health which is defined as theosis or deification. The patristic tradition, says Fr. Romanides, closely resembles medicine, especially psychiatry. As a spiritual hospital the Church becomes the instrument of theosis.

St. John Chrysostom would agree with the concept of the Church as hospital, for he wrote, "Enter into the Church and wash away your sins. For this is a hospital for sinners and not a court of law."

The patristic tradition of the *Philokalia*, in dealing with the passions greatly emphasizes the importance of the Church as a spiritual hospital.

St. Nicodemos of the Holy Mountain describes two of the effective medicines used by the Church for the healing of those enslaved by passions:

If it is necessary to confess and do penance to receive forgiveness of sins, Holy Communion is just as necessary for the remission of sins. As with a festered wound, first one removes any worms, afterwards one cuts away the putrified flesh and lastly puts on an ointment, that it might be healed; and if you do this you are restored to your former condition. Thus if you sin, with confession you remove the worms, and with penance you cut away the putrid parts and you follow this with Holy Communion, which is the ointment—and you are healed. For if he is not given Holy Communion, the wretched sinner will return to his former state and will become, in the end, someone worse than before.

St. Ambrose of Milan adds, "He that has a sickness needs medicine. It is a sickness that we are subject to sin. The medicine is the heavenly and venerable sacrament (the Eucharist)."

Speaking of Jesus as the Great Healer, the same St. Ambrose wrote,

Thus, in Christ we possess everything. Let every soul approach him, be it sick with sins of the flesh, infixed by the nails of worldly desires, admittedly still imperfect, progressing by intense meditation, or already perfect in its many virtues. Everyone is in the Lord's power, and Christ is all things to us. If you desire to heal your wounds, he is your doctor; if you are on fire with fever, he is your fountain; if you are burdened with iniquity, he is your justification; if you need help, he is your strength; if you fear death, he is your life; if you desire heaven, he is your way; if you are fleeing from darkness, he is your light; if you are seeking food, he is your nourishment: Taste and see that the Lord is good. Happy is the man who takes refuge in him.

Church Fathers on the Passions

St. Justin the Martyr proclaims,

To yield and give in to our sinful desires is the lowest form of slavery. To rule over such desires is the only true freedom.

Commenting on the passions, Tertullian wrote,

We read that "the flesh is weak," and we thereby soothe our consciences at times. Yet, we also read that "the spirit is strong" (Matt. 26:41). For both expressions occur in the same sentence. Flesh is an earthly material. Spirit is a heavenly one. Why then are we so prone to make excuses for ourselves? Why do we offer our weak part as our defense? Should we not rather look at our strong part? Why shouldn't it be the earthly that yields to the heavenly? Since the spirit is stronger than the flesh, being of a nobler origin, it is our own fault if we follow the weaker of the two.

CHAPTER THIRTEEN

The Gift of Tears

The flood of tears which we shed after our Baptism, that is, after the former infant Baptism, is yet more powerful than Baptism itself—bold as this assertion may appear. For Baptism cleanses only from offenses previously committed, tears from offenses after Baptism ... If God, in His mercy, had not granted to men this second baptism, then few indeed would be saved.

– St. John Climacus

CHAPTER THIRTEEN

The Gift of Tears

Many ask about the phenomenon of weeping icons in the Orthodox Church, "What does it mean? Why do tears flow from the eyes of the Theotokos on the icon? Is God trying to tell us something? If so, what?"

To get the answer to these questions we need to look at tears and their meaning in Scripture as well as in the Sacred Tradition of the Church. For, the Eastern Church has a rich theology of tears.

God Gives Adam and Eve a Gift

According to an ancient story from the Talmud when Adam and Eve sinned, the holy and just God could not let them remain in His perfect paradise. They were expelled. As Adam and Eve trudged from paradise to their new "real" world, God looked down from heaven and felt sorry for them. He knew what was ahead for His children. So, in His compassion, God decided to give Adam and Eve a gift that would ultimately lead them back to paradise. He gave them the gift of tears.

A Gift of God

Tears are indeed a gift of God. St. John Climacus wrote, "God in His love for mankind gave us tears." In fact, the gift of tears is one of the 30 rungs on the famous ladder to heaven of St. John Climacus. It is Step 7 on "joy-creating" sorrow. The gift of tears is viewed as the renewing of the grace of baptism.

More Powerful Than Baptism

St. John Climacus does not hesitate to write some astounding statements about the importance of tears, such as the following:

The flood of tears which we shed after our Baptism, that is, after the former infant Baptism, is yet more powerful than Baptism itself— bold as this assertion may appear. For Baptism cleanses only from offenses previously committed, tears from offenses after Baptism... If

God, in His mercy, had not granted to men this second baptism, then few indeed would be saved...When our soul departs from life, we shall not be accused because we have not worked miracles...but we shall all certainly have to give account to God because we have not wept unceasingly for our sins.

The Fruit of Baptismal Grace

Commenting on these words of Climacus, Vladimir Lossky wrote,

This judgment (that tears are greater than baptism) may appear paradoxical and even scandalous, if it be forgotten that repentance is the fruit of baptismal grace; it is indeed the same grace when it has been acquired, appropriated by the human person, and become in him "the gift of tears"—the infallible sign that the heart has been overwhelmed by the love of God... These charismatic tears, which are the consummation of repentance are at the same time the first-fruits of infinite joy: "Blessed are ye that weep now: for ye shall laugh." Tears purify our nature, for repentance is not merely our effort, our anguish, but it is also the resplendent gift of the Holy Spirit, penetrating and transforming our hearts.*

St. John Chrysostom on Tears

St. John Chrysostom describes what a great blessing the soul receives through the gift of tears:

Just as clouds when they gather begin by making the day dark, then, once they have poured out all the water they contained, the atmosphere is serene and light; so anguish, as it builds up in our heart, plunges our thoughts into darkness, but then, when it has vented all its bitterness through prayer and accompanying tears, it brings to the soul a great light. God's influence irradiates the soul of the one who is praying, like a ray of sunlight.

Tears: The Baptism of the Holy Spirit

The gift of tears is connected with baptismal grace. St. John of Damascus lists tears among the forms of baptism. St. Symeon the New Theologian looks upon tears as the Baptism of the Holy Spirit. He goes so far as to say that sins committed after baptism cannot be

---

* "Mystical Theology of the Eastern Church." V. Lossky. James Clarke and Co. Ltd. Cambridge, England. 1957. p. 205.

forgiven without tears. If anyone doubts the efficacy of tears, let him listen to Nicetas Stethatos who says that "tears can even restore lost virginity."

St. Theodore the Studite invites us to "go in the Spirit to the Jordan...and let us receive baptism with Him, I mean the baptism of tears."

"The fruits of the inner man begin with the shedding of tears," wrote St. Isaac of Syria.

"The fire of sin is intense," wrote St. John Chrysostom, "but it is put out by a small amount of tears, for the tear puts out a furnace of faults, and cleans our soul of sin."

Penthos

There is a Greek word for penitential sorrow for which there is simply no good English equivalent. It is the word *penthos*. It means a broken and contrite heart, being filled with godly sorrow. It means blessed mourning, a deep inner compunction for sin. Above all, *penthos* means the tears of penitence, inner sorrow for the sins we have committed.

St. Photios on Tears

St. Photios speaks of the fountain of tears, that most excellent and most beneficial blessing which drips down the cheeks, yet washes splendidly the soul...and waters paradise to bear fruits for us. Tears offer "a sweet fragrance" and they "blot out the stains and scars" of our souls.

Soap for the Soul

A proverb says, "What soap is for the body, tears are for the soul." Bishop Ignatios Brianchaninov writes, "A dirty garment cannot be washed without water: and without tears it is impossible for the soul to be washed and cleansed of its defilements and impurities."

St. Symeon the New Theologian describes the cleansing power of tears as follows:

To wash a soiled garb without water is impossible; to purify a rusty, stained soul without tears is even more inconceivable. Let us not summon useless pretexts that are pernicious to the soul and only good enough to lead us to perdition. Let us wholeheartedly seek out this queen of virtues (that is, compunction). First, it cleanses all those who practice it. Then, it also rubs away the passions and makes them chaste, removing them like scabs from wounds... This is not all: like a creeping fire it eliminates the passions by burning them like brambles by consuming them. This is what the divine fire of compunction achieves with tears, or better, through tears. As was said before, however, without tears nothing of the sort ever happened or will happen either to us or to anyone else.

Tears that Lead to Joy

The tears of sorrow lead to joy. "Weeping may endure for a night, but joy cometh in the morning," says the psalmist. "These tears," writes St. John Chrysostom, "do not bring sorrow; they bring more joy than all the laughter of the world can gain for you." "Those who sow in tears shall reap with joyful shouting," says the psalmist (126:5). Archim. Sophrony writes, "Stemming originally from bitter repentance, weeping develops into tears of rapture with Divine love. And this is a sign that our prayer is heard and through its action we are led into new imperishable life."

A Spiritual Rainbow

Tears of sorrow are tears that glisten with hope for a better tomorrow. Such tears are, in fact, like a rainbow, a God-given sign of hope. This spiritual rainbow is caused by the rays of the Son of God striking the tears of penitence and transforming them into sparkling droplets of joy and hope.

"Fear produces tears, and tears joy. Joy brings strength, through which the soul will be fruitful in everything," writes St. Ammonas, a disciple of St. Anthony.

St. John Climacus describes the joy that comes from the tears of repentance:

One who goes on his way to God with interior tears never ceases keeping festival.

One who is clothed with blessed tears for a wedding dress knows the soul's spiritual smile.

Mary Magdalene's Tears

The first recorded words of Jesus after His resurrection have to do with tears. They were the words He spoke to Mary Magdalene, "Woman, why are you weeping?" Mary was heartbroken, crushed, overcome with sorrow. Not only was Jesus dead, but now His body was missing. So she wept.

When Jesus asked, "Why are you weeping?" she answered, "Because they have taken away my Lord and I know not where they have laid Him. If you tell me, I shall take care of Him." She thought the person she was speaking to was a gardener.

Then Jesus spoke just one word to her. He spoke her name, "Mary."

This beautiful story tells me that when I weep tears of sorrow, I need to listen to hear the voice of Jesus speaking my name. If I am still and listen, I will hear it—not in an audible voice but in the quietness of the soul, the Risen Christ will come to comfort and console me. For the Christian, the time of sorrow is a bittersweet time in life. It is bitter because of the pain of loss and the suffering of separation. But it is also sweet in the experience of the nearness of God and the reality of His power. As someone so well said, "The soul can have no rainbow if the eyes have no tears."

Tears: The Answer to Guilt

One of man's greatest problems is guilt. It can take a person to the border of insanity and far beyond. It can lead to physical ailments of all kinds. It can produce an anguish far more distressing than physical pain. It can fashion sleepless nights and cheerless days without end. Guilt is one of our greatest tormentors.

God's answer to guilt is to be found in tears—the tears of repentance. In Luke 7:38 we read of the sinful woman who came to Jesus. "Weeping... she began to wet our Lord's feet with her tears and wiped them with the hair of her head." To this woman who grieved so much for her sinful life Jesus said, "Thy sins are forgiven thee." Her guilt was washed away by the tears of repentance.

Peter's Tears

Of our Lord's apostles perhaps none was more devoted to Jesus than Peter. He boasted that he would under all circumstances remain loyal to his Lord and Master, even at the threat of death. Yet this same Peter vehemently denied his Lord. Three times he swore that he didn't know Jesus. Then suddenly "Peter remembered the saying of Jesus, 'Before the cock crows you will deny Me three times.' And he went out and wept bitterly." He didn't just weep, says the Gospel, he wept *bitterly*. He was baptized a second time; this time by his own tears of repentance. Because he wept so bitterly, his sin was forgiven and he was commissioned by Jesus to "feed my sheep."

If Peter's tears brought him such great forgiveness, surely our tears can do the same for us. Whether it be your heart that cries or your eyes, let your tears be not tears of despair, not tears of self-pity, not tears of hurt pride, but tears of repentance that lead to salvation. When we look at the cross we see what sin did to God. We see also what sin made God do to save us. If nothing else moves us to shed tears of repentance, certainly the sight of God on the cross should.

The Tears of Jesus

Tears were consecrated and made sacred when the Son of God and the Son of Man, Jesus the Christ, wept three times: once over death in the case of Lazarus; once over the unbelief of Jerusalem; and once for the sins of humanity as He made red the olive roots of Gethsemane with the tears of His blood.

The answer to the question, "Why is the Theotokos weeping in her icon?" could very well be that she is weeping for the same reason her Son wept: for our unbelief, for our sins, and for the wages of sin: separation from God and eternal death.

We should be the ones to be weeping. Perhaps the tears of the Theotokos are designed to help lead us to tears; tears of repentance that will make us forsake our sins and return to God. "Do not weep for me," said Jesus to the women of Jerusalem who were weeping for Him at His Passion; "weep rather for yourselves and for your children."

Hezekiah's Tears

Elsewhere the Bible tells us that Hezekiah the king was restored to health and given extra years of life and service because God heard his prayers and saw his tears. We read in Isaiah 38:5, "Thus says the Lord...I have seen your tears, behold, I will add fifteen years to your life." Picking up on this, the hymnographer says the following on the eve of the Sunday of the Pharisee and the Publican:

Almighty Lord, I have known how effective are tears; for they snatched Hezekiah from the doors of death, and saved the sinning woman from the chronic iniquities. And as for the Publican they justified him more than the Pharisee. Wherefore, I implore Thee to number me among them and have mercy upon me.

David's Tears

In Psalm 56:8 David says to God about his tears, "You have noted my lamentation; put my tears in Your bottle; are they not recorded in your book?" Our penitential tears are so precious to God, says David, that He gathers them up and bottles them in a wine-skin lest any one of them be lost.

St. John Chrysostom said of David's tears:

Do you wish to see what makes a bed truly beautiful? I will show you now the splendor of a bed, not of a citizen or a soldier, but of a king...the blessed David. What kind of a bed did he have? Not adorned all over with silver and gold, but with tears and confessions. He himself tells of this, when he says, "I shall wash my bed every night; I shall water my couch with my tears." He fixes his tears like pearls everywhere on his bed...When everyone was quiet and at rest, he met God alone...as he wept and mourned and told of his private sins. You also ought to make a bed like this for yourself...

"Blessed are Those Who Mourn..."

Speaking of tears Jesus said in the Beatitudes, "Blessed are they who mourn for they shall be comforted" (Matt. 5:4). Those who are comforted; those who are truly happy, says Jesus, are those who are sorry; those who weep for their sins, for they are the ones upon whom God bestows His forgiveness and, together with it, His peace which passes all understanding.

Father Christoforos Stavropoulos adds, "This mourning is the cause of holy tears. These tears give wings to our soul; they become one with it; they brighten and cleanse it."[*]

---

[*] "Partakers of Divine Nature." C. Stavropoulos. Translated by S. Harakas. Light and Life Publ. Co. Mpls, MN. 1976. p. 70.

The Prostitute's Tears

On the fifth Sunday of Lent, just before Palm Sunday, the Church holds up before us the example of St. Mary of Egypt, who repented of her sins and with her tears of penitence found her way to newness of life in Christ. The Church holds her up as an example on the last Sunday of Lent in order to give us one last opportunity to repent before Lent is over.

Seeing the depth of sin within herself and the evil she shared with a broken world, St. Mary of Egypt, together with countless other fathers and mothers of the desert, cried out tearfully day after day, hour after hour, minute after minute, "Lord Jesus Christ, Son of God, have mercy on me, the sinner!" In the bittersweet tears of repentance they discovered the sweetness of God's forgiveness.

Abba Joseph used to relate what Abba Isaac said about Godly sorrow:

One day I was sitting near Abba Poimen and I saw him in ecstasy, and as I enjoyed great freedom of speech with him, I prostrated myself and besought him saying, "Tell me, where were you?" And he replied in embarrassment, "My thoughts were there where Mary was, the holy Mother of God, weeping over the cross of the Savior. And for my part I wish I could always be thus weeping."

It is said that St. Arsenius the Great always carried a handkerchief on his lap. While his hands were busy with work, his mind was occupied in penitential prayer, releasing tears continually on his handkerchief.

The Most Precious Thing on Earth

There is an old legend according to which God said to one of His angels: "Go down to earth and bring back the most precious thing in the world."

One angel brought a drop of blood from a person who had sacrificed his life to save another. God said, "Indeed, O Angel, this is precious in my sight, but it is not the most precious thing in the world."

Another angel caught the last breath of a nurse who died from a dread disease she contracted in nursing others to health. God smiled at the angel and said, "Indeed, O Angel, sacrifice in behalf of others is very precious in my sight, but it is not the most precious thing in the world."

Finally one angel captured and brought a small vial containing the tear of a sinner who had repented and returned to God. God beamed upon the angel as He said, "Indeed, O Angel, you have brought me the most precious thing in the world—the tear of repentance which opens the gates of heaven."

No More Tears

We look forward to the day when there will be no more tears of any kind. It is the time when Jesus will come again. At that time, we read in Rev. 7:17, "God will wipe away every tear from their eyes."

What the Church Fathers Say About Tears

The soul is dead because of sin...Tears falling on a corpse cannot bring it back to life; but if they fall on a soul, they do revive and bring it back to life again (St. Ephrem).

Pray first for the gift of tears so that by means of sorrow you may soften your native rudeness (Evagrius).

St. Symeon the New Theologian calls tears "the baptism of the Holy Spirit." He considers that sins committed after baptism cannot be forgiven without tears. Next to St. Isaac the Syrian, no other father emphasized more than St. Symeon the necessity of receiving this gift of tears from the Holy Spirit. He writes:

No one will ever prove from the divine Scriptures that any person was ever cleansed without tears and constant compunction. No one ever became holy or received the Holy Spirit, or had the vision of God or experienced His dwelling within himself, or ever had Him dwelling in his heart, without previous repentance and compunction and constant tears ever flowing as from a fountain. Such tears flood and wash out the house of the soul; they moisten and refresh the soul that has been possessed and inflamed by the unapproachable fire (cf. I Timothy 6:16).

The expression "baptism of tears" was coined by St. Gregory of Nazianzen who wrote:

They (tears) are the deluge falling on sins, the purification of the world...Weep, sinner, weep; you have no recourse but this.

A brother once asked St. Anthony, "What should I do about my sins?" The saint replied, "Whoever seeks deliverance from sins will find it in tears and weeping, and whoever wishes to advance in building up virtue will do so through weeping and tears.

Tell me, my soul, why do you bathe your face...If you wish to wash your face, wash it, flood it with tears so that it may shine with glory before God and His holy angels. A face bathed with tears has an undying beauty (St. Basil).

When asked, "How can I wash away my stains?" St. Barsanuphius replied, "If you wish to wash your stains, wash them with tears, for they do indeed wash every spot."

St. John Chrysostom wrote,
Think of his (St. Paul's) face streaming with tears. Day and night for three years he never ceased his weeping. Imitate his weeping. Make your face bright with tears. Weep for your sins: your anger, your loss of self-control, your love of revelry. Imitate Paul's tears, and you will laugh to scorn the vanities of this passing life. Christ blessed these tears, when He said, "Blessed are you that weep now, for you shall laugh." Nothing is sweeter than these tears; they are more to be desired than any laughter. Pray earnestly for these tears, so that when others sin, your heart may be broken for them. Raise your sons and daughters in the same way; weep for them when you see them led astray. Remember the psalmist's words: "The Lord has heard the sound of my weeping; the Lord accepts my prayer."

> *Sadness weighs us down,*
> *self-disgust is unbearable.*

But tears before God are stronger than either (Evagrius of Pontus).

Tears are the mother and daughter of prayer (St. John Climacus).

Never receive communion without tears (St. John Climacus).

Tears are proof that the human soul has won divine mercy. It has been accepted by God through repentance and has now entered upon the phase of purity (St. Isaac the Syrian).

We shall not be accused of not having performed miracles ... but we shall surely have to answer to God for not having wept ceaselessly for our sins (St. John Climacus).

CHAPTER FOURTEEN

The Ladder to Heaven

Enter eagerly into the treasurehouse (the heart) that lies within you, and so you will see the treasurehouse of heaven. For the two are the same, and there is but one single entry to them both. The ladder that leads to the Kingdom is hidden within you, and is found in your soul. Dive into yourself, and in your soul you will discover the rungs by which you are to ascend.

— St. Isaac the Syrian

CHAPTER FOURTEEN

The Ladder to Heaven

On the Fourth Sunday of Lent the Orthodox Church calls attention to St. John of the Ladder (Climacus) who lived in the seventh century. He is held up before us during the season of Lent as an example of penitence. St. John (580-650 A.D.) was the saintly abbot of the Monastery of St. Catherine at Mt. Sinai. Although his feast falls on March 30, the custom of celebrating it on the Fourth Sunday of Lent came into being because his famous spiritual work, *The Ladder of Divine Ascent*, was read—and still is—at table in monasteries around the middle of Lent. From this work he came to be known as St. John Climacus (from the Greek word *klimax*: ladder). This famous work, reminiscent of the ladder in Jacob's dream that extended from heaven to earth, is made up of 30 steps leading toward the spiritual perfection of man. Each step represents one year in the life of Christ to the age of His baptism and offers directions to those who would follow the injunction of Jesus: "Be perfect as your heavenly Father is perfect." The book consists of spiritual exercises through which the Christian can reach the highest point of spiritual perfection and thus become a partaker of divine life receiving the fullness of life in Christ. *The Ladder of Divine Ascent* includes a detailed classification of the passions. It is a remarkably successful attempt to produce a directory of monastic spirituality. The focus of its monastic spirituality is the invocation of the name of Jesus. St. John places monasticism in proper perspective when he writes that it has no value if it is not an expression of love. Thus the hymn says of him at vespers: "Thus it is that Thou dost entreat us: love God so that ye may live His eternal goodwill, and let nothing be set higher than this love."

The hymns of his feast extol him as "an angel in human body" who by "fasting, vigilance and prayers received heavenly gifts to heal the sick and the souls who come to him in faith." "As thy body became thin through abstinence," we sing, "so didst thou renew the power of thy soul, enriching it with heavenly glory." A hymn from vespers calls him, "the pride of ascetics, an angel on earth, the man of

God in heaven, the adornment of the world, the flower of virtue and good deeds. Planted in the house of God, he blossomed with justice like a cedar tree in the wilderness. He helped the flock of Christ grow in holiness and righteousness and justice." The *Philokalia* contains works that are both earlier and later than the time of St. John Climacus, but they are all part of the same spiritual tradition.

Jacob's Ladder

Since *The Ladder of Divine Ascent* is based on Jacob's dream of a ladder, let us briefly review that famous dream; how he laid himself down to sleep in the wilderness one night with a stone for a pillow and dreamed of seeing a ladder set up between heaven and earth; how he saw angels ascending and descending on the rungs of the ladder; and how God spoke to him in that dream from the top of the ladder. And how Jacob said when he woke, "Surely the Lord is in this place and I knew it not."

Jacob had committed a terrible sin. He had betrayed his brother and his father, lied, connived, cheated. He had thus cut himself off from God. He could not on his own build a ladder by which to climb back into his broken communion with God. Yet a ladder there had to be, between God in heaven and this sinful, frail child of dust on earth. God builds the ladder in Jacob's dream and comes down to him. In this dream we see God taking the initiative, making it possible for us to come to Him and for Him to come to us.

The dream was the turning point in Jacob's life. From then on he was God's man. He dedicated himself to the service of the Lord. For he had seen the God who hears and answers prayer; the God who built a ladder from heaven to earth to speak to him; the God who in speaking to a sinner like Jacob had proven Himself kind and merciful beyond comprehension.

It would be many long years before Jacob's dream would come true; for the coming of Christ was many long ages in the future. But in Jacob's dream of the ladder, God promises to bridge the gap between heaven and earth, between God and man. One day the dream would come true in the flesh.

The Fulfillment of Jacob's Dream

We leave the Old Testament and we come now to the New Testament. We hear Jesus saying in St. John's Gospel 1:51, *Verily, verily, I say unto you, hereafter ye shall see heaven open, and the angels of God ascending and descending upon the Son of man.* With these words, Jesus recalls Jacob's dream of the ladder and tells His disciples that they are about to see the ancient dream fulfilled before their very eyes—in the Son of Man; for Christ Himself is the ladder, linking heaven and earth.

No longer then do we need to dream of a ladder between heaven and earth whereby God might come to us and we might climb to Him. Now in Christ we have Jacob's dream come true. Because Jesus paid the price for our salvation, the great gulf is bridged. Our fellowship with Him is restored. Jesus is Emmanuel, i.e., God with us. He is the Ladder.

Man's sin had severed us from God, but Jesus became the mediator between God and man. He is the way by which the glory of God comes down to us and we ascend to the glory of God.

The ladder that God built from heaven to earth leads directly to your heart and mine. It is here that the Lord Jesus wishes to dwell more than anywhere else. God is present everywhere in the universe but his favorite dwelling place is in your heart and mine. "Behold, I stand at the door and knock," says Jesus, "if anyone hears my voice and opens the door I will come in to him..." (Rev. 3:20).

A Continuing Ascension

Christ's coming into the world marks the opening of heaven. He came down the ladder from heaven and ever since then heaven has remained open. As the ladder, Jesus is the only way to communion with the Father and the Holy Spirit. There is a constant stream of traffic on that ladder. Those angels ever going up and coming down are our prayers. Up to gain help and inspiration—down to bring a little bit of heaven, a breath of Godly air into this world of struggling humanity. "Prayer," writes St. John of the Ladder, "is a continuous ascension to heaven." We may add, so is the liturgy and the reading of God's word—a continuous ascension to where God is.

Metropolitan Emilianos Timiadis likens the Church unto a ladder: "The Church...is the mystical ladder on which man ascends to God and God descends, so that a real ascent and descent (*anabasis* and *katabasis*) takes place, resulting in the blessed meeting between Creator and creature."*

The Mystic Ladder

Jesus is the mystic ladder. No matter where you are, on a bed of pain, or wherever, the ladder who is Jesus, will be right there by your bedside, speaking to you, taking you by the hand to lead you closer to His presence.

The Ladder is Still There

Several years ago an interesting cartoon appeared in one of the newspapers on Lincoln's birthday. It represented a log cabin close to the base of a high mountain. On the mountain-top was shown the White House. Against the side of the mountain rested a ladder, its foot touching the cabin at the bottom, its uppermost rung touching the White House. The cartoon bore the caption:

"The Ladder Is Still There."

It is a sermon in one sentence.

It was as a ladder that God came to us in Christ. He bridged the distance between God and man. He came down to earth to raise us to heaven. He became human that we might become divine, "partakers of divine nature." He came to elevate us from mere existence to fullness of life. He came to lift us from ignorance of God to such personal familiarity with Him that we could address Him as "Our Father." He came to raise us from weakness to power: "...you shall receive power when the Holy Spirit has come upon you" (Acts 1:8). He came as a ladder to raise us from the inner hell of sin and guilt to the heavenly joy of God's forgiveness. He came to raise us from the grave of sin and death to freedom and life.

Jesus came as a ladder to connect us with God. And...

The ladder is still there.

Interesting cartoon isn't it? A log cabin at the bottom, the White House at the top with a ladder in between. The "log cabin" represents our poverty, our weakness, our sinfulness, our emptiness, our hell, our death. The "White House" represents all that God craves for us to

---

* "The Nicene Creed: Our Common Faith." E. Timiadis. Fortress Press. Philadelphia, PA. 1983. p. 121.

have: forgiveness, fullness of life, a personal love relationship with Him, free access to His presence, power, peace, joy, theosis. Christ is the ladder that leads us from emptiness to fullness, from weakness to power, from death to life.

Not a Ladder of Worthiness

It was not Jacob who built the ladder to God. It was God Who let down the ladder from heaven and came to where sinful Jacob was. It is impossible for us to earn salvation by climbing the ladder to God and meeting Him on the topmost rung of the ladder of worthiness. The only way to get to God is for God to come to us through the incarnation and meet us as sinners on the bottommost rung of the ladder. The Gospel begins not with our erecting a ladder of reasoned argument or moral achievement and trying to climb from earth to heaven. It begins with God letting down the ladder and coming to where we are, entering our lives, casting out our devils, and destroying our death.

So, God is no longer at the top of the ladder. He is with us at the bottom of the ladder; nay, He is with us on the ladder itself. There are those who look upon Christianity as an impossible ideal. They conceive of Christ as standing on top of a Mt. Everest, calling out to us to struggle and climb to where He is. But Christ does not stand at the top of the ladder of Mt. Everest calling on us to follow Him to the top. He comes down to the bottom of the ladder, to where we are, and climbs the ladder with us, step by step. There is traffic on the ladder—more than just angels ascending and descending. In the words of Fr. Dumitru Staniloae: "...not only do we ascend to communion with the Supreme Person, but that Person descends to us, too. For love requires the movement of each one of those who love each other toward the other. God gives Himself to man through everything, and man to God."

The Upward Climb

The Ladder of Divine Ascent shows us that an upward journey begins at baptism. To be baptized marks the first step or rung on the ladder to heaven. We must not remain on the first rung of the ladder to heaven, but proceed to the next and the next. There are those who will object and say that we Orthodox are denying that salvation is a gift of God when we begin talking about climbing a ladder to God. This is obviously false since we do not make or climb our own ladder. The Ladder is a Gift; it is Christ Himself. Let us use an example. If a poor young man is given a scholarship by a rich benefactor, the lad is given something he could never achieve on his own: a very great gift. But the young man has to be prepared to work, study and toil hard as a student if he is to realize the full benefit of what he has been given. This then is why it is necessary for us to climb the ladder that God has given us in Christ. God gives us the ladder as a gift. The ladder is none other than Christ, but once we are baptized and accept Jesus as Lord, the task of climbing the ladder, or following Christ, begins.

There is a story of a religious man who dreamed he was building a ladder to heaven. When he did a good deed, the ladder went up one more step. When he gave a dollar to charity, he added another step. When he joined the church, the ladder went up 10 steps. Higher and higher went the ladder 'til it reached beyond the clouds and out of sight. As the end of his life neared, the man thought that surely the ladder would extend clear up into heaven by then. So, confidently stepping off the top of the ladder, thinking it was heaven, he found nothing there and went tumbling head over heels to his ruin. Awakening from his dream, he remembered the words of Jesus, "He that...climbeth up some other way, the same is a thief and a robber" (John 10:1). The ladder is the gift of God's grace. It can never be built by our virtues or good deeds.

Grow By Climbing

The very meaning of ladder associates itself with progress and growth. As Thomas Huxley wrote, "The rung of the ladder was not meant to rest upon, but only to hold a man's foot long enough to enable him to put the other somewhat higher." This is why the ladder is projected as a meaningful symbol of spiritual growth during Lent. Thus, spirituality according to St. John Climacus, is not mere perfectionism ("I have arrived! I have made it!") but a never-ending process of climbing and growth leading to new levels of knowledge of God and holiness. Our walk with God in Christ following baptism is a journey onward and upward toward the goal of theosis, i.e., union with Christ. It is steady progress one rung at a time. St. John Climacus himself warns: "You will be rejected if you have the effrontery to leap to the top of the ladder of love."

Professor Panagiotes Chrestou speaks of the never-ending spiritual climb when he writes, "Gregory of Nyssa had earlier indicated that he recognized only one limitation in perfection, that it has no limit. When we climb the ladder of spiritual progress, we will never be able to stop ascending; for there is always a step above the step we occupy and there is no summit. Man continuously becomes more spiritual and his spiritual food continuously increases, without his growth ever ending."*

The Four Steps of the Ladder

St. Theophan the Recluse has written on the four steps of the ladder:

Remember the wise teaching of St. John of the Ladder. He describes the way of our ascension to God in the form of a ladder with four steps. Some people, he says, tame their passions; others sing, that is, pray with their lips; the third practice inner prayer; finally the fourth rise to seeing visions. Those who want to ascend these four steps cannot begin from the top, but must start from the bottom; they must step onto the first rung and so ascend to the second, then to the third, and finally to the fourth. By this ladder everyone can ascend to heaven. First you must work on taming and reducing passions; then practice psalmody—in other words, attain the habit of oral prayer; after this, practice inner prayer; and so at last reach the step from which it is possible to ascend to visions. The first is the work of the novice; the second is the work of those who are progressing; the third, of those who have progressed to the end; and the fourth is reserved for those who have achieved perfection.

In Orthodox theology salvation is not static but dynamic; it is not a state of being, a state of having arrived, a state of having made it, but a constant movement or climbing toward theosis, toward Christ-likeness, toward receiving the fullness of God's life.

Where is the Ladder?

St. Isaac the Syrian answered this question when he wrote:

Enter eagerly into the treasurehouse (the heart) that lies within

---

* "Partakers of God." P.K. Chrestou. Holy Cross Orthodox Press. Brookline, MA. 1984. p. 64.

you, and so you will see the treasurehouse of heaven. For the two are the same, and there is but one single entry to them both. The ladder that leads to the Kingdom is hidden within you, and is found in your soul. Dive into yourself, and in your soul you will discover the rungs by which you are to ascend.

Where are the Rungs?

In describing the rungs on St. John's *Ladder of Divine Ascent*, M. Heppell writes: "His thirty progressive steps may perhaps be regarded as falling into two sections. Steps 1-26 are mainly concerned with an analysis of the principal vices which must be mastered if progress is to be made in the spiritual life, and with suggestions as to how they are combated, followed by the virtues of spiritual warfare. Steps 27-30 speak, on the other hand, of solitude, prayer, dispassion (*apatheia*) and love, the virtues of the victor's positive achievement." [1]

Some of the other rungs on the *Ladder of Divine Ascent* are: repentance, remembrance of death, mourning which causes joy, meekness, poverty, bodily vigil, humility, holy solitude, prayer: the mother of virtues.

The Jesus Prayer is one such rung. Henri Nouwen writes about it: "Such a simple, easily repeated prayer can slowly empty out our crowded interior life and create the quiet space where we can dwell with God. It can be like a ladder along which we can descend into the heart and ascend to God." [2]

Another important rung of *The Ladder of Divine Ascent* is inner desire and perseverance. St. Gregory of Nyssa stresses this when he writes, "Having once put your foot on the ladder..., go on climbing... every rung leads up to the beyond.... Finding God means looking for Him tirelessly.... To see God means never to cease to desire Him."

One Rung at a Time

Each rung on the ladder is there to hold your foot just long enough to step higher. It wasn't put there for you to park on it permanently. As someone said, "You have to climb all the steps to get to the top, but you don't have to build a nest on them." The purpose of the ladder is to help you keep climbing upward and onward. The one who

---

[1] "Ladder of Divine Ascent." Translated by Lazarus Moore. Faber and Faber. 1959. p. 19.
[2] "The Way of the Heart." H. Nouwen. The Seabury Press, NY. 1981. p. 82.

succeeds is the one who perseveres; the one who fights just one more round. When we consider that our goal in life is theosis, becoming like God in Christ, the goal on the very top of the ladder of divine ascent may seem formidable, sometimes even impossible. But remember the image of the ladder. It speaks to us. It tells us that the way to the goal is one small rung at a time. It can be fatal to try to leap several rungs on a ladder. One sure step at a time makes it to the top, always remembering that Jesus is not waiting for us at the top of the ladder. He is on the ladder itself, helping us each step of the way.

There is an ancient icon of the Heavenly Ladder at the Monastery of St. Catherine at Mt. Sinai. It portrays monks climbing a ladder to heaven. Winged devils interfere to impede the ascent of some monks, dragging them down into the open mouth of hell. They are shown being pulled off the ladder and falling into hell. Christ is shown as standing in heaven at the top of the ladder welcoming St. John Climacus who stands at the topmost rung of the ladder. As effective as the icon is, it does not tell the whole story. Christ does not remain at the top of the ladder. His presence should also be portrayed on the ladder itself. We are not at the mercy of the devil. Emmanuel—God with us—is on the ladder with us. His strengthening presence enables us to resist the onslaughts of the evil one.

Climbing an Extension Ladder

Climbing an extension ladder is a scary experience. When you begin, the ladder seems wobbly and unsteady. But the higher you climb, the more you begin to discover that the weight of your body combines with gravity to steady the ladder. So, the higher you climb, the safer you feel.

Is it not the same when you first begin to climb the ladder of faith? You feel scary at the beginning, shaky and insecure. But the higher you climb, one day of trust at a time, the more you discover that the weight of your trust in God combines with His love for you to give you a steady and secure feeling.

Another Ladder

The image of the ladder held up before us by St. John Climacus speaks loudly and clearly to modern man. Every one of us is climbing some kind of ladder in this age of "upward mobility." People today spend a whole lifetime, sacrificing even family and health, in order to climb a ladder—not the ladder of divine ascent but another ladder—the ladder of worldly success. Yet how often we come to discover in the end that all was in vain because we placed the ladder against the wrong building. The goals for which we sacrificed our all remain unfulfilled. We end up with an inner emptiness and void that is terribly painful and so unbearable that it often leads to suicide.

The only real ladder of success is the one about which Jacob dreamed in the Old Testament and which Jesus actually established through His incarnation, death, resurrection and ascension. It is the ladder that God let down to sinful Jacob in the wilderness to assure him of God's Presence, His love and forgiveness. He comes to us again and again piercing the darkness of sin and death. He descends to us to help us ascend to Him. He descends to the very door of our soul and knocks, seeking entrance.

God first let this ladder down into your soul when you were baptized. It is still there. God will never remove it. So, dive into your soul and start climbing it one step at a time using the rungs of faith, love, hope, prayer, humility, repentance, gentleness, kindness, self-control, joy, peace, obedience. It is truly a ladder of divine ascent for it leads to the God of peace and glory.

Spiritual Gems from St. John Climacus

M. Heppell says that "reading the Ladder offers a rich reward. There are many passages of profound insight, often vividly expressed; sometimes these occur unexpectedly in the middle of a series of almost trite remarks, like gleams of spiritual light. Here, in such passages, all who are humble and sincerely desire to "know themselves" as the first step towards inner harmony and spiritual progress can find help and enlightenment..."[*]

Here are some of those spiritual gems:

It is the property of men to fall and to rise again as often as this may happen. But it is the property of devils and devils alone, not to rise once they have fallen...

Repentance is the daughter of hope and the denial of despair...

Prayer is a continuous ascension to heaven...

---

[*] "Ladder of Divine Ascent." Translated by L. Moore. Faber and Faber, London. 1959. p. 32.

Repentance is the renewal of baptism. Repentance is a contract with God for a second life...

A servant of the Lord is he who in body stands before men, but in mind knocks at heaven with prayer...

Asked about how he prays he said,

I have the habit...at the very beginning, of collecting my thoughts, my mind and my soul, and summoning them, I cry to them: O come, let us worship and fall down before Christ, our king and God...

He likens humility to *a veil which hides from us our good deeds to keep us from the terrible sin of pride...*

Whip your enemies with the name of Jesus, for there is no weapon more powerful in heaven or on earth...

Solitude (hesychia) is worship and uninterrupted service of God. May the name of Jesus be united with your breath; then you will understand the value of solitude...

When you pray do not try to express yourself in fancy words, for often it is the simple repetitious phrases of a little child that our Father in heaven finds most irresistible.... One phrase on the lips of the tax collector was enough to win God's mercy; one humble request made with faith was enough to save the good thief...

The tears that come after baptism are greater than baptism itself, though it may seem rash to say so. Baptism washes off those evils that were previously within us, whereas the sins committed after baptism are washed away by tears. The baptism received by us as children we have all defiled, but we cleanse it anew with our tears. If God in His love for the human race had not given us tears, those being saved would be few indeed and hard to find...

Let them take courage who are humbled by their passions. For even if they fall into every pit and are caught in every snare, when they attain health they will become healers, luminaries, beacons and guides to all, teaching about the forms of every sickness and through their own experience saving those who are about to fall...

I have seen impure souls crazed for physical love; but when these same souls have made this grounds for repentance, as a result of their experience of sexual love they have transferred the same eros to the Lord. They have immediately gone beyond all fear and been spurred to insatiable love for God. This is why the Lord said to the chaste harlot not that she had feared, but that she had loved much, and was readily able to repel eros through eros...

If anyone could see his own vices accurately without the veil of self-love, he would worry about nothing else in his life...

A horse when it is alone often imagines that it is galloping, but when it is with others it finds out how slow it is...

CHAPTER FIFTEEN

Spiritual Synergy

We receive salvation by grace and as a divine gift of the Spirit. But to attain the full measure of virtue we need also to possess faith and love, and to struggle to exercise our free will with integrity. In this manner we inherit eternal life as a consquence of both grace and justice. We do not reach the final stage of spiritual maturity through divine power and grace alone, without ourselves making any effort; but neither on the other hand do we attain the final measure of freedom and purity as a result of our own diligence and strength alone, apart from any divine assistance. If the Lord does not build the house, it is said, and protect the city, in vain does the watchman keep awake, and in vain do the laborer and builder work (Ps. 127:14).

– St. Macarius

CHAPTER FIFTEEN

Spiritual Synergy

A very important word in Orthodox spirituality is the word synergy. Orthodox theologians use the New Testament Greek word *synergy* to express the Biblical teaching that God does not force His grace upon us, but guides and strengthens us when we submit to His will. Synergy is derived from the word *synergoi,* fellow workers with God, used by Paul in I Corinthians 3:9. It comes from two Greek words: *syn*, meaning "with" and *ergon,* meaning "work". We cooperate. He works with us. We work with Him.

As St. Isaac the Syrian said:

For the Christian no thought, no feeling, no action can come from the Gospel without the help of God's grace. Man, for his part, brings the desire, but God gives the grace, and it is from this mutual activity, or synergy, that Christian personality is born.

God wants free-will partners. He created us to be His sons and daughters not His blind slaves. Once we come to know Him, however, we do become His servants, but we do it willingly, out of love. God offers us the gift of eternal life, but it is up to us either to accept it or reject it. "It is for God to grant His grace," said St. Cyril of Jerusalem (d. 386), "your task is to accept that grace and guard it." "The will of man is an essential condition," said St. Macarius of Egypt, "for without it God does nothing." "Draw near unto God and He will draw near unto you" (James 4:8).

The Philokalia on Synergy

The *Philokalia* offers the means by which we can cooperate with God to achieve theosis. These are nepsis, vigilance, askesis, fasting, stillness, tears, repentance, the sacraments, prayer, scripture, struggle against the passions, etc. Thus the *Philokalia* fosters a very clear synergy between the grace of God and human effort which is described as follows by St. Macarius:

We receive salvation by grace and as a divine gift of the Spirit. But to attain the full measure of virtue we need also to possess faith and love, and to struggle to exercise our free will with integrity. In this manner we inherit eternal life as a consequence of both grace and justice. We do not reach the final stage of spiritual maturity through divine power and grace alone, without ourselves making any effort; but neither on the other hand do we attain the final measure of freedom and purity as a result of our own diligence and strength alone, apart from any divine assistance. If the Lord does not build the house, it is said, and protect the city, in vain does the watchman keep awake, and in vain do the laborer and builder work (Ps. 127:14).

Grace and Free Will

To see what this word synergy means, let us turn first to I Cor. 15:10:

By divine grace, however, I am what I am, and His grace toward me was not ineffective. In fact, I have worked harder than any of them, that is, not really I but the grace of God that is with me.

St. Paul is telling us in this verse that both he and the grace of God were operative in his life and ministry. He seems to be saying that he worked harder than anyone else. Yet, at the same time, he says that he owes it all to God.

Not Victims but Co-Creators

The great doctrine or teaching behind this verse is that man is not a robot and God, on the other hand, is not a manipulator who pulls strings and pushes buttons to get people to do things. Endowed by God with free will, man cooperates with God's grace. We are not masters of our fate, but neither are we victims of it. We are, indeed, co-creators and cooperators with God and His grace.

Fellow Workers with God

When Paul says, *I labored harder than any of them*, he shows the effort of his own will. But when he adds the words, *Yet not I, but the grace of God*, he points to the role God played in his life. And when he adds that the grace of God is *with me*, he affirms that God's grace cooperates with him. But when? Exactly when he does not sit back idly but labors as best he can do God's will. What Paul is saying here is what he said in I Corinthians 3:9, *For we are fellow workers with God.*

God's grace is not irresistible. We can reject it. We can say no to it. Neither does God allow us to sit back and do nothing while He does everything for us. He cooperates with us, as we cooperate with Him. We are *fellow workers* (*synergoi*) with Him. An example of this is I Corinthians 3:6-7 where Paul writes, *I planted, Apollos watered, but God gave the growth. So neither he who plants nor he who waters is anything, but only God who gives the growth.* Thus, one plants, another waters (both the planting and the watering represent our effort) but God is the One Who gives the growth. We cooperate with Him. We do the planting and watering: He gives the growth. We do our part; God more than does His part; His part, of course, being far greater than ours. God will take nine steps to come to us but He will not take the tenth.

This reminds me of the story of the tourist who was driving through unfamiliar countryside and lost his way. He came upon a farmhouse. Spotting the farmer nearby he asked for directions. Then, looking out on the beauty of the cultivated fields, he said, "God has certainly provided bountifully for you with this farm." "Yes," responded the farmer, "and I am grateful." Then he added with a grin, "But you should have seen this place when God had it all to Himself."

Not Valid Until Accepted

A gift is not valid until it is accepted.

Early in the 19th century, a man named George Wilson killed a government employee who had caught him robbing the mail. He was tried and sentenced to hang. However, President Andrew Jackson sent him a pardon. But Wilson for some unknown reason refused to accept it and no one knew what to do. The case went to the United States Supreme Court. Chief Justice Marshall wrote the decision: "A pardon is a slip of paper, the value of which is determined by the acceptance of the person to be pardoned. If it is refused, it is no pardon. George Wilson must be hanged." And he was.

The acceptance of God's forgiveness does not become valid until it is accepted and passed on to others. We must ask for salvation. We must want it. We must seek it. That is our part in the synergy of God's grace with our free will.

Does He Save All?

A student once asked his seminary teacher, "Do you mean that Christ saved even a man like Adolph Hitler?" Without hesitation the professor replied, "Yes, Christ saved even a man like Adolph Hitler—but Hitler never accepted Christ's salvation."

This is what synergy is: accepting, receiving, claiming, appropriating the gift of God's Son. We have to "come and see". We have to "taste" and experience the sweetness of God's mercy. Then we have to go and tell the good news of Christ to the world. That is what synergy is all about. "It is God Who saves us," says St. John Chrysostom, "but us who are willing."

He Had a Hand In It!

A minister was once being tried in a heresy trial. He believed in synergy whereas his official church did not. Some Protestant churches believe that we can contribute absolutely nothing to our salvation—not even our free will and the acceptance of God's Gift. The defendant was asked if the man with the withered hand, whom Jesus healed, had any part in his healing. After a moment of silence, he replied, "At least you can say that he had a hand in it!" We all have a "hand" in our salvation. We must all open the door to let Jesus come into our lives.

What Synergy is Not

In speaking of synergy, we must be careful to say what it is not. It is not, as Father Peter Gillquist has said, "God is my co-pilot. Under that precarious system, I'm in the left-hand seat as pilot, with the Lord over on the right-hand side as my back-up." That is not what synergy is. "By synergy we mean that the actual living out of our union with Jesus Christ as Lord requires the cooperation of two unequal but equally necessary persons: Christ and me."[*]

99.9% is God's

Synergy does not mean that God does one-half of the saving work and I do the other half. For God always takes the crucial initiative. We love because He first loved us. All we do is respond to His initiative. He alone provides the saving grace. God does all of the saving work; we merely respond. He stands knocking and calling at

---

[*] "The Physical Side of Being Spiritual." Peter Gillquist. Zondervan. Grand Rapids, MI. 1979. p. 147.

the door of our soul. Yet, He will not break down the door. We have to open it freely. That effort on our part of opening the door and then taking up our cross to follow Jesus is our part in God's plan of salvation. If we were to use percentages here, we would say that God does 99.9% of the work of salvation. Our response to God in accepting the Gift would amount to one-tenth of one percent. Yet that one-tenth of one percent is crucial. It represents our free response, our acceptance of His great gift.

God does not say to us, "Rest in Me and I will do it," rather He says to us, "Rest in Me, and I will help you, so that we will do it together." He respects our free will. Yet, we are still helpless without His grace. God gives us the ingredients for our daily bread, but He expects us to do the baking.

The Word "Synod"

The word *synod* expresses the doctrine of synergy very effectively. Derived from two Greek words *syn* (with) and *odos* (way), it means walking on the same road. God and man walk together. For example, the bishops of the Church meet in an ecumenical synod. They meet under the leadership and guidance of the Holy Spirit. If the Holy Spirit does not inspire, nothing will happen. The bishops walk with God the Holy Spirit on the same road *synodoi*, as the disciples did with Jesus on the road to Emmaus. They depend on Him for guidance. They pray. They offer their open minds and hearts. He comes to lead and guide, to fill their emptiness. Thus, the word *synod* serves as a good example of synergy.

Synergy in Worship

The concept of synergy is expressed in the way Orthodox Christians worship. For example, the laity cannot celebrate the liturgy without the priest. Neither is the priest allowed to celebrate without the presence of the laity. When the priest prays the epiclesis, invoking the presence of the Spirit upon us and the gifts of bread and wine, the faithful ratify this invocation with their *amens*. In this respect they are concelebrants of the liturgy.

Synergy is also practiced in the administration of the Church. For example, Canon 22, Fourth Council of Carthage, forbids any bishop from ordaining anyone without the advice of his clergy, so that through them and together with them, he might keep in touch accurately with the sense of the people in his parishes.

The Hands of Grace and Faith

Before salvation and union with God can take place, two things must happen. First, God must reach out to us. This is the divine initiative and it is called *Grace*. Grace is God's hand stretched out to us in baptism. Then, there must be our response to God's reaching out, and the name of the response is *Faith*. Faith is our hand reaching out to clasp God's hand. Paul brought these two words—grace and faith—together when he described salvation in Ephesians 2:8, *By grace are you saved through faith*. When God's hand of grace is grasped by our hand of faith, the result is salvation, wholeness, union with God.

Two Keys

Another example of synergy comes to mind from the fact that when one has a safe deposit box, one realizes that there are two keys. The bank holds one key, and you hold the other. Similarly, the Bible speaks of the keys of the Kingdom of heaven.

Jesus has already turned the first key. When Jesus said on the cross, "It is finished," He meant it. He had finished God's plan of salvation to wash away our sins and make us by grace partakers of God's nature.

Jesus has turned the top key; now we need to turn the bottom key. When we turn the bottom key (our key), the door comes open and God enters. The second key is the key of synergy, man's opening the door to Jesus; man's response to God's invitation to the Kingdom.

Another example of synergy is found in the sea gull that soars and glides with such ease. But we must remember that without the air under its wings, the sea gull would be bound to the ground, unable to fly. We discover a sense of true freedom when we know that we do not have to do anything on our own. The *I* of us, like the wing of a sea gull, can do nothing alone. The spirit of God within us, like the air beneath the wing, lifts us over all obstacles and challenges. Together wings and air produce freedom of flight. So it is with our relationship with God. We have the wings. God provides the Spirit under the wings enabling us to fly in freedom.

Synergy Does Not Gain Us Merit

In no way must it ever be imagined that our free response to God earns us merit. As Bishop Kallistos Ware points out, "God's gifts are always free gifts, and man can never have any claim upon his Maker. But man, while he cannot "merit" salvation, must certainly work for it, since "faith without works is dead" (James 2:17).*

The gift of God is not a wage He pays us but a free gift (Romans 6:23). Our work and our efforts are simply a feeble response on our part for this great gift. Though we work hard, we know that, no matter how long or diligently we work, we can never earn the gift.

Orthodoxy believes that man cannot be saved apart from the action of God in Jesus Christ and the Holy Spirit. Man cannot save himself, but neither is he a robot. Having been endowed by God with free will, he has a real, though limited part to play in his salvation.

It must be emphasized at this point that the Orthodox Church has never been bedeviled with "merit" theology whereby each good deed earns credit(s) toward one's salvation. Latin theology has been heavily stained by "merit" theology which indeed provoked the Protestant reformation. Ever since then there has been a strong aversion among some of our Protestant brethren to anything that smacks of "merit" or "works" righteousness. For Orthodoxy, no person can ever earn merits toward one's salvation which is totally a Gift of God. All we are called upon to do is to respond, to accept the Gift, by freely opening the door behind which Jesus stands knocking and calling out to us; then to take up our cross and follow Him through askesis, nepsis, prayer, etc.

St. John Chrysostom writes,

For (it is) not by laboring and sweating, not by fatigue and suffering, but merely as being loved of God (that), we received what we have received.

Under no condition does synergy mean that man becomes his own co-redeemer and co-Savior with Jesus. Our part is limited to the offering of our will, opening the door (Rev. 3:20). "Open your mouth and I will fill it," says the Lord (Ps. 80:10). He cannot fill it if we do not open it. God does not force feed His children.

---

* "The Orthodox Church." T. Ware. Penguin Books. Baltimore, MD. 1963. p. 227.

Unworthy Servants

Jesus points this out to us powerfully in Luke 17:10 where He says that no matter how much good we do, we are unworthy servants:

So you also, when you have done all that is commanded of you, say, "We are unworthy servants; we have only done what was our duty."

Thus, when we have done all that Christ asks of us, we have done nothing of which to be proud. The wonder of it all is that God condescends to take us into partnership with Himself (John 13:13-16).

The Liturgy Speaks of our Unworthiness

St. John Chrysostom says in one of the prayers of the divine liturgy:

You brought us into being out of nothing, and when we fell, You raised us again. You did not cease doing everything until You led us to heaven and granted us Your kingdom to come.

It is clear from these words that God has done all for our salvation. Nothing we can ever do can in any way cause us to earn that which is clearly a gift. St. Basil adds in his liturgy:

Wherefore, all Holy Lord, we also Thy sinful and unworthy servants...not for our righteousness for we have done no good thing on earth, but for Thy mercy and the bounties which Thou has shed on us abundantly, we presume to draw nigh unto Thy holy altar...

God Offers Not a Reward But a Gift

No matter how many good works we do in the name of Jesus, we remain unworthy servants, beggars of His mercy. St. Mark the Ascetic (5th century) wrote:

(For us) to fulfill every commandment is a duty, whereas sonship is a gift given to human beings through His (Christ's) blood...The kingdom of heaven is not a reward for works but a gift of the Lord prepared for His faithful servants.

The works of love that we do for Christ, although they earn us no merit, have their own reward.

Paul Evdokimov writes:

One could say, paradoxically, "It is God who works, and man who sweats." There is no question here of any meritorious work, but of human action within the divine action—this is the most precise definition of synergism. There is never a question of any reward. God is our creator and savior; he is not the one who measures, and weighs the price of our works" (Mark the Ascetic). *If God regarded merits, then no one would enter the Kingdom of God. It is God who works in us virtue, knowledge, victory, wisdom, goodness.**

Thus, when correctly interpreted, synergy means that while God had completed all the work of salvation ("It is finished!"), we who are created in His image must respond freely with our whole being, which includes both faith and works, in order to share in the fruits of salvation.

What the Bible Says

Besides the verses we have already mentioned, the Bible contains many other references to synergy. Let us look at some of them.

St. Paul says, *I can do all things through Christ who strengthens me* (Phil. 4:13). Who is it who does all things? I! Where do I receive the strength? From Christ! God gives me the power to do all things as His cooperative worker in union with His Son. To quote from the Orthodox Theological Symposium of the World Council of Churches on the Sixth Assembly theme:

When we are united with Christ our actions become the actions of Christ, and thus divine-human acts; there is here no idea of cooperating with God as equals, or of salvation by works.

Philippians 2:13, *It is God who works in you both to will and to do for His good pleasure.* Both *to will and to do* are from God. But where is the will and the doing planted? *In you!* In us! We are His workmanship, created in Christ Jesus for good works. But while *we* are doing these good works, we smile, for we know that we can do them *only* in union with Christ.

Mark 16:20, *And they went out and preached everywhere, the Lord working with them (the actual Greek verb "synergy" is used here) and confirming the word through the accompanying signs.*

Philippians 2:12, *Therefore, my beloved...work out your own salvation with fear and trembling.* Notice that the text does not say, "Work *for* your salvation"; or "Work *toward* your salvation"; or

---

* "The Sacrament of Love." P. Evdokimov. SVS Press. Scarsdale, NY. 1985. p. 78-79.

"Work *at* your salvation"; but "Work *out* your salvation. God, in His grace, has worked it *in*. Now you and I, in His strength, must work it *out*. "When we work out our salvation," writes Father Theodore Bobosh, "we are not earning it, but rather we allow it to be active in our daily lives."

The words "with fear and trembling" are added: *Work out your salvation with fear and trembling.* These awesome, terrifying words are used to head off trifling with grace. Don't ever play on God's grace! Don't ever presume on God's mercy! Be in earnest about your salvation! But remember always what St. Paul says in the second half of this verse, "Work out your salvation... *for God is at work in you, both to will and to work for his good pleasure.*" It is not you; it is God in you! This truth is expressed in the icon of St. George slaying the dragon. The dragon, of course, represents evil. But it isn't St. George who slays the dragon. If you look at his hand, you will notice that he isn't really holding the spear, just touching it lightly. This expresses what we mean by synergy. It is not by our own strength that we overcome evil, but by the strength of God.

Be What You Are!

Be true to what you are! By grace, God has made you His saint. Now *be* one! By grace He has implanted His life in you. Express it! His love is spread abroad in your heart. Show it in what you do and say! Grace has made you lovely, graceful. Let every word and act express that graceful loveliness. *You are washed, you are anointed, you are sanctified*, says the prayer of baptism. Now *be* what you are! *Work out your salvation with fear and trembling.*

The Vine and the Branches

Another excellent example of synergy is to be found in John 15 where Jesus speaks of the vine and the branches: *I am the vine, you are the branches. He who abides in me and I in him, he it is that bears much fruit, for apart from me you can do nothing* (John 15:4-5). Is not the vine abiding in the branch an example of synergy? The fruit is borne by the branch, not the vine. Hence the great responsibility we have to abide, to remain connected with the vine that we may bear fruit richly for God.

Salvation is something God has accomplished for us in Christ "once and for all," yet it is also something that needs to be reaffirmed constantly from our side. *We have died with Christ*, and yet we must constantly *put to death* the old nature in us. Thus Jesus warns us to *abide* in Him constantly. He is our source of strength. Without Him we can do nothing. This "abiding" in Christ through prayer, nepsis, ascesis, etc. is part of what we mean by synergy.

"Take My Yoke Upon You"

In Matthew 11:28-30, Jesus says, *Come unto me; take My yoke upon you, and learn of Me; for My yoke is easy and My burden is light.* A yoke is an instrument that ties together two oxen so that they may work in concert with one another, sharing the burden. Jesus asks us to take His yoke upon us so that He may walk beside us, under the same yoke, to help us carry the heavy burdens of life.

We!

In John 6:5, we read, *Then Jesus lifted up His eyes, and seeing a great multitude coming toward Him, He said to Philip, "Where shall we buy bread that these may eat?"* Notice that little pronoun *we*! Jesus could have fed the multitudes alone, without the assistance of the disciples. But He calls them into fellowship with Him. He tells them, in effect, "The needs of the world are not a matter for Me alone, or for you alone, but for us together! I am the Vine, you are the branches." *We* shall feed them!

In John 15:15, Jesus said, *No longer do I call you servants...but I have called you friends.* Paul Evdokimov writes, "Beyond the slave and mercenary ethic, the Gospel proposes the ethic of the friends of God." God and man: friends working together!

In Revelation 3:20, Jesus said, *Behold, I stand at the door and knock; if anyone hears My voice and opens the door, I will come in to him, and will dine with him, and he with me.* Here is synergy at its best! God knocks seeking entrance. Man responds either by opening the door to fellowship with God or by keeping it closed. Respecting the gift of free will He has given us, Jesus will never force open the door against our will.

The Sails and the Wind

The third century writer, Origen of Alexandria, describes the relationship between man's effort and God's grace by using the metaphor of the sails of a ship with the wind that propels them and the sailors. The wind will not take matters into its own hands to sail the ship without the attention and cooperation of the human sailor. Both are needed. This is synergy. The wind will provide the power if man will channel and direct that power. Similarly, praying to God to make us loving people, without any other effort on our part to love, will not make us love. Both God's grace and man's effort are needed. We can do nothing without the grace of God, but neither will God do anything without us, for He wants to leave us free.

Bishop Theophanes, a 19th century Russian ascetic, wrote:

The Holy Ghost, acting within us, accomplishes with us our salvation.

St. John Chrysostom:

God never draws anyone to Himself by force and violence. He wishes all men to be saved, but forces no one.

J.N.D. Kelly writes:

Our salvation comes, stated Gregory Nazianzen, both from ourselves and from God. If God's help is necessary for daily good and if the good will itself comes from Him, it is equally true that the initiative rests with man's free will. Chrysostom similarly teaches that without God's aid we should be unable to accomplish good works; nevertheless, even if grace takes the lead, it cooperates with free will.*

The grace of God alone will never save us without the cooperation of our free will. This cooperation (synergy) has Old Testament types in the example of Moses praying while Joshua leads Israel in the battle with Amalek (Exodus 17). Another example is that of David using his sling against Goliath while he depended on the name of the Lord (I Samuel 17).

David and Goliath: Synergy

Who fought the battle? David did! Who gave the victory? God did! David could not do God's part, but neither would God do David's part. It was a cooperative effort from start to finish, with God provid-

---

* "Early Christian Doctrines." J.N.D. Kelly. Harper and Row. NY. 1978. p. 352.

ing the power and protection, and David actually casting the stone and smiting the enemy. For David to go forth in his own strength, or sit idly by and expect the job to get done by God's strength, would have proven disastrous. But teaming up with God, David was invincible.

The attitudes, "God, you don't need me" and "God, I don't need you", are twin formulas for disaster. We need God, and God needs us. As St. Augustine said, "Without God we cannot. Without us God will not."

A person said once:

I used to ask God to help me. Then I asked if I might help Him. I ended up by asking God to do His work through me.

The Theotokos

Another great Biblical example of synergy that is often used by the Fathers of the Church is the Theotokos. St. Nicholas Cabasilas has written:

The Incarnation was not only the work of the Father, of His Power and His Spirit...but it was also the work of the will and faith of the Virgin....Just as God became incarnate voluntarily, so He wished that His Mother should bear Him freely and with her full consent.

Mary stands as the great example of man's free response to God's offer of salvation. She stands as an example of synergy, or cooperation between man and God. God does not force His will on Mary but waits for her free response which she grants with the beautiful words:

Behold the handmaid of the Lord; be it done to me according to Your word (Luke 1:38).

Father George Florovsky expressed it this way:

The initiative was of course divine. Yet, as the means of salvation chosen by God was to be an assumption of true human nature by a divine Person, man had to have his active share in the mystery. Mary was voicing this obedient response of man to the redeeming decree of the love divine, and so she was representative of the whole race. She exemplified in her person, as it were, the whole of humanity. This obedient and joyful acceptance of the redeeming purpose of God, so beautifully expressed in the Magnificat, was an act of freedom. Indeed, it was freedom of obedience, not of initiative and yet a true freedom, freedom of love and adoration, of humility and trust—a freedom of cooperation (cf. St. Irenaeus, Adv. Haeres., III, 21,8; "Mary cooperating with the economy")—this is just what human freedom means. The grace of God can never be simply superadded, mechanically as it were. It has to be received in a free obedience and submission.

God Borrows Us

As God used the Theotokos so He uses us. When Jesus was on earth He was always asking people to loan Him something. He borrowed a crib in which to be born. He borrowed Peter's boat from which to preach to those on shore. He borrowed a donkey to make His entry into Jerusalem on Palm Sunday. He borrowed the loaves and the fish to feed the multitude. He borrowed the sponge of a soldier to slake His thirst. He borrowed the spear of a Roman centurion to reveal His loving heart. So, He asks to borrow us—lumps of clay though we be—to do His work in the world today—but never against our will. He waits to hear from us the words He heard from the Theotokos, "Let it be done to me according to your will."

Both Grace and Free Will Needed

Thus, both grace and free will are needed for our salvation. As St. Maximus the Confessor said:

Man has two wings, freedom and grace.

St. Theophan writes:

Exert all your strength, but rest your concern with success on God.

It is up to us to make the effort, yet the result is always in the hands of God and there we must leave it.

A person cannot return to God by his own ability alone: *No one can come to Me unless the Father...draws him* (John 6:44). Yet God draws those who seek Him.

Great care needs to be taken lest giving too much attention to grace, we appear to destroy man's free will, or lest giving too much attention to free will, we appear to weaken the power of God's grace.

Bishop Kallistos Ware writes:

We are told to hold in balance two complementary truths: with-

out God's grace we can do nothing; but without our voluntary cooperation God will do nothing...Our salvation results from the convergence of two factors, unequal in value yet both indispensable: divine initiative and human response. What God does is incomparably more important, but man's participation is also required.[1]

God Needs You!

One of the great corollaries of synergy is that God has paid us an immense compliment. He has chosen to work through us, the members of His Body. Incorporated into the Body through Baptism and nourished regularly through the Holy Eucharist, we the members of the Body become the instruments through which God works. "Christ is the Head of the Body, the Church," writes St. Chrysostom, "but what can the head do without hands, without feet, without eyes, without ears, without tongue?" "Without God, we cannot. Without us, God will not," said Augustine. And he went on to say, "Pray as if everything depends on God. Work as if everything depends on you."

We read in the document drawn up by Orthodox theologians for the Sixth W.C.C. Assembly theme "Jesus Christ—the Life of the World":

Synergy means that God has chosen to work through us. God calls us to surrender ourselves to Christ in order that He may unite us to Himself and work through us... It is precisely in our weakness that the strength of God is manifested. When we acknowledge our natural limitations in humility and repentance, then God takes us and does His mighty acts through us. Where there is faith, God works through the feeble and the powerless. The apostles were not chosen because they were wise or learned, wealthy or powerful... Not many of us Christians were chosen because we were wise and strong...transcendent power is not limited by our limitations, but only waits for our repentance and faith to receive that power.[2]

The same Jesus Who said, "Apart from Me you can do nothing" (John 15:5), also said, "I chose you to go and bear fruit" (John 15:16). Of course, God could accomplish His purposes without you and me, but that is not His plan. He wants us to share in His work. He has chosen you and me to be His partners, his co-workers, His fruitbearers.

---

[1] "The Orthodox Way." K. Ware. SVS Press. Scarsdale, NY. 1979. p. 149-150.
[2] "Jesus Christ—The Life of the World." Edited by Ian Bria. W.C.C. Press. Geneva, Switzerland. 1982. p. 9-10

Faith as Synergy

Just before Jesus raised Lazarus from the dead, he said to Lazarus's sister, Martha, "Did I not say to you that if you would believe you would see the glory of God?" (John 11:40). He insisted that her faith was an essential condition in the raising of her brother to life. God cooperates with man's faith to produce miracles.

Prayer as Synergy

Prayer is synergy, or cooperation with God. In prayer we align our desires, our will, our life to God. Prayer is not trying to get God to do our will. It is the getting of our will into line with God's will. "Thy will be done on earth as it is in heaven."

Repentance as Synergy

The task of repentance is also synergy. God is constantly calling us to forsake sin and to return to Him. But it is up to each of us to choose to respond, to repent and return to Him. This prompts St. John of the Ladder to write:

We will not be condemned at the end of our lives because we did not perform miracles. Nor because we failed to theologize. Neither will we be condemned because we have failed to achieve the divine vision. But because of one reason only; that we did not repent continuously.

God in Me

"It is no longer I who live, but Christ Who lives in me" (Gal. 2:20). If this be true, then I can proceed to say, "It is no longer I who loves, but Christ Who loves in me. It is no longer I who forgives, but Christ Who forgives in me. It is no longer I who overcomes, but Christ Who overcomes in me."

The alcoholic who has been restored leads a *we* life. He has learned to say, "I cannot overcome drinking, Lord...but *we* can!"

A widow once had a rough go of it. She was left with twelve children. But she managed to do a splendid job. Someone asked her how she was able to do so well. She replied, "I entered into a partnership." "A partnership?" asked a friend. "Yes," said the widow, "some years ago I entered into a partnership with God. I made a deal with

Him. I said I would do the work if He would do the worrying. And I've gotten along well ever since." *We*—God and I! Synergy!

How?

How is it possible to live the WE life in synergy with God?

We know that nothing gets anywhere until it is connected.

The electric outlet, for example, is the source of tremendous power. It can produce heat and light, cut down trees, brew coffee, toast bread, mow grass, open cans, turn on radios, refrigerate and freeze food, cook meals, etc., but first we must plug in; we must connect.

There is no greater source of power than God. We connect with that power through prayer. Prayer is not only conversation with God; it is hearing the knock of Jesus on the door of our soul and opening to let Him in. It is meditating on the name of Jesus through the Jesus Prayer until the heart swallows the Lord and the Lord the heart. It is a constant *epiclesis*, or petition that God the Holy Spirit may come to dwell in us with His wisdom and power. For the Orthodox Christian such personal prayer is combined with the corporate prayer of the Eucharist through which God gives us a divine transfusion whereby the Precious Blood of Jesus comes to flow in our very veins giving us here and now the life of God. "He who eats my flesh and drinks my blood abides in me and I in Him," said Jesus.

Personal prayer, the Jesus Prayer, prayer to the Holy Spirit, the Sacrament of Communion—these are the ways we *connect* with God to live the WE-life so that we may say with St. Paul, "It is no longer I who live but Christ Who lives in me. The life I now live in the flesh, I live by faith in the Son of God Who loved me and gave Himself for me." This is synergy!

Does God Need Our Help?

I conclude with the story of a European driver who careened down a two-lane road in the Dolomite Mountains at top speed, only occasionally drifting into the correct lane. His American passenger was terrified.

"I know what you are thinking," he said to his American friend, as he nipped the wheel a millimeter to the right to miss a hill-climbing truck. "But you are wrong. God will protect us till He is ready to take us to His side." "Is it against the rules to give God a little help?" asked the American passenger. "Give *Him* help?" said the European. "You are a typical American! To think that God needs *your* help?!! Shame on you for such thoughts!"

But God does need our help! Without our help, without our free commitment and decision, without our obedience, without our repentance, God cannot lead us; cannot guide us; cannot forgive us; cannot empower us; cannot work through us; cannot save us. For we are indeed fellow-workers, *synergoi* with Him! Our response and cooperation are crucial.

Once we yield our life to Him to allow Him to work through us synergistically then we can pray the beautiful prayer by Francis of Assisi:

> *Lord, make me an instrument of your peace.*
> *Where there is hatred, let me sow love.*
> *Where there is injury, let me sow pardon.*
> *Where there is friction, let me sow union.*
> *Where there is error, let me sow truth.*
> *Where there is doubt, let me sow faith.*
> *Where there is despair, let me sow hope.*
> *Where there is darkness, let me sow light.*
> *Where there is sadness, let me sow joy.*
>
> *O Divine Master, grant that I may not so much seek*
> *to be consoled as to console,*
> *to be understood as to understand;*
> *to be loved as to love,*
> *For it is in giving that we receive.*
> *It is in pardoning that we are pardoned.*
> *It is in dying that we are born to eternal life.*

CHAPTER SIXTEEN

Hesychasm—The Practice of Silence

All human beings are alone. No other person will completely feel like we do, think like we do, act like we do. Each of us is unique, and our aloneness is the other side of our uniqueness. The question is whether we let our aloneness become loneliness or whether we allow it to lead us into solitude. Loneliness is painful; solitude is peaceful. Loneliness makes us cling to others in desperation; solitude allows us to respect others in their uniqueness and create community.

Letting our aloneness grow into solitude and not into loneliness is a lifelong struggle. It requires conscious choices about whom to be with, what to study, how to pray, and when to ask for counsel. But wise choices will help us to find the solitude where our hearts can grow in love.

– Henri Nouwen

CHAPTER SIXTEEN

Hesychasm—The Practice of Silence

The heart of Eastern Orthodox prayer teaches inner silence. Body and mind are brought to solitude and quietness in order to experience the peace and silence that surround the presence of God. The ultimate aim is a mystical union with God within a context of silence. As Bishop Kallistos Ware writes, "The hesychast, the person who has attained *hesychia*, inward stillness or silence, is *par excellence* the one who listens. He listens to the voice of prayer in his own heart, and understands that this voice is not its own but that of Another speaking within him."

The way to know God in the Orthodox Tradition is called *hesychasm*. It is closely associated with *nepsis* and *katharsis* (watchfulness and cleansing of the heart). For God cannot be known unless the heart is purified through (*katharsis*) tears of repentance. "Blessed are the pure in heart for they shall see God," said Jesus. *Hesychasm, nepsis* and *katharsis* together define Orthodoxy. Without these three pillars, Orthodoxy would be inconceivable, patristically speaking.

Stillness or silence is one of the rungs on *The Ladder of Divine Ascent*, as described by St. John Climacus.

Inner Attention

Hesychia is defined as quietness, stillness, tranquility. It is one of the central considerations in the prayer of the desert fathers. It signifies not just the individual living as a solitary but the possession of inner quiet and peace. It may be used to describe not just the hermit but anyone who guards the mind, practices constant remembrance of God, and possesses inner prayer.

The hesychastic Fathers, like St. Paul, affirmed and taught that man is a Temple of the Holy Spirit. God is present within. What is needed is constant inner attentiveness to the Holy Spirit Who is constantly speaking within our hearts of the Father's infinite love for us. For this they teach the necessity of inner stillness, of *hesychia,* or resting in active self-surrender to God's love.

Hesychia as Listening

Bishop Kallistos Ware speaks of *hesychia* as active listening, "Silence is not merely negative—a pause between words, a temporary cessation of speech—but, properly understood, it is highly positive: an attitude of attentive alertness, of vigilance, and above all of listening."[1] Archbishop Anthony Bloom describes a woman who discovers a presence as she is practicing prayerful stillness. She says, "I perceived that this silence was not simply an absence...of something but the presence of something... All of a sudden I perceived that the silence was a presence. At the heart of the silence there was (the One) who is all stillness, all peace, all poise."[2]

The goal of *heyschia*, inner stillness, is not mystical silence but *nepsis* or listening to the voice of God.

Henri Nouwen described the voice we need to hear by contrasting it with the many other kinds of voices that vie for our attention:

Many voices ask for our attention. There is a voice that says, "Prove that you are a good person." Another voice says, "You'd better be ashamed of yourself." There also is a voice that says, "Nobody really cares about you," and one that says, "Be sure to become successful, popular and powerful." But underneath all these often very noisy voices is a still, small voice that says, "You are my Beloved, my favor rests on you." That's the voice we need most of all to hear. To hear that voice, however, requires special effort; it requires solitude, silence, and a strong determination to listen.

That's what prayer is. It is listening to the voice that calls us "my Beloved."[3]

One of the primary purposes of *hesychia* or stillness is not the silence itself but communication: to truly hear God, to hear ourselves and others, and, indeed, the whole creation more deeply.

Hesychasm Is for All

The practice of *hesychia* is not just for the monk or hermit. It is meant to be practiced by all. St. Nicholas Cabasilas was a layman who lived in the 14th century. Yet he lived the same hesychastic life in the world as the monastics did in the monasteries. He described this as follows:

And everyone should keep his art or profession. The general

---

[1] "The Power of the Name." Bishop Kallistos of Diokleia. SLF Press. Oxford, England. 1986. p. 1.
[2] "Beginning to Pray." Anthony Bloom. Paulist Press. Mahwah, NJ.
[3] "Bread for the Journey." Henri Nouwen. Harper Collins. NY. 1997.

should continue to command; the farmer to till the land; the artisan to practice his craft. And I will tell you why. It is not necessary to retire into the desert, to take unpalatable food, to alter one's dress, to compromise one's health, or to do anything unwise, because it is quite possible to remain in one's own home without giving up all one's possessions, and yet to practice continued meditation.

A Prayer of Rest

The word *hesychia* in Greek also means rest. Thus the prayer of the hesychasts is a prayer of inner peace; a peace that comes from the total relinquishment of one's life to the Triune God. It is not a Utopian Nirvana-type of peace, but a peace in God in the midst of intense daily struggle. Thus, the Fathers teach us that *hesychia* or inner quietness and tranquility proceed from unceasing prayer. Hesychastic prayer leads to true rest where the soul can dwell with God in utter inner peace despite outer storms.

St. Gregory Palamas (+1359) describes hesychastic prayer as follows:

Let us work with the body and pray with the soul. Let our outer man perform bodily tasks, and let the inner man be entirely dedicated to the service of God. As Jesus, God and man, commanded us, saying, "But when you pray, enter into your closet, and when you have shut your door, pray to your Father which is in secret" (Matt. 6:6). The closet of the soul is the body; our "doors" are the five bodily senses. The soul enters its closet when the mind does not "roam" among the things of this world and the affairs of this world, but stays within—in our heart. Our senses become closed and remain closed when we do not let them be attached to external sensory things. In this way, our mind remains free from every worldly attachment; and, by secret mental prayer, unites with God its Father.

Dr. Gabriele Winckler comments on the deeper meaning of the silence that is part of hesychastic prayer:

The hesychastic prayer teaches inner silence as the fundamental and original state of being. Hesychia is perceived as the highest realization of spiritual life, a life where body and mind are brought to absolute inner recollection and peace in order to become aware of the awesome peace and silence of which God is surrounded.

Hesychia as Contemplation

Hesychastic prayer is very much like contemplation which may be defined as enjoying the Lord in silence. It is a relaxing love relationship. The mind rests and the heart is full of joy. Contemplation begins where prayer leaves off. In contemplation there are no words, no actions, no thoughts. Our heart is completely open before God. We receive His love and enjoy His presence. Contemplation, enjoying the Lord in silence, is as close to heaven as we can get here on earth. Nay, it is heaven. For, hesychastic prayer, according to St. Theophan the Recluse, leads us into the very presence of God: "To pray is to descend with the mind into the heart, and there to stand before the face of the Lord, ever-present, all-seeing, within you."

"Silence is the sacrament of the world to come; words are the instrument of this present age," wrote St. Isaac the Syrian.

Noise! Noise! Noise!

We live in a noisy world. The roar of traffic has grown so overwhelming that now cars are being soundproofed. And because cars are soundproofed, auto horns have to be made louder for motorists to hear them. Now we have portable transistors with earplugs constantly bombarding our eardrums with noise. An AP dispatch from Los Angeles told of a huge sixty-pound dog dropping dead of a heart attack when two smaller dogs barked at him. Noise permeates our lives. And we're paying the price.

As far back as 1927, noise was identified as a slow agent of death. Studies have repeatedly linked noise pollution not only to hearing problems but also to insomnia, ulcers, high blood pressure, and heart disease.

One of our greatest needs is the need for silence. James Truslow Adams the American historian said, "Perhaps it would be a good idea, fantastic as it sounds, to muffle every telephone, halt every motor, and stop all activity some day, to give people a chance to ponder for a few minutes on what it is all about, why they are living and what they really want." Solitude gives us the power not to win the rat race, but to ignore it altogether. The rat race is for rats not humans.

Soren Kierkegard, the great Danish philosopher, wrote about such genuine silence and the urgency on our part to attain it when he stated:

The present state of the world and the whole of life is diseased. If I were a doctor and were asked for my advice, I should reply: Create silence! Bring men into silence. The Word of God cannot be heard in the noisy world of today. And even if it were blazoned forth with all the panoply of noise so that it could be heard in the midst of all the other noise, then it would no longer be the Word of God. Therefore, create silence.

Intervals of Silence

A famous music master often told students that the rests were just as important in music as the notes. New students thought that he was exaggerating, but soon learned that without careful attention to the intervals between music phrases, however brief, the music lost half its beauty.

What is true of music is also true of life. For without daily intervals of silence and prayer, however brief, life loses much of its beauty and meaning. Even the heart that beats 70 years, rests during 35 of those years.

When the human mind is agitated, it's like the surface of the sea in a storm. No insight can emerge from the depths. But when the mind is calmed by the great hand of the Lord, then insight comes, and understanding, and wisdom. It's much like a computer. In using a computer, the operator must clear the machine of the previous problem before undertaking a new one. Otherwise, parts of the old problem carry over into the new situation, and the result is a wrong answer.

Ernesto Cardenal wrote, "Modern man always tries to flee from himself. He can never be silent or alone, because that would mean to be alone with himself, and this is why the places of amusement and the cinemas are always filled with people. And when they find themselves alone and are at the point where they might encounter God, they turn on the radio or the television set."

Hesychasm is Not the Silence of Emptiness but of Fullness

For many people silence is to be avoided at all costs. For them silence is emptiness and boredom. Since they are empty inside, their silence is empty. It confronts them with their inner emptiness and is thus very painful. Feeling restless, they will do anything to fill the void with busyness, entertainment, etc. As with death, they are terrified by silence. For death, too, is silent. As absolute emptiness, death exposes the utter futility of one's empty life. This is not the kind of silence that constitutes the content of hesychasm, Christian stillness.

On the contrary, Christian stillness is a silence not of emptiness but of fullness. The hesychast places himself in the presence of God and waits for God to fill him with His presence.

Thus the stillness of hesychasm is never empty but always full. It is filled with expectation for God to come, standing before Him with full attention and vigilance (*nepsis*).

It is a stillness not only of the mind and heart but also of the entire body. We become silent, for example, with our eyes, restraining them from impure glances that incite impure thoughts. We become silent with our ears as we flee from foul language and gossip. We seek to fill the inner silence and emptiness with God through sacred readings and the Jesus Prayer.

St. Augustine spoke of three kinds of silences that bring us in touch with God: first, the silence of the body; second, the silence of the tongue; third, the silence of the soul.

Abraham of Nathpar, a Syrian Father, wrote,

Thus there is a silence of the tongue, there is a silence of the whole body, there is the silence of the soul, there is the silence of the mind, and there is the silence of the spirit. The silence of the tongue is merely when it is not incited to evil and cruel speech, or to utter something full of anger, or liable to stir up trouble, or some calumny or accusation. The silence of the entire body is when all its senses are not occupied by a propensity to evil deeds or improper actions; or when the body is in a sort of death, unoccupied by anything. The silence of the soul is when there are no ugly thoughts bursting forth within it, hindering anything good.

A Stillness of Repentance

In stillness we come to know ourselves. "If a man cannot be alone, he doesn't know who he is," said Thomas Merton. Yet, in seeing ourselves as we really are, much of what we see is not pleasant. This is part of the reason many people flee silence. They do not want to be confronted with their shadow side, their false self. They realize that the only way to real life is a death to self, to the false, sinful self, and no one wants to die. This is the great value of *hesychia*, divine stillness. This is what makes St. Isaac of Syria say, "If you love repentance, love silence. For outside of silence repentance does not reach perfection."

A Stillness of Self-Knowledge

The Desert Fathers tell of a monk who poured some water into a bowl and said to his fellow monks, "Look at the water," and it was disturbed. After a little while he said to them again, "Look how still the water is now," and as they looked into the water, they saw their own faces reflected in it as in a mirror. Then he said to them, "It is the same for those who live among men; disturbances prevent them from seeing their faults. But when a man is still, especially in the desert, then he sees his failings."

A Stillness of Love

Hesychia reaches its summit in love. Since divine stillness is filled with an expectant waiting for the living God, who is love, it involves love of God and love of neighbor. It involves losing ourselves in God and in our neighbor that we may find ourselves. When we reach the point of true love for God, as we see Him in our neighbor, then we have reached the true meaning and purpose of stillness.

Great Discoveries Made in Silence

It is in silence that some of the world's greatest discoveries have been made. Archimedes discovered the law of specific gravity while relaxing in silence in his bath. Galileo discovered the principle of the pendulum while praying silently in the cathedral of Pisa. When the scientist of today would wrest some secret of nature's mystery, he does not set up his apparatus in the midst of a noisy and crowded street, but in some quiet and remote laboratory, where he waits for nature to speak. It is so when man waits for God to speak. He must shut the door on the world.

Out of the such silences have come the great prophets—Moses from the desert, Amos from the hillside, Paul from Arabia, John the

Baptist from the wilderness, Anthony from the desert, and Jesus from the seclusion of Nazareth and from His forty days and nights in the wilderness.

It was during the fourteen years of vowed silence that the great icon painter and monk, Rublev, produced some of his greatest works. Silence had released his creative genius.

Mother of Prayer

Elijah found that the Lord was not in the whirlwind, nor in the earthquake, nor in the fire, but in the still small voice. It was in silence that God spoke to him. Isaiah learned that "in quietness and confidence" lay the sources of his strength. The saints and mystics of every age unite in testifying that silence is an indispensable condition of spiritual knowledge, that without it we cannot call our souls our own, that "a man does not see himself in running water but in still water," that spiritual realities do not shriek or shout but that God is waiting in the depths of our being to talk to us if we will only "wash our souls with silence." "Silence," writes St. John of the Ladder, "is the mother of prayer...a continuous ascension to heaven." "Love silence diligently," said St. Isaac the Syrian, "for in it your soul finds life."

Jesus Practiced Solitude

Jesus practiced quietness in spite of all His activities. St. Mark, for example, tells how Jesus spent a typical day in Capernaum. Entering the town he taught in the synagogue. Then He restored health to a man with an unclean spirit. After that He went to Simon's house where He healed Peter's mother-in-law. In the evening He ministered to the sick of the city. Where did He get the strength for all this activity? St. Mark provides the answer. The next morning, he writes, "a great while before day, He (Jesus) rose and went out to a lonely place, and there He prayed." Jesus went out often to lonely places to pray. For Him they were places of power, places of strength and peace. Before His crucifixion, He poured out His soul in prayer in the lonely corner of a garden. He emerged from Gethsemane with a feeling of strength and peace. The night before He chose His own disciples He went out on the mountainside and "passed the whole night offering prayer to God."

If Jesus found it necessary to guard carefully the time for quiet and reflection, if He had to be alone to keep His soul steady, how much more do we? It is not only the health of body and soul and the state of our nerves that depend on it; something much deeper is at stake. Until we know God and are sure of Him, we have no fixed point in life, no wall, amid the pressure of things, against which to put our back. We cannot know God if we are always in motion, caught up and held prisoners by the rush and pace of life. It is when we go into our closet and shut the door that God has an opportunity to become real to us.

Keeping the Inner Flame Alive

Hesychia, stillness, is the inner warmth of God's presence. This inner heat is the life of the Holy Spirit in us. Thus, *hesychia* is the discipline by which the inner fire of God is tended and kept alive in us.

Diadochus of Photiki offers a very concrete image:

When the door of the steambath is continually left open, the heat inside rapidly escapes through it; likewise the soul, in its desire to say many things, dissipates its remembrance of God through the door of speech, even though everything it says may be good. Thereafter the intellect, though lacking appropriate ideas, pours out a welter of confused thoughts to anyone it meets, as it no longer has the Holy Spirit to keep its understanding free from fantasy. Ideas of value always shun verbosity, being foreign to confusion and fantasy. Timely silence, then, is precious, for it is nothing less than the mother of the wisest thoughts.[*]

We live in a day when people are made to feel that feelings, emotions, and even inner stirrings of the soul have to be shared with everyone. The door of our steambath is kept open most of the time. We come away from these sharing sessions feeling that something precious has been taken away from us and that holy ground has been trodden upon.

James Hannay, commenting on the sayings of the Desert Fathers, writes of this excessive sharing:

The mouth is not a door through which any evil enters. The ears are such doors as are the eyes. The mouth is a door only for exit. What was it that they [the Desert Fathers] feared to let go out? What was it which someone might steal out of their hearts, as a thief takes the steed from the stable when the door is left open? It can have been nothing else than the force of religious emotion.*

By "religious emotion" he means the inner warmth of the life of the Holy Spirit in us.

God Makes Silences for Us

Perhaps this is the reason God makes silences in every life: the silence of sleep, the silence of sickness, the silence of sorrow, and then the last great silence of death. One of the hardest things in the world is to get little children to keep still. They are in a state of perpetual activity, restless, eager, questioning, alert. And just as mother says to her child, "Be still," and hushes it to sleep that it may rest, so God does sooner or later with all of us. What a quiet, still place the sick-room is! What a time for self-examination! What silence there is in a house where a loved one has died! How the voices are hushed, and every footstep soft. Had we the choosing of our own affairs we would never have chosen such an hour as that; and yet how often it is rich in blessing. All the activities of our years may not have taught us quite so much as we learned in the silence of sickness, sorrow and death. So God comes, in his irresistible way, which never ceases to be a way of love, and says, "Be still, and know that I am God."

It must be understood that silent prayer cannot stand alone. It is intimately related to public worship. As one of the saints said, "There can be no closet prayer without common prayer." It is common prayer—the liturgy— that gives us the inspiration and the motivation to practice closet prayer.

Silence: The Mother of Knowledge

Fr. Thomas Hopko said once, "In order to pray you've got to be quiet. In order to get to know your children, you've got to be quiet. In order to get to know your spouse, you've got to be quiet. In order to get to know yourself, you've got to be quiet. In order to get to know God, you've got to be quiet."

How few of us there are who can be still enough to hear God

---

* "Wisdom of the Desert." James O Hannay. London. 1904. p. 206.

speak. For before we can hear Him, we must learn to go into the closet and shut the door.

Henri Nouwen writes, "We have to fashion our own desert where we can withdraw every day, shake off our compulsions and dwell in the gentle, healing presence of our Lord. Without such a desert, we will lose our own soul while preaching the gospel to others."*

Describing the stillness he found on the Holy Mountain, one visitor wrote:

This stillness, this silence, is everywhere, pervades all, is the very essence of the Holy Mountain. The distant sound of a motorboat serves only to punctuate the intensity of the quietness; a lizard's sudden rustling among dry leaves, a frog plopping into a fountain, are loud and startling sounds, but merely emphasize the immense stillness. Often as one walks over the great stretches of wild country which form much of this sacred ground, following paths where every stone breathes prayers, it is impossible to hear a sound of any kind. Even in the monastery churches, where silence is, as it were, made more profound by the darkness, by the beauty and by the sacred quality of the place, it seems that the reading and chanting of priests and monks in the endless rhythm of their daily and nightly ritual is no more than a thin fringe of a limitless ocean of silence.

But this stillness, this silence, is far more than a mere absence of sound. It has a positive quality, a quality of fullness, of plenitude, of the eternal Peace which is there reflected in the Veil of the Mother of God, enshrouding and protecting her Holy Mountain, offering inner silence, peace of heart, to those who dwell there and to those who come with openness of heart to seek this blessing.

"If you have silence, you will have peace wherever you live," said Abba Poemen.

The Church Fathers on Silence

The highest form of prayer is to stand silently in awe before God.   – St. Isaac the Syrian.

When Arsenius prayed, *Lord, lead me into the way of salvation,* he heard a voice saying, *Arsenius, flee, be silent, pray always, for those are the sources of sinlessness.*

---

* "The Way of the Heart." H. Nouwen. Seabury Press. NY. 1981. p. 30.

May the name of Jesus be united with your breath; then you will understand the value of solitude. – St. John Climacus

Speech is the organ of this present world. Silence is the mystery of the world to come. – St. Isaac the Syrian

I have often repented of having spoken, but never of having remained silent. – Abbot Arsenius

The desert fathers tell of the time Archbishop Theophilus went to the desert to visit Abba Pambo. But Abba Pambo did not speak to him. When the brethren finally said to Pambo, *Father, say something to the archbishop so that he may be edified*, he replied, *If he is not edified by my silence, he will not be edified by my speech.*
– Sayings of the Desert Fathers

A brother once came to visit Abba Moses and asked him for a word of advice. The old man said to him, *Go, sit in your cell, and your cell will teach you everything.*
– Sayings of the Desert Fathers

When the sea is calm, the eyes of the fisherman can penetrate to the point where he can distinguish different movements in the depth of the water, so that hardly any of the creatures who move through the pathways of the sea escape him, but when the sea is agitated by the wind, she hides in her dark restlessness what she shows in the smile of a clear day.
– Diadochus of Photice

Behold, my beloved, I have shown you the power of silence, how thoroughly it heals and how fully pleasing it is to God. Wherefore I have written to you to show yourselves strong in this work you have undertaken, so that you may know that it is by silence that the saints grew, that it was because of silence that the power of God dwelt in them, because of silence that the mysteries of God were known to them.
– Ammonas

Talkativeness is the throne of vainglory on which it loves to preen itself and show off. Talkativeness is a sign of ignorance, doorway to slander, a leader of jesting, a servant of lies, the ruin of compunction, a summoner of despondency, a messenger of sleep, a dissipation of recollection, the end of vigilance, the cooling of zeal, the darkening of prayer. Intelligent silence is the mother of prayer, freedom from bondage, custodian of zeal, a guard on our thoughts.

– St.John Climacus

Climacus urged monks, "Once outside your cell, watch your tongue, for the fruits of many labors can be scattered in a moment."

– St. John Climacus

A certain brother asked Abba Poemen: "Is it better for someone to speak, or to be silent?" The Elder said to him: "Whoever speaks for the sake of God does well. And whoever keeps silent for the sake of God again does well." – The Desert Fathers

The silence of the soul is one of the mysteries of the coming age.

– St. Isaac of Nineveh

An old man was asked, "What is it necessary for the monk to be?" He answered, "According to me, alone with the Alone."

Many are avidly seeking but they alone find who remain in continual silence.... Every man who delights in a multitude of words, even though he says admirable things, is empty within. If you love truth, be a lover of silence. Silence like the sunlight will illuminate you in God and will deliver you from the phantoms of ignorance. Silence will unite you to God himself....

More than all things love silence: it brings you a fruit that tongue cannot describe. In the beginning we have to force ourselves to be silent. But then there is born something that draws us to silence. May God give you an experience of this "something" that is born of silence. If only you practice this, untold light will dawn on you in consequence...after a while a certain sweetness is born in the heart of this exercise and the body is drawn almost by force to remain in silence. – St. Isaac of Nineveh

Secret meditation wounds devils, and drives away thoughts of wickedness. He who arms himself with this secret meditation, making his inner man resplendent, is strengthened by God, fortified by the angels, and glorified by men. Secret meditation and reading turn the soul into an impregnable stronghold, an invincible fortress, a peaceful haven, and they preserve it undisturbed and unshaken. The devils are greatly disturbed and troubled when the monk arms himself with this secret meditation and reading. Secret meditation is a mirror for the mind and a light for the conscience; it tames lust, calms fury, dispels wrath, drives away bitterness, puts irritability to flight, and banishes injustice. Secret meditation illuminates the mind and expels laziness. From it is born the tenderness that warms and melts the soul. Through it the fear of God enters and dwells within you, touching you to tears. By secret meditation a monk is given true humility of mind, untroubled prayer, a vigil blessed by tenderness and warmth. Secret meditation disperses evil thoughts, flogs the demons, sanctifies the body, teaches us long-suffering and self-restraint, and keeps us mindful of Gehenna. Secret meditation preserves the mind free of distractions and helps it to reflect upon death. Secret meditation is full of every kind of good work, adorned with every virtue; and it is far removed from every evil deed. – Abba Isaias

Silence like sunlight will illuminate you in God, and will deliver you from the phantoms of ignorance. Silence will unite you with God Himself. – St. Isaac of Nineveh

We are never less alone than when alone. – St. Jerome

Who sits in solitude and is quiet has escaped from three wars: hearing, speaking, seeing; yet against one thing shall he continually battle: his own heart. – St. Anthony

"Be Still and Know..."

"Be still and know that I am God, " says the Lord. Be still! Stop your rushing about all tensed up, acting as if everything depends on you, acting as if you are God. Stop! "Be still and know that I am God." In stillness as we practice God's presence, we discover who

God is and who we are. The noises and disturbances of the world serve to hide our faults and our true selves from us. The desert fathers were disciples of Jesus in honest search for their true selves in Christ.

"Silence. All human unhappiness comes from not knowing how to stay quietly in a room," said Pascal.

It was Paul Tillich who said, "Language has created the word *loneliness* to express the pain of being alone, and the word *solitude* to express the glory of being alone with God."

Commenting on Mary who was sitting at the feet of Jesus listening to His words of eternal life, while Martha, her sister was busy working in the kitchen, St. Augustine wrote, "Martha is who we are. Mary is who we hope to be."

The Place of Our Salvation

Henri Nouwen explains what happens in solitude, "Solitude is not a private therapeutic place. Rather, it is the place of conversation, the place where the old self dies and the new self is born, the place where the emergence of the new man and the new woman occurs.... In solitude I get rid of my scaffolding: no friends to talk with, no telephone call to make, no meetings to attend...just me—naked, vulnerable, weak, sinful, deprived, broken—nothing. . . The wisdom of the desert is that the confrontation with our frightening nothingness forces us to surrender ourselves totally and unconditionally to the Lord Jesus Christ. ...Solitude is not simply a means to an end. Solitude is its own end. It is the place where Christ remodels us in His own image and frees us from the victimizing compulsions of the world. Solitude is the place of our salvation."[*]

As Mother Euphrasia, mother superior of the monastic community of Deolu of the Romanian Orthodox Patriarchate, wrote: "*Hesychia* is the supreme mark of the ascetic life and of our victory over our passions. For St. John Climacus *hesychia* is the sum of the virtues, paradise restored, heaven in our hearts. It is a different way of speaking of the gifts of the Spirit mentioned by the apostle Paul (Gal. 5:22). The hesychast possesses these gifts and exhales them in all directions like the fragrance of the knowledge of Christ (II Cor. 2:14), as a flower gives off its scent or the sun sheds abroad its kindly light."

---

[*] "The Way of the Heart." H. Nouwen. Seabury Press. NY. 1981. pp. 27, 28, 32.

The Purpose of Stillness

The purpose of stillness according to the desert fathers is to descend with the mind into the heart and stand in the presence of God. It is not just a time of silence, of not speaking, but of listening to God Who dwells in the inner temple of the soul and standing in His presence.

Fr. John Meyendorf has written,

Since the incarnation, our bodies have become "temples of the Holy Spirit who dwells in us" (I Cor. 6:19); it is there, within our own bodies that we must seek the Spirit, within our own bodies sanctified by the sacraments and grafted by the Eucharist into the Body of Christ. God is now to be found within; He is no longer exterior to us. Therefore, we find the light of Mt. Tabor within ourselves.*

The purpose of solitude is to celebrate the liturgy in the inner chapel of the heart which is the temple of the Holy Spirit. For in reality there are three liturgies: the liturgy celebrated in the chapel of the heart for which stillness is so necessary. The corporate liturgy celebrated in church. And the liturgy after the liturgy, the *diakonia* or service rendered to Christ in the world. "I was hungry and you fed me."

Archbishop Anthony Bloom said, "It is not the desert that makes a desert father...the desert is everywhere." It is portable. It is within. It is such stillness that creates an inner desert, an inner monastery, as it were, where we stand in His presence and where God is constantly listened to, remembered and praised.

Don't Lose Him in Your Heart

Let me share with you a folk tale from India:

"A neighbor found Nasruddin on his knees searching for something. 'What are you searching for, Mullah?' 'My key. I've lost it.' Both men got on their knees to search for the lost key. After a while the neighbor said, 'Where did you lose it?' 'At home.' 'Good Lord! Then why are you searching for it here?' 'Because there is more light here.'"

Of what use is it to search for God in holy places if you have lost Him in your heart?

How can we find Him in the heart so as to stand constantly in His presence? Following are some ways.

---

* "St. Gregory Palamas and Orthodox Spirituality." John Meyendorff. St. Vladimir's Press. Crestwood, NY. 1974. p. 113.

How to Shut the Door on the World

The early Church Fathers speak of their private prayer life as *krypti ergasia* (secret work) or *noera meleti* (the work of the intellect). This is what they called their constant inner awareness and conversation with God. God was in the inner temple of the soul and man was in constant communion with Him. Part of this "secret work" was the recitation over and over again to oneself, either quietly or more loudly, of certain prayers such as the Jesus Prayer or Scripture verses or entire Psalms.

St. John Climacus mentions this inner prayer activity when he writes, "Not even in the refectory did they (the monks) stop *noera ergasia*, but according to certain customs, these blessed men reminded one another of interior prayer by secret signs and gestures. And they did that not only in the refectory, but at every encounter and gathering."

To silence the mind is an extremely difficult task. It is hard to keep the mind from thinking, thinking, thinking, forever producing thoughts in a never-ending stream. The Church Fathers have taught us the way to control the mind. It is by using one thought to rid ourselves of all other thoughts that crowd the mind. That one thought is the Jesus Prayer. By fastening the mind on the name of Jesus we are enabled to keep the mind open to the voice of God, keeping at bay all other voices that seek to intrude. "He who has achieved stillness has arrived at the essence of the Christian faith," wrote St. John Climacus.

A Time Set Apart

In order to have quiet time with God we need to set apart a time and a place to be alone with God. It could be in the early morning or late night or in the middle of the night. As Fr. Maloney writes, "...the living God of Abraham, Isaac and Jacob waits for us in the desert of our silent selves to reveal Himself to us in His own time and in His own words."

A successful businessman once shared his secret for preventing tensions. He had a short period of silence every day at 10 o'clock and at 3 o'clock. This did not take the usual form of prayer for he did not think about his problems but dwelt upon God's power and peace. He placed himself deliberately in God's presence and he thought of the spiritual strength of Christ flowing into him. He reported that those few minutes a day spent in God's presence resulted in complete renewal of energy and clarity of mind. "Thou wilt keep him in perfect peace, whose mind is stayed on Thee, because he trusteth in Thee," said the Prophet Isaiah (26:3).

One woman has learned to rise early each morning and spend one hour silently in the presence of God. It wasn't easy, she says. It took time and persistence to get it started. But she now feels "the warm presence of love. I know no other way to describe it.... Through every crisis, I have found a quietness of soul in that hour with God. It gives me time to put things in perspective, to find God in every circumstance. Once I find Him, there seems to be no problem that cannot be resolved. Because of it, my life is better. Starting my day with an hour of prayer has filled the empty space within me—to overflowing."

Other "Little Solitudes"

There are other "little solitudes" that fill our day. We can take advantage of those early morning hours in bed before the family awakens. Or the solitude of the early morning cup of coffee before leaving for work. Or the solitude of bumper to bumper traffic during the freeway rush hour. Or the solitude of waking up in the middle of the night and talking to the Shepherd instead of counting sheep. Or the solitude of a minute's silence at 6 a.m. to thank Him for the physical light of the sun and for the spiritual light of the other sun, the Son of God. At 9 a.m. to pause quietly and remember that this was the hour of Pentecost and to pray for the presence of the Holy Spirit within us. At noon to remember Jesus nailed to the cross and to thank Him for His love. At 3 p.m. to pause and remember His death on the cross at this hour and to pray the penitent thief's prayer, "Lord, remember me when You come into Your Kingdom." And at 6 p.m. when the coming darkness reminds us of the darkness of sin and death, to remember Jesus Who came into the world as Light to destroy the oppressive darkness of sin and death.

A Silence Zone

There is no doubt that we live in a noisy world among crowds of hurrying, pushing mortals. The pressure is harder. The pace is quicker.

The noise is louder. We owe it to ourselves to set up a *silence zone* somewhere in every day. When the Bible talks of one day in seven being set aside for worship, it emphasizes the need for a break in the noise. We need this break in the noise, this silent zone, every day. We need to go into our room, shut the door, and pray to our Father in secret. We need it physically; we need it mentally; we need it spiritually. Dr. Paul Tournier, the eminent Swiss psychiatrist, wrote, "One day, almost a year ago, I realized I was doing myself harm because I had begun to read the newspaper before my morning meditation, the time when God was asking me to listen to Him before listening to the world. Correcting that was simple, but it was enough to brighten again the climate of my life."

> *Dear God*
> *Help me to be still and know*
> *That You are there.*
> *I was making so much noise*
> *That I couldn't hear You.*
>
> – J.B. Turber

The Fruit of Hesychasm

St. Symeon said of Moses, "Moses went up to the mountain as a mere man; he came down carrying God with him." St. Anthony went into the desert a mere man. He came out of it carrying God. So did the other saints. So can we if we daily descend with the mind into the heart, there to stand in God's presence. This is the fruit of hesychasm, of our solitude: to carry God into the world.

The climate of your life, too, can be brightened if you will take time to be alone with Jesus, to go into your room, shut the door against the noise of the crowd, and listen to the still, small voice of God. It speaks of forgiveness and new life. It speaks of the never-failing love of God. It speaks of this life and blessed fellowship with God eternally. It speaks of peace and pardon, of courage and strength, of life and hope through Christ Jesus, our Savior. We need to pause and to be silent from time to time, quietly to unwrap God's gift of life in Christ Jesus.

The whole purpose of the spiritual life is to descend with the mind into the heart through inner prayer and silence and to discover there the Kingdom of God (the grace of baptism and the Holy Spirit). The heart is the Lord's reception room. Meet Him there. "The Kingdom of God is within you," said Jesus.

Fr. Basil Pennington sums up the purpose of hesychasm:

By deep prayer, with the help of the Holy Spirit, we can hope to so establish this deep inner quiet that even in the midst of everyday activities, this lively sensitivity will remain and all activities will be guided by the call of grace and the leading of the Holy Spirit. This is really the fruit of hesychasm.*

Some Thoughts on Silence

Stillness is a state of inner tranquility or mental quietude and concentration. Not simply silence, but an attitude of listening to God and of an openness to God.

– Bishop Kallistos Ware

Hesychia (silence) is worship and uninterrupted service to God.
– St. John Climacus

The silence I am speaking of is the silence of the sentry on duty at a critical moment; alert, immobile, poised and yet alive to every sound, every movement. This living silence is what discipleship requires first of all, and this is not achieved without effort. It requires from us a training of our attention, a training of our body, a training of our mind and our emotions.

– Metropolitan Anthony of Sourozh

Stillness initiates the soul's purification.
– St. Basil the Great

When you pray, you yourself must be silent...let the prayer speak.
– Tito Colliander

---

* "O Holy Mountain." Basil Pennington. Doubleday and Co. NY. 1978. p. 64.

The mind is filled with thoughts that create a gulf between man and God. Empty the mind; in the stillness you will find union with God.

– Fr. Basil Pennington

Every man who delights in a multitude of words, even if he says admirable things, is empty within.

– St. Isaac of Nineveh

CHAPTER SEVENTEEN

Kyrie Eleison, Lord, Have Mercy

"Never say that God is just. If He were just, you would be in hell. Rely only on His injustice which is mercy, love, and forgiveness."

– St. Isaac the Syrian

CHAPTER SEVENTEEN

Kyrie Eleison; Lord, Have Mercy

A woman once hired an artist to paint her portrait. When he finished, the woman complained that the portrait did not do her justice. The artist laughed and said, "Lady, you don't need justice. You need mercy."

The prayer that the Fathers of the *Philokalia* emphasize greatly and is most expressive of Orthodox spirituality is a plea for God's mercy. It is the Jesus Prayer: "Lord Jesus, Son of God, have mercy on me." *Kyrie eleison*, "Lord, have mercy," is a contraction, a shortened version of the Jesus Prayer. Used extensively in Orthodox worship services, it is a prayer that pleads for nothing but God's mercy.

Psalm 51 is used most extensively in Orthodox worship services. In this penitential psalm, David asks God's mercy for his sins and proclaims that God's steadfast love and mercy are greater than all the sins of His creatures. St. Paul agreed when he wrote, "Where sin abounds, grace (God's mercy) superabounds" (Rom. 5:20).

The theme of God's mercy runs through many of the Gospel readings and worship services of the Orthodox Church.

The Pharisee and the Publican

On the Sunday of the Pharisee and the Publican, the Church offers us the example of two persons who go to the temple to pray. One, the Pharisee, brags about his virtues and sets himself apart from others as the paragon of virtue. The other—a tax collector—stands alone in a corner. He does not dare lift his eyes to heaven; he is too full of shame. Instead, he looks down to the ground, and beating his breast penitently he prays, *"God, be merciful to me the sinner."* He may have been a kind father and a good friend, but it does not occur to him to mention that. He sees himself in God's sight only as God sees him. He prays, *"God, be merciful to me, the sinner."* The Greek text says not *a* sinner but *the* sinner. He regards himself as the sinner *par excellence*. As the Pharisee singles himself out as the only holy one in the world, so the tax collector singles himself out as the greatest of sinners. In the end this man who knew his own sin got nearer to God than the Pharisee who could see nothing but his virtue. Instead of justifying himself, as did the Pharisee, the tax collector accused himself in order that God might justify him.

"God, be merciful to me, the sinner." He has nothing to trust but the mercy of God. He looks nowhere but to God's mercy for help. He knows that people as personified by the Pharisee are unmerciful, but he believes God to be merciful. His only plea is, "God, be merciful!"

Keep Your Sins Before You

The Desert Fathers tell the story of a monk who took a sack, filled it with sand, and carried it on his back over his shoulder. He also put a little sand into a tiny bag which he carried in front of him. When asked what this meant, he said, "In the sack over my shoulder there is much sand. These are my sins and they are many. I have put them behind me so as not to see them, not to be troubled by them, and not to weep for them. And in this tiny bag in front of me I keep the sins of my brothers and sisters. I keep judging them all the time. But this is not right. I ought to carry my sins in front of me where I can see them and do something about them, and the sins of my brothers and sisters on my shoulder behind me." When the other fathers heard this they said, "Truly, this is the way of salvation." And this was the way of the publican, who kept his own sins constantly before him: *"Lord, be merciful to me, the sinner."* "The prayer of the publican— 'Lord have mercy on me, the sinner'—will accompany the just even to the gates of the kingdom," said Vladimir Lossky. And it will even open those gates for us!

The Prodigal Son

The same theme of God's mercy is expressed again in the Gospel lesson of the Prodigal Son. Read the following words from one of the hymns of the Vesper service:

As the Prodigal Son I come to you, merciful God. I have wasted my whole life in a foreign land; I have scattered the wealth which You gave me, O Father. Receive me in repentance, O God, and have mercy upon me.

One of the most beautiful examples of God's mercy is the prodigal son, who leaves home, wastes his father's resources in sin, ends up living with pigs, remembers his father, repents, and returns home where he is embraced by the waiting father, who then declares a feast to celebrate his return. That is God's mercy in action.

The same theme of mercy is emphasized in the Gospel reading which deals with the Second Coming of Christ. The following hymn is from the Matins service:

Have mercy, O Lord, have mercy upon me. I cry to you, when you come with your angels to give to every person due return for his/her deeds.

From the Matins Services of Lent

After the Gospel reading at matins on each Sunday of Lent, we hear the following beautiful hymns beseeching God's mercy:

Open to me the doors of repentance, O Life-Giver... But in your compassion purify me by the loving kindness of your mercy.

When I think of the many evil things I have done, wretch that I am, I tremble at the fearful day of judgment, but trusting in Your loving kindness, like David I cry out to You. Have mercy on me, O God, according to your great mercy.

These hymns are preceded by the reading of Psalm 51 in which David asks God's mercy for his sins and proclaims that God's steadfast love and mercy are greater than the sins of His creatures:

Have mercy on me, O God, according to thy steadfast love. According to Thy abundant mercy, blot out my transgressions. Wash me thoroughly from my iniquity, and cleanse me from my sin (Ps. 51:1-2).

From the Penitential Canon of St. Andrew of Crete

Another place where the call to God for mercy is heard strongly is the penitential canon of St. Andrew of Crete sung during compline. Here are some of the hymns:

I have sinned, Lord, I have sinned against you.
Be merciful to me
though there is no one whose sins I
have not surpassed.

I cry to You, O Lord:
Have mercy, have mercy on me!

When you come with Your angels
to give due reward to each person for his deeds.
I have sinned as no other person before,
I have transgressed more than any other, O Lord.
Before the Day of Judgment comes
be merciful to me, O Lover of Man.
Have mercy on me, O God, have mercy on me!

David once showed us the image of true repentance in a psalm he wrote exposing all that he had done. "Be merciful to me and cleanse me! he wrote, "For against You only have I sinned, the God of our fathers."
Have mercy on me, O God, have mercy on me!
I have distorted Your image, O Savior,
   and broken Your commandments.
The beauty of my soul has been spoiled,
   and its light extinguished by my sins.
But have pity on me and, in David's words,
   "Restore to me the joy of Your salvation."
Have mercy on me, O God, have mercy on me!

Return! Return! Uncover what is hidden!
Say to God who knows all things:
"You are my only Savior and know my terrible secrets.
Yet in David's words I cry to You:
'Be merciful to me, O God, according to Your steadfast
   love.'"
Have mercy on me, O God, have mercy on me!

The gateway to God's mercy is repentance. That is why St. John of Kronstadt said, "Let us hasten to call forth His mercy by repentance and tears."

Kyrie eleison is indeed an effort to call forth God's mercy. It has become one of the most repeated petitions in the liturgy. It is repeated again and again, ten , twenty, thirty, forty, a hundred times.

The Meaning of Kyrie Eleison

St. Symeon of Thessaloniki writes about the *Kyrie Eleison* prayer: "'Have mercy upon us, O God, according to your great mercy, we beseech you...' This expression is appropriate, since we should not ask for anything except for mercy, as we have neither boldness nor access to offer anything as our own... So as sinners and condemned through sin we cannot, nor dare not, say anything to our Loving Master except 'have mercy.'"

The excellent book *Orthodox Worship* describes the meaning of the word mercy as follows:

The word mercy in English is the translation of the Greek word eleos. *This word has the same ultimate root as the old Greek word for oil, or more precisely, olive oil; a substance which was used extensively as a soothing agent for bruises and minor wounds. The oil was poured onto the wound and gently massaged in, thus soothing, comforting and making whole the injured part. The Hebrew word which is also translated as* eleos *and mercy is* hesed, *and means steadfast love. The Greek words for "Lord have mercy", are "Kyrie eleison"—that is to say, "Lord, soothe me, comfort me, take away my pain, show me your steadfast love." Thus the mercy does not refer so much to justice or acquittal—a very Western interpretation—but to the infinite loving-kindness of God, and his compassion for his suffering children! It is in this sense that we pray "Lord, have mercy," with great frequency throughout the Divine Liturgy.**

From the Liturgy

The following prayer from the liturgy reminds us that God's awesomeness, His majesty, and His power are exceeded only by His mercy:

O Lord our God, Whose power is unimaginable and Whose glory is inconceivable, Whose mercy is immeasurable and Whose love for mankind is beyond all words, in Your compassion, Lord, look down on us and on this holy house, and grant us and those who are praying with us the riches of Your mercy and compassion. For to You are due all glory, honor and worship, to the Father and to the Son and to the Holy Spirit, now and ever and unto ages of ages.

---

* "Orthodox Worship." B. Williams and H. Anstall. Light and Life Publ. Co. Mpls, MN. 1990.

From the Scriptures

Think of the people in the gospels who approached Jesus with this simple prayer: *Kyrie eleison*, Lord, have mercy:

- The Canaanite woman whose daughter was tormented by a devil. She persisted in her plea for mercy until her daughter was healed.

- The man whose son was possessed by an evil spirit that threw him into the fire. He came to Jesus with the plea *Kyrie eleison*. The prayer was answered and his son was healed.

- The two blind men sitting by the road outside Jericho who cried out to Jesus, *Kyrie eleison*. That cry was heard by Jesus who healed both of them.

- The ten lepers who came to Jesus pleading mercy. They were healed.

- A final example. Jesus is left alone with the adulteress. Misery is left alone face to face with mercy. And she hears from the mouth of Jesus the words, "Neither do I condemn thee. Go and sin no more." That is God's mercy in action!

In all these instances *Kyrie eleison* was not a prayer that people recited unthinkingly and mechanically, but a cry of sincere faith that came from their hearts, a cry of desperate need and dependence on Jesus. Such a prayer God will not despise.

Not What We Deserve

A precious story pictures a mother pleading with Napoleon to spare her condemned son's life. The emperor called the crime dreadful; justice demanded his life. "Sir," sobbed the mother, "Not justice, but mercy." "He does not deserve mercy," was the answer. "But, sir, if he deserved it, it would not be mercy," said the mother. "Ah yes, how true," said Napoleon. "I will have mercy." And he spared her son.

Mercy! No one deserves it. Everyone needs it.

We dare not stand before the throne of God and ask that we be given what we deserve. Our only cry is, "Lord, be merciful". And the miracle is that there is mercy. At the very heart of the universe beats the heart of God's love.

Not My Rights

C.S. Lewis tells an interesting story in his book *The Great Divorce*. A busload of ghosts is making an excursion from hell to heaven with a view of remaining there permanently. They meet the citizens of heaven and one very big ghost from hell is astonished to find there a man, who on earth, had been tried and executed for murder.

"What I would like to know," he explodes, "is what are you doing here, you a murderer, while I, a pillar of society, a self-respecting decent citizen am forced to walk the streets down there in smoke and fumes and must live in a place like a pigsty." His friend from heaven tries to explain that he has been forgiven, that both he and the man he had murdered have been reunited before the judgment seat of Christ. But the big ghost from hell replies, "I just can't buy that!" "My rights!" he keeps shouting, "I have got to have my rights the same as you!" "Oh no!" his friend from heaven keeps reassuring him, "It's not as bad as all that! You don't want your rights! Why, if I had gotten my rights, I would never be here. You'll not get your rights, you'll get something far better. You will get the mercy of God."

This is why we pray so often in the liturgy: "Lord, have mercy." This prayer, uttered with the least particle of faith, will open the way to God's forgiveness and for the coming of His kingdom in our hearts.

Rely Only On God's Injustice Which is Mercy

St. Isaac the Syrian said once, "Never say that God is just. If He were just, you would be in hell. Rely only on His injustice which is mercy, love and forgiveness."

St. Isaac continues as he contrasts God's justice with His mercy:

How can you call God just when you read the gospel lesson concerning the hiring of the workmen in the vineyard? How can someone call God just when he comes across the story of the prodigal son who frittered away all his belongings in riotous living—yet merely in response to his contrition his father ran and fell on his neck, and gave him authority over all his possessions?

In these passages it is not someone else speaking about God; had that been the case, we might have had doubts about God's goodness. No, it is God's own Son who testifies about him in this way.

Where then is this "justice" in God, seeing that, although we were sinners, Christ died for us? If he is so compassionate in this, we have faith that he will not change.

Have mercy upon me, O God...according to the multitude of thy tender mercies blot out my transgressions.

One person said, "This is what I felt Jesus was saying to me as He looked down from the cross: 'You don't need justice. You need mercy. Here is the mercy you need. It's being poured out for you by the love of God. In spite of your tainted past, God loves you and wants to cleanse you.'"

Let us then with confidence draw near to the throne of grace, that we may receive mercy and find grace to help in time of need (Heb. 4:16).

"Why Should I Let You Into Heaven?"

What if you die suddenly and appear before God? This can happen at any moment since we are but a heartbeat away from Him. And God asks you, "Why should I let you into heaven?" What would you say?

One person replied, "Like the publican I would fall to my knees, beat my breast, and with my eyes cast on the ground, I would plead, 'Lord, be merciful to me, the sinner.'"

Or, I would say with the prodigal son, "Father, I have sinned against heaven and before you; I am no longer worthy to be called your son; treat me as one of your hired servants."

"Even if we reach the summit of virtue, we are saved only by God's mercy," said St. John Chrysostom.

St. Macarius adds:

Never cease being active. But do not hope to achieve much for your own salvation either by your works or by your merits. It is only the mercy of our Lord that saves us.

The Apostle Paul writes,

But God who is rich in mercy, out of the great love with which He loved us, even when we were dead through our trespasses, made us alive together with Christ (by grace you have been saved) and raised us up with Him, and made us sit with him in the heavenly places in Christ Jesus (Eph. 2:4-6).

Be Merciful as God is Merciful

We cannot pray for mercy without being willing to extend mercy to others. That is the point of Jesus' parable about the two debtors (Matt. 18:23-35). Matthew uses a form of the same Greek word *eleison* in presenting Jesus' teaching, "Should you not have had mercy on your fellow servant, as I had mercy on you?" "Blessed are the merciful, for they shall receive mercy," said Jesus.

The mercy we ask for is the mercy we must give to others. Lord, have mercy—and make us merciful.

A dying Christian was asked on his death bed, "Are you going to God now to receive your reward?" "No, no!" he breathed. "I go to receive not my reward but God's mercy."

No Room for Despair

Because of God's mercy there is no room for despair. A Eucharistic prayer says, "I know that neither the magnitude of my faults nor the host of my transgressions surpass the infinite tenderness and immense love of my God for mankind..."

For as the heavens are high above the earth, so great is His steadfast love toward those who fear Him; as far as the east is from the west, so far does He remove our transgressions from us. As a father pities his children, so the Lord pities those who fear him. For he knows our frame; he remembers that we are dust (Ps. 103:11-14).

"Nothing attracts God to us so much as His mercy," said St. John Chrysostom.

The Ultimate Sin

"The mercy of God has no limits, nothing is too great for it. That is the reason why anyone who despairs of it is the author of his own death," said St. John Climacus.

Olivier Clement adds, "The ultimate sin is to despair of God's mercy. That is to limit it, to make our ego its limit, whereas it is boundless."

Never should we despair or fear to come to God even though we sin. For we know that being human, sin we shall but, provided that after each fall, we stumble to our feet again, beg God's mercy and continue our walk with God, God will instantly forgive us and come to meet us.

God's Greatest Attribute

God's greatest attribute is mercy. His true majesty is indeed His mercy. God declares His majestic power chiefly by showing mercy.

If St. Basil is in heaven, it is only because of God's mercy and forgiveness. If St. John Chrysostom is in heaven, it is only because of the mercy and forgiveness of Jesus. If any saint is in heaven, it is only because of the mercy and forgiveness of Jesus. If you and I get to heaven, it will be only because of *metanoia*, repentance, and God's mercy; certainly not by our efforts. "God judges our *metanoia* not by our efforts but by our humility," said St. John Climacus.

Penitential Yet Joyful

Kyrie eleison is a penitential prayer, but it is never to be separated from joyful hope because of our faith in Christ's mercy. For, in Christ sin is the only evil that can always be wiped out with repentance. St. Isaac of Nineveh says, "As a handful of sand in the boundless ocean, so are the sins of the flesh in comparison with God's providence and mercy."

Elder Macarius of Optina said, "No sin can claim victory over God's mercy; repent, and He will accept your repentance, as He did that of a fornicator and a harlot."

"I am the foremost of sinners but I received mercy..." said St. Paul (I Tim. 1:15-16).

The Fathers Speak of God's Mercy

St. Symeon the New Theologian said of God's mercy:

You know, Master, I have never counted on works or deeds for the salvation of my soul. I took refuge in Your mercy, O Lover of mankind, in the assurance that You, All-merciful One, will save me freely and have pity on me, as You, who are God, showed mercy to the adulterous woman and to the prodigal son who said, "I have sinned."

Diadochos of Photike believed that, if at the hour of his death, his confidence in God's mercy is unfaltering, he would pass the frontier, without trouble, by the grace of God and the Precious Blood of Christ the Lamb of God.

Abba Poemen said, "When the time comes for us to stand before God, then what shall we be anxious about?" The brother replied, "Our sins." Poemen replied, "And so let us go into our huts, and there in solitude let us recall our sins in repentance, and the Lord will hear us."

St. Makarios of Egypt said once that his life was like an onion. He kept peeling off layers of skin each day. He called these layers: anger, envy, fear, anguish, anxiety, hate, lust, slothfulness, avarice, judgmentalism, overindulgence—you name it. One by one these layers had to be shed before one could reach the innermost chamber of one's heart. There, in the innermost chamber, one finds a crawling serpent nestled in comfort. The serpent's name is self-love and self-pity. This serpent has invaded and wounded the soul's most vital organ, the heart. The snake cannot be killed, says St. Makarios, it can only be controlled through *ascesis*, watchfulness, prayer, and the Holy Spirit. St. Makarios was so busy shedding the many layers of sin from his life, so busy coping with the snake of self-love and self-pity in his heart that he had no time to focus on the sins of others; all he could say was, "Lord, be merciful to me, the sinner."

Death-Bed Repentance

There was a man once who led an evil life. Yet he boasted that he needed never worry about his soul. When the time came, he could save it with just three words, "Lord, have mercy." He was counting on a deathbed conversion. Yet he never got to say those words. As the horse threw him over the cliff, his last words were, "Well, I'll be damned."

Settle in Advance

Jesus said in Luke 12:58-59,

As you go with your accuser before the magistrate, make an effort to settle with him on the way, lest he drag you to the judge, and the judge hand you over to the officer, and the officer put you in prison. I tell you, you will never get out until you have paid the last penny.

Jesus is saying here that, when you are threatened with a lawsuit, come to an agreement with your adversary before the matter goes to court, for if you do not, you will face imprisonment and a fine. "Every man," Jesus implied, "has a bad case in the presence of God, and if a person is wise, he will make his peace with God while there is yet time."

Only One Plea

Who wants to quarrel with God's way? Would you or I want to appear before Him and His high court and plead for justice: "God be fair with me. Give me what I have coming, no more and no less." We may be audacious enough to ask this of some human court and engage an attorney to see that we do get justice. But not before God. If we are at all honest, we will join the publican who cried, *God, be merciful to me, the sinner!* In the presence of God there is only one plea to make, the plea for mercy.

Someone said, "Grace is getting something you don't deserve. Mercy is not getting something you do deserve."

Lord, grant me your grace which I do not deserve and your mercy that I may escape the hell that I do deserve.

Kyrie eleison, the plea for God's mercy, is one of the cornerstones of Orthodox spirituality according to the Scriptures and the Fathers of the *Philokalia*.

CHAPTER EIGHTEEN

Descend With the Mind Into the Heart

The head seeks God but it is the heart that finds Him. "For man believes in his heart and so is justified ..." writes St. Paul (Rom. 10:10). When the head descends into the heart, the head faith becomes a heart faith. It becomes not just a head faith, or just a heart faith, but a head-in-the-heart faith. Just as love, charity and other important virtues cannot exist only in the mind but are primarily of the heart, so it is with our faith and trust in God. We are not to let Jesus remain in the mind and give Him only a cold intellectual allegiance. He must descend into the heart where we shall be able to see his presence and yield our will to Him.

CHAPTER EIGHTEEN
Descend with the Mind Into the Heart

St. Theophan the Recluse defines prayer:

To pray is to descend with the mind into the heart, and there to stand before the face of the Lord, ever-present, all-seeing, within you.

Elsewhere he writes,

The principal thing is to stand before God with the mind and heart and to go on standing before Him unceasingly night and day.

The Fathers of the *Philokalia* place great emphasis on descending with the mind into the heart when praying. What is this practice? Why is it important? How can it be achieved?

The Mind: A Crowded Rag Market

St. Theophan the Recluse calls the head (mind) "a crowded rag market: it is not possible to pray to God there." He tells us that life is in the heart and that we must descend there with the mind:

I remember your writing to tell me that you get a headache when you try to hold fast your attention. Yes, if you work only with the head, that is what will happen; but when you descend into the heart there will be no strain at all. The head will become empty and there will be an end to thoughts. They are always in the head, chasing one another, and it is not possible to control them. But if you enter the heart, and are able to remain in it, then every time thoughts begin to confuse you, you have only to descend into the heart and the thoughts will flee. It will be a comforting and safe haven. Do not be lazy about descending. In the heart is life, and you must live there. Do not think that this is something to be attempted only by the perfect. No. It is for everyone who has begun to seek the Lord.

Why is it necessary to descend with the mind into the heart?

What is the Heart?

1. God's Spirit dwells in the heart and there it is that the encounter with God must take place. Henri Nouwen wrote about the heart in

the Jewish-Christian tradition:

From the heart arise unknowable impulses as well as conscious feelings, moods, and wishes. The heart, too, has its reasons and is the center of perception and understanding. Finally, the heart is the seat of the will: it makes plans and comes to good decisions. Thus the heart is the central and unifying organ of our personal life. Our heart determines our personality, and is therefore not only the place where God dwells but also the place to which Satan directs his fiercest attacks. It is this heart that is the place of prayer. The prayer of the heart is a prayer that directs itself to God from the center of the person and thus affects the whole of our humanness.[*]

St. Theophan describes the heart as follows:

The heart is to be understood here, not in its ordinary meaning, but in the sense of "inner man". We have within us an inner man, according to the Apostle Paul, or a hidden man of the heart, according to the Apostle Peter. It is the Godlike spirit that was breathed into the first man, and it remains with us continuously, even after the Fall. It shows itself in the fear of God, which is founded on the certainty of God's existence, and in the awareness of our complete dependence on Him, in the stirrings of conscience and in our lack of contentment with all that is material.

According to the biblical understanding of the heart, it is the seat and center of various functions of the Spirit. It is considered as the seat of wisdom and the real center of life. St. Theophan says, "If the heart is at the center of the human person, then it is by the heart that man enters into relation with all that exists."

2. One of the most profound insights accorded us by the Desert Fathers is that to enter the heart is to enter the kingdom of God. The way to God is through the heart. In the words of Isaac of Syria:

Try to enter the treasure chamber...that is within you and then you will discover the treasure chamber of heaven. For they are one and the same. If you succeed in entering one, you will see both. The ladder to this Kingdom is hidden inside you, in your soul. If you wash your soul clean of sin you will see there the rungs of the ladder which you may climb.

It is for this reason that St. Macarios the Great said that, "The

---

[*] "The Way of the Heart." Henri Nouwen. Seabury Press. NY. 1981. p. 77.

chief task of the athlete (the monk) is to enter into his heart."

When prayer descends from the mind into the heart, the two are so united that the prayer becomes truly a *prayer of the heart*. "Always keep your mind collected in your heart," said St. Theophan the Recluse.

"Find the door of your heart and you will find the door to the Kingdom of Heaven," wrote St. John Chrysostom.

The Heart is Christ's Palace

In his *Homilies* St. Macarios develops the idea of the heart as the center of life when he writes:

The heart governs and reigns over the whole bodily organism; and when grace possesses the ranges of the heart, it rules over all the members and the thoughts. For there, in the heart, is the mind, and all the thoughts of the soul and its expectation; and in this way grace penetrates also to all the members of the body... Within the heart are unfathomable depths. There are reception rooms and bedchambers in it, doors and porches, and many offices and passages. In it is the workshop of righteousness and of wickedness. In it is death; in it is life.... The heart is Christ's palace; there Christ the King comes to take His rest, with the angels and the spirits of the saints, and He dwells there, walking within it and placing His Kingdom there.

The heart is but a small vessel: and yet dragons and lions are there, and there poisonous creatures and all the treasures of wickedness; rough, uneven paths are there, and gaping chasms. There likewise is God, there are angels, there life and the Kingdom, there light and the apostles, the heavenly cities and the treasures of grace: all things are there.

To descend into the heart, some ascetics say, is to climb Mt. Sinai where God revealed Himself to Moses.

This descent into inner space (the heart) is a profound mystery. For, as we descend into the depths of our being, we begin to ascend to the heights of heaven. We descend in order to ascend.

A Personal Encounter with God

Bishop Kallistos Ware describes what happens when the one who prays descends with the mind into the heart: "It is now possible to understand, in some small measure, what Theophan means when he describes prayer as 'standing before God with the mind in the heart.' So long as the ascetic prays with the mind in the head, he will still be working solely with the resources of the human intellect, and on this level he will never attain to an immediate and personal encounter with God. By the use of his brain, he will at best know *about* God, but he will not *know* God. For there can be no direct knowledge of God without an exceedingly great love, and such love must come, not from the brain alone, but from the whole man—that is, from the heart. It is necessary, then, for the ascetic to descend from the head into the heart. He is not required to abandon his intellectual powers—the reason, too, is a gift of God—but he is called to descend with the mind into his heart.

"Into the heart, then, he descends—into his natural heart first, and from there into the 'deep' heart—into that 'inner closet' of the heart which is no longer of the flesh. Here, in the depths of the heart, he discovers first the 'godlike spirit' which the Holy Trinity implanted in man at creation, and with this spirit he comes to know the Spirit of God, who dwells within every Christian from the moment of baptism, even though most of us are unaware of His presence. From one point of view the whole aim of the ascetic and mystical life is the rediscovery of the grace of baptism. The man who would advance along the path of inner prayer must in this way 'return into himself', finding the kingdom of heaven that is within, and so passing across the mysterious frontier between the created and the uncreated."[*]

Enter Your Closet

St. Dimitri of Rostov considers praying with the mind in the heart a fulfillment of Christ's command to "enter the closet" when we pray:

The mind in the heart stands consciously before the face of God, filled with due reverence, and begins to pour itself out before Him... The essence or the soul of prayer is within a man's mind and heart... The Savior commanded us to enter into our closet and there pray to God the Father in secret. This closet is the heart.

St. Theophan explains how we must pray when we descend with the mind into the heart:

---

[*] "The Art of Prayer." Chariton. Faber and Faber. London. 1966. p. 20-21.

You must pray not only with words but with the mind, and not only with the mind but with the heart, so that the mind understands and sees clearly what is said in words, and the heart feels what the mind is thinking. All these combined together constitute real prayer, and if any of them are absent your prayer is either not perfect, or is not prayer at all.

Bishop Ignatii teaches that descending with the mind into the heart helps us grow in discernment:

You wish to grow wise in discernment of thoughts? Descend from the head into the heart. Then you will see all thoughts clearly, as they move before the eye of your sharp-sighted mind. But until you descend into the heart, do not expect to have due discrimination of thoughts.

How are the Mind and the Heart United?

St. Theophan explains how the mind and the heart can be united through the Jesus Prayer:

All your inner disorder is due to the dislocation of your powers, the mind and the heart each going their own way. You must unite the mind with the heart: then the tumult of your thoughts will cease, and you will acquire a rudder to guide the ship of your soul, a lever with which to put all your inner world in movement. How can this union be achieved? Make it your habit to pray these words with the mind in the heart: "Lord Jesus Christ, Son of God, have mercy upon me." And this prayer, when you have learnt to use it properly, or rather, when it becomes grafted to the heart, will lead you to the end which you desire: it will unite your mind with your heart, it will quell the turbulence of your thoughts, and it will give you power to govern the movements of your soul.

Collect your Mind

The Fathers of the *Philokalia* explain how we may descend with the mind into the heart:

Collect your mind, lead the mind into the path of the breath along which the air enters in, constrain it to enter the heart...and keep it there listening to your natural breathing of the heart, while saying the Jesus Prayer.

We Bow in Perpetual Adoration

We descend with the mind in the heart and there we bow in perpetual adoration and worship before God. The union of the mind with the heart unites the spiritual thoughts of the mind with the spiritual feelings of the heart so that the complete person stands before God. "The principle thing is to stand with the mind in the heart before God, and to go on standing before Him unceasingly day and night, until the end of life" (St. Theophan). Many monks, for example, pray with the head bent, almost touching the heart to express physically what is going on spiritually: they are descending with the mind into the heart.

A-Head-in-the-Heart Faith

The head seeks God but it is the heart that finds Him. "For man believes in his heart and so is justified..." writes St. Paul (Rom. 10:10). When the head descends into the heart, the *head* faith becomes a *heart* faith. It becomes not just a *head* faith or just a *heart* faith, but a *head-in-the-heart* faith. Just as love, charity and the other important virtues cannot exist only in the mind but are primarily of the heart, so it is with our faith and trust in God. We are not to let Jesus remain in the mind and give Him only a cold intellectual allegiance. He must descend into the heart where we shall be able to feel his presence and yield our will to Him.

St. John Chrysostom says that God hears our prayers more loudly when we are praying with the mind in the heart.

A Union of Mind and Heart

The over-intellectual scholars in Constantinople criticized St. Gregory Palamas and his way of prayer. Faith to them was only a matter of the mind not of the heart. For Gregory Palamas it was both. And the Church supported his view.

"You must descend with your mind into your heart," Theophan insists. "At present your thoughts of God are in your head. And God himself is, as it were, outside you, and so your prayer and other spiritual exercises remain exterior. Whilst you are still in your head, thoughts will...always be whirling about like snow in winter, or clouds of mosquitoes in the summer... All our inner disorder is due to the dislocation of our powers, the mind and the heart each going its own way. The mind must come to an initial concord with the heart, growing eventually into a union of the mind with the heart."

Thus it is that the Fathers of the *Philokalia* invite us through prayer to dive into the fathomless depths of the heart, the Lord's reception room, there to discover the kingdom of God.

CHAPTER NINETEEN

The Inner Closet

Man needs to enclose himself in the inner closet of his heart more often than he need go to church: collecting all his thoughts there, he must place his mind before God, praying to Him in secret with all warmth of spirit and with living faith.

– St. Dimitri of Rostov

CHAPTER NINETEEN
The Inner Closet

Jesus said, "The Kingdom of God is within you." Masters of the inner life, the Fathers of the *Philokalia* seized upon these words to remind us that God is to be found in the "inner closet" of the heart. Even though we may be unaware of it, the Spirit of God dwells within us from the moment of baptism. The whole purpose of the spiritual life is to rediscover the grace of baptism or the Holy Spirit within us. This is done through inner prayer as we descend into the heart with the mind to discover there the kingdom of God.

St. Makarios of Egypt

St. Makarios of Egypt writes,

The heart is a small vessel, but all things are contained in it; God is there, the angels are there, and there also is life and kingdom, the heavenly cities and the treasures of grace.

St. Dimitri of Rostov

Commenting on these words, St. Dimitri of Rostov says,

Man needs to enclose himself in the inner closet of his heart more often than he need go to church: and collecting all his thoughts there, he must place his mind before God, praying to Him in secret with all warmth of spirit and with living faith.

The heart is the bridal chamber where we are to meet our Lord and Savior, the Bridegroom of our soul.

Where else but in our heart shall we find the Garden of Eden where Adam walked with God?

Man's heart is a chapel where continuous prayer can be offered to God. This is part of the image of God in us. This is why St. Paul calls us "temples of the Holy Spirit."

The Lord's Reception Room

Theophan the Recluse says,

You seek the Lord? Seek, but only within yourself. He is not far from anyone. The Lord is near all those who truly call on Him. Find a place in your heart and speak there with the Lord. It (the heart) is the Lord's reception room. Everyone who meets the Lord, meets Him there. He has fixed no other place for meeting souls.

Strive to enter within your inner chamber and you will see the chamber of heaven. For the two are the same and one entrance leads to both.

In Orthodox spirituality the monk is asked to become conscious of the actual presence of Jesus in the interior of his being without any images. The Presence is there through the life of God received in prayer and the Sacraments.

Nicephoras says,

The kingdom of God is within us, and for a man who has seen it within, and having found it through true prayer...everything outside loses its attraction.

The Light of Mt. Tabor is Within

Fr. John Meyendorff explains how the kingdom becomes a reality in us:

Since the Incarnation, our bodies have become "temples of the Holy Spirit within us" (I Cor. 6:19); it is there, within our own bodies, that we must seek the Spirit, within our bodies sanctified by the sacraments and engrafted by the Eucharist into the Body of Christ. God is now to be found within. He is no longer exterior to us. Therefore, we find the light of Mt. Tabor within ourselves.*

St. Isaac the Syrian

St. Isaac the Syrian wrote,

Enter eagerly into the treasure-house (the heart) that lies within you, and so you will see the treasure-house of heaven... The ladder that leads to the Kingdom is HIDDEN WITHIN YOU, AND IS FOUND IN YOUR SOUL. DIVE INTO YOURSELF, and in your soul you will discover the rungs by which you are to ascend.

St. Augustine

Where can we find Him? Not on earth, for he is not here. And not in heaven, for we are not there. But in our own hearts we can find him.

---

* "St. Gregory Palamas and Orthodox Spirituality." John Meyendorf. SVS Press. Crestwood, NY. p. 113.

He ascended to heaven openly so that He could come back to us inwardly, and never leave us again.

St. Ephraim

The kingdom of God is within you. In so far as the Son of God dwells in you, the Kingdom of Heaven lies within you, also. Here within are the riches of heaven, if you desire them. Here, O sinner, is the Kingdom of God within you. Enter into yourself, seek more eagerly and you will find without great travail. Outside you is death, and the door to death is sin. ENTER WITHIN YOURSELF AND REMAIN IN YOUR HEART, FOR THERE IS GOD.

John Karpathios

It takes great effort and struggle in prayer to reach the state of mind which is free from all disturbance; it is heaven within the heart, the place, as the Apostle Paul assures us "where Christ dwells in us" (II Cor. 13:5).

Thus, the purpose of descending with the mind into the heart is to be completely present to the Lord as we enter His reception room in the inner closet of the heart.

CHAPTER TWENTY

The Inner Flame

In anyone pours out water or dirt upon the light of a lamp, it goes out, and this also happens if they simply pour all of the oil out of it—in the same manner the gift of grace is extinguished. If you have filled your mind with earthly things, if you have given yourself up to the cares of daily business, you have already quenched the Spirit. The flame goes out when there is not enough oil, that is, when we do not show charity. The Spirit came to you by God's mercy; and so if it does not find corresponding fruits of mercy in you, it will flee away from you. For the Spirit does not make its indwelling in the unmerciful soul.

– St. John Chrysostom

CHAPTER TWENTY

The Inner Flame

The Fathers of the *Philokalia* speak much of an "inner flame" that burns in the heart.

St. Theophan the Recluse writes,

Learn to perform everything you do in such a way that it warms the heart instead of cooling it. Whether reading or praying, working or talking with others, you should hold fast to this one aim—not to let your heart grow cool. Keep your inner stove always hot by reciting a short prayer, and watch over your feelings in case they dissipate this warmth.

What is the flame that keeps the "inner stove" hot?

It is the Holy Spirit whom we receive at baptism. Like a fire He burns within us. Depending on how much fuel we provide, the fire can be as faint as a tiny matchstick or as huge as a bonfire. It can even go out if it is not tended. St. Nicodemos urges us to rescue the spark that remains in the embers since baptism; to fan it into a flame through prayer, inner attention, and askesis.

St. Dimitri of Rostov

St. Dimitri of Rostov describes how we can fan the inner spark into a flame:

To kindle in his heart such a divine love, to unite with God in an inseparable union of love, it is necessary for a man to pray often, raising the mind to Him. For as a flame increases when it is constantly fed, so prayer, made often, with the mind dwelling ever more deeply in God, arouses divine love in the heart. And the heart, set on fire, will warm all the inner man, will enlighten and teach him, revealing to him all its unknown and hidden wisdom, and making him like a flaming seraph, always standing before God within his spirit, always looking at Him within his mind, and drawing from this vision the sweetness of spiritual joy.

St. Theophan

St. Theophan agrees that the inner flame burning within us is the Holy Spirit Whom we received at baptism:

We all received grace in Baptism and Chrismation. Therefore we should burn in our spirit, which is animated by the grace of the Holy Spirit. Why is it, then, that we do not burn in the spirit? Because we are occupied largely or even exclusively with our own personal affairs, with worldly business and public life, so that the spirit, although it still makes itself felt, is choked. In order to kindle the spirit, we must be aware of the unsatisfactory direction of our activities, especially their orientation towards earthly and worldly things; and we must enter deeply into the contemplation of what is divine, holy, heavenly, eternal. The most important thing is to begin to act in a manner that is truly spiritual. And then the spirit will start to burn: for as a result of all this, the gift of grace which lives within us will begin to grow in warmth.

How to Keep the Inner Flame Alive

How is the inner flame kept alive?

St. Theophan explains,

Cast aside everything that might extinguish this small flame which is beginning to burn within you, and surround yourself with that which can feed and fan it into a strong fire. Isolate yourself, pray... Your solitude must become more collected, your prayer deeper, and your meditation more forceful.

According to the Fathers of the *Philokalia* silence (*hesychia*) is important because it guards the inner flame which is the life of the Holy Spirit within us. *Hesychia* is the discipline by which the inner fire of God is fanned and the small spark grows into a flame.

What Quenches the Flame

St. John Chrysostom tells us that what quenches the flame of the Spirit within us is an impure life:

If anyone pours out water or dirt upon the light of a lamp, it goes out, and this also happens if they simply pour all of the oil out of it— in the same manner the gift of grace is extinguished. If you have filled your mind with earthly things, if you have given yourself up to the cares of daily business, you have already quenched the Spirit. The flame goes out when there is not enough oil, that is, when we do not show charity. The Spirit came to you by God's mercy; and so if it does not find corresponding fruits of mercy in you, it will flee away from you. For the Spirit does not make its indwelling in the unmerciful soul.

What the Inner Flame Produces

St. Theophan describes what happens to us when the inner flame is kept burning within us:

According to St. Barsanouphrios, when we receive in our heart the fire which the Lord came to send on earth (Luke 12:49), all our human faculties begin to burn within. When by long friction fire is ignited and logs begin to burn with it, the logs thus kindled will crackle and smoke until they are properly alight. But when they are properly alight they appear to be permeated with fire, and produce a pleasing light and warmth without smoke and crackling. So it happens within men. They receive the fire and begin to burn—and how much smoke and crackling there is only those who have experienced it can know. But when the fire is properly alight the smoke and crackling cease, and within reigns only light. This condition is a state of purity; the way to it is long, but the Lord is most merciful and all powerful. Thus it is clear that when a man has received the fire of conscious communion with God, what lies before him is not peace but great labor. But from this point onwards he will find the labor sweet and full of fruit, whereas before the work was bitter and bore little fruit or none.

The Ceaseless Burning Within

St. Theophan continues as he describes a ceaseless burning within:

As soon as this warmth is kindled, your thoughts will settle, the inner atmosphere will become clear, the first emergence of both good and bad movements in the soul will become plainly apparent to you, and you will acquire power to drive away the bad. This inner light also extends to outside things and makes clear the distinction between right and wrong, giving you the strength to establish yourself in what is right, despite any kind of obstacles. In a word, you now begin true, active spiritual life, for which hitherto you were still searching; and if it appeared, it appeared in you only fitfully...

The Lord will come to shed His light on your understanding, to purify your emotions, to guide your actions. You will feel in yourself forces which until now were unknown to you. This light will come: not apparent to the sight and senses, but arriving invisibly and spiritually—yet none the less effectively. The symptom of its advent is the engendering at this point of a constant burning of the heart: as the mind stands in the heart, this ceaseless burning of the heart infuses it with the remembrance of God, so that you acquire the power to dwell inwardly, and consequently all your inner potentialities are realized. You accept all that is pleasing to God, while all that is sinful you reject. All your actions are conducted with a precise awareness of God's will regarding them; strength is given you to govern the whole course of your life, both within and without, and you acquire mastery over yourself.

Our purpose in life, that is, life according to the Fathers of the *Philokalia,* is to keep tending the inner flame of the Holy Spirit which burns before the image (icon) of God in the chapel of our heart. Whenever we feel that the warmth is fading, we need to make an effort to re-kindle it through prayer, inner attention, repentance, *ascesis, hesychia*, Scripture reading, the Eucharist, almsgiving, acts of charity, etc.

Reading or listening to the word of God can often touch the heart and set it on fire. When that happens we must pause and let the fire spread by meditating on what we heard or read. Origen says,

When a saying of the Lord's kindles the imagination of a hearer of the Word and makes him enamored of the Wisdom that bursts into flames at the sight of any beauty, then "the fire of the Lord is come down upon him."

There is a story from the Desert Fathers that illustrates what can happen to us if, instead of quenching the Spirit, we keep fanning it into a flame:

Abba Lot went to see Abba Joseph and said to him, "Abba, as far as I can, I say my little office, I fast a little, I pray and meditate, I live in peace and as far as I can, I purify my thoughts. What else can I do?" Then the old man stood up and stretched his hands toward

heaven. His fingers became like ten lamps of fire and he said to him, "If you will, you can become all flame."

We, too, can become "all flame" shining as lights for Jesus in a sin-darkened world, offering warmth and light to those who have lost their way.

CHAPTER TWENTY-ONE

The Fathers of the Philokalia and the Bible

As when God became man in Bethlehem the eternal Word became flesh, so in the Bible the glory of God veils itself in the fleshly garment of human thought and human language.

– St. John Chrysostom

CHAPTER TWENTY-ONE

The Fathers of the Philokalia and the Bible

What did the Fathers of the *Philokalia* think of the Bible? Did they encourage its reading? Was it part of their *askesis*, their daily Christian discipline?

The answers to these questions will truly inspire us. Perhaps no other group of Christians has emphasized the importance of reading the Scriptures more than the Fathers of the *Philokalia*. In fact, it has been said that most of the writings of these Fathers are mere commentaries on the Bible.

A great many of the spiritual counsels of the Fathers of the *Philokalia* are accompanied by Scripture verses. Here is an example:

If God sees that the intellect flees towards Him (with unceasing prayer) with all its strength and does not have any other help except Him then He strengthens the intellect saying: "Fear not, my child Jacob, the least of Israel" and again "fear not, for I have redeemed you; I have called you by name, you are mine. When you pass through the waters I will be with you; and through the rivers, they shall not overwhelm you; when you walk through fire you shall not be burned and the flame shall not consume you. For I am the Lord your God, the Holy One of Israel, your Savior" (Isa.: 41:13-14, 43:1-3) (*Philokalia* Vol. 1)

St. John Chrysostom says, *The reading of the Holy Scriptures is like the opening of heaven.*

St. John Damascene:

To search the Scriptures is a work most fair and profitable for souls. For just as the tree planted by the channels of waters, so also the soul watered by the Scriptures is enriched and gives fruit in its season....

St. Isaac the Syrian:

Constant meditation upon the holy Scriptures will perpetually fill the soul with incomprehensible ecstasy and joy in God.

St. Basil the Great:

The voice of the Gospels is much more magnificent than the other teachings of the Holy Spirit. In the other teachings God spoke to us through his servants the prophets, but in the Gospels he spoke to us personally through his Son and our Lord...Read the Scriptures for your own sake, for you will find there the remedy for every one of your ailments.

St. John Chrysostom:

Insatiable is the sweetness of spiritual thoughts. Just as the earth that is not watered cannot bring forth wheat even though it may hold within itself thousands of seeds, so also the soul cannot show forth any spiritual fruit unless it is first enlightened by the Holy Scriptures. Again, as wine when drunk helps to put an end to our sorrow and brings gladness to the heart, so also the spiritual wine brings joy to the soul.

St. Nicodemos of the Holy Mountain:

From the meadow of Holy Scripture you can select, like a bee, the flowers of all the virtues. From Abraham we select the virtue of faith and the virtue of hospitality and assistance to strangers; from Job we receive the virtue of courage and patience; from Joseph we receive prudence; from Moses and David, meekness and the absence of malice; from the Evangelists we receive our faith in Christ; from St. John we receive theology; from St. Peter the confession; from St. Paul the fervent zeal, and so forth. In general, we receive from Scripture and learn all the traditions and teachings of all the virtuous deeds and promises and warnings all of which help to make mature and perfect the person who believes in Christ, as St. Paul wrote: "All scripture is inspired by God and profitable for teaching, for reproof, for correction, and for training in righteousness, that the man of God may be complete, equipped for every good work" (II Tim. 3:16).

St. Isaac of Nineveh:

Nevertheless the fountainhead for all these things is the reading of Scripture: from it comes the mind's beauty. All these things are born out of the reading of Scripture: even pure prayer itself is born from such reading.

St. John Chrysostom likens the Bible to entering a garden to admire and pick a variety of flowers. He also speaks of reading the

Bible as entering a perfume shop, attracted by the aromatic scents, and leaving the shop with an ethereal fragrance.

Upon selling his treasured copy of the gospels, a monk in fourth-century Egypt said, "I have sold the book that told me to sell all that I have and give to the poor."

St. Nicodemos of the Holy Mountain:

A source of spiritual delight is the word of God contained in Holy Scripture because there is to be found ultimate truth that enlightens the mind, which, being mind, has truth as its object. Moreover, there is ultimate sweetness and grace in the words of Scripture, which draw like a great magnet the hearts of the readers to agree with them and to be convinced. This is only natural. After all, the words of Scripture are the words of God and of the Holy Spirit. This is to say that they are the words of truth itself and grace itself.

Martyrius (6th century):

It is from the Scriptures that we learn how to travel on the road of virtuous conduct, for in them all the fine deeds of the just life are delineated. Just as one cannot see anything without light, for it is light that enables us to see, as it is written "By your light we see light," similarly, without the light of the Scriptures we are unable to see God, who is Light, or his justice, which is filled with light.

St. John Chrysostom:

As when God became man in Bethlehem the eternal Word became flesh, so in the Bible the glory of God veils itself in the fleshly garment of human thought and human language.

Abba John:

The nature of water is soft, that of stone is hard; but if a bottle is hung above the stone, allowing the water to fall drop by drop, it wears away the stone. So it is with the word of God; it is soft and our heart is hard, but the man who hears the word of God often, opens his heart to the fear of God.

Evagrius, a Desert Father:

May the sun, on rising, find you with a Bible in your hand.

St. John Chrysostom:

What on earth are you saying? It's "not your business to read the Bible" because you've got too many other things to bother about? But that's the very reason why you need to read the Bible! The more wor-

ries you have, the more you need the Bible to keep you going! People like monks and nuns who have left the troubles of the world behind are quite safe; they are like ships sailing on a calm sea, or moored in a quiet harbor. But you are in the middle of this godless world's stormy sea, and so you need spiritual help and sustenance far more urgently. They live far from the battlefield, out of the sound of gunfire; but you are in the front line, face to face with the enemy, and you are bound to suffer frequent blows and be severely wounded. So you need the medicine-chest close at hand.

St. Clement of Alexandria:

For those who have chosen to major in holiness, there is special training in the Word.

St. Ambrose of Optino:

Read a chapter of the Gospel every day and when anxiety seizes you, read again until it passes away. If it returns, read the Gospel once more.

St. Jerome:

One should rise two or three times a night to go over parts of the Scripture that one knows by heart.

St. Ephrem the Syrian:

I read the opening verses of the book, and was full of joy, for its verses and lines spread out their arms to welcome me, the first rushed out and kissed me, and led me onto the next.

St. John Chrysostom:

Your wife irritates you, you worry about your children, your enemies are waiting to catch you, someone you thought was your friend is jealous of you, your neighbor spreads rumors about you or picks quarrels with you, your colleague acts behind your back, someone sues you, you suffer from poverty, you lose your nearest and dearest, success gives you a boost and then trouble brings you down to the depths again... Where can you find a suit of armor, or a castle from which to defend yourself? Where can you find ointment for your wounds, but in the Bible?...

John the Solitary:

Toil at reading the Scriptures more than anything else: for in prayer the mind frequently wanders, but in reading even a wandering mind is recollected.

St. John Chrysostom:

Haven't you noticed how a smith, mason or carpenter, or any other craftsman, however much his back is against the wall, will never sell or pawn the tools of his trade? If he did, how could he earn his living? That is how we should think of the Bible, just as mallets, hammers, saws, chisels, axes, and hatchets are the tools of the craftsman's trade, so the books of the prophets and the apostles, and all scripture inspired by the Holy Spirit, are the tools of our salvation.

St. Athanasius:

In the words of Scripture the Lord is found, whose presence the demons cannot stand.

St. Isaac:

The constant meditation on the Word is the light of the soul.

Origen:

In truth, before Jesus, Scripture was like water, but since Jesus it has become for us the wine into which Jesus changed the water.

St. John Chrysostom:

The Scriptures were not given merely that we might have them in books, but that we might engrave them on our hearts.

St. Gregory the Theologian:

The Bible is like a river, shallow and deep, in which a lamb can cross, but in which an elephant can swim.

The "In Trullo" Council (692 A.D.) urges priests to lead their flocks into a greater intimacy with the Bible. They emphasize that especially children must be helped to develop the habit of reading the Scriptures daily.

They "Ate" the Word of God

Since the reading of Scripture provides spiritual food, many Church Fathers speak of "eating" Scripture. St. Jerome wrote, "We eat the flesh and drink the blood of the Divine Savior in the Holy Eucharist, but so do we in the reading of the Scriptures." The Desert Fathers were saturated with Scripture. It was their food. They lived by it. St. Seraphim of Sarov read the entire New Testament once a week. The ascetics memorized the psalms and other parts of Scripture which they quoted from memory, repeating them "from the heart" with deep and simple concentration. Paul Evdokimov writes, "While reading

Scripture, the Fathers read not words, but the living Christ, and Christ spoke to them. They consumed words in the manner of the Eucharistic bread and wine, and the word appeared to them in its Christ dimension."

The Fathers of the *Philokalia* preserved the seed of the word of God as the verbal icon of Christ not just in their memory, but, above all, in their living and burning hearts from which it sprouted and brought forth rich fruit.

How to Read the Bible

The Fathers of the *Philokalia* have much to say about how we should read the Scriptures:

St. Nicodemos of the Holy Mountain:

When you read the Scriptures, do not have in mind to read page after page, but ponder over each word. When some words make you go deep into yourself, or stir you to contrition, or fill your heart with spiritual joy and love, pause on them. It means that God draws near to you.

St. Irenaeus:

Read the Scriptures with the presbyters of the Church, for they, as we have shown, have the teaching of the apostles.

Philemon:

Without interruption, whether asleep or awake, eating, drinking, or in company, let your heart be inwardly and mentally meditating on the Psalms, at other times be repeating the prayer, "Lord Jesus Christ, Son of God, have mercy on me."

St. Mark the Monk:

He who is humble in his thoughts and engaged in spiritual work, when he reads the holy Scriptures, will apply everything to himself and not to his neighbor.

St. John Chrysostom:

Let each one of you, on some day of the week, even on the Sabbath itself, take in your hands the selection of the Gospels that is going to be read to you [at our next meeting].

Read it frequently as you sit at home in the time intervening, and often ponder with care the thoughts stored up in it and examine them well.

Note what is clear and what obscure, and which thoughts seem to be contradictory, though they really are not.

And when you have finally sampled all of it, thus prepared come to the sermon.

Reading the Bible Along With The Holy Fathers

St. Ignatii Brianchaninov:

You ask: Why is it necessary to read the Holy Fathers? Is it not enough to be guided by the Holy Scriptures as the pure Word of God, without any admixture of human words? And I reply: Reading the Holy Writ, one also has to read the Holy Fathers of the Eastern Church. St. Peter says this concerning Scripture: "No prophecy of the scripture is of any private interpretation. For the prophecy came not in old time by the will of man: but holy men of God spake as they were moved by the Holy Ghost" (II Peter 1:20,21). So how do you wish to interpret arbitrarily the spiritual words which were uttered not from one's own will, but as prompted by the Spirit and which, as such, prohibit any arbitrary interpretation. It is the Spirit who uttered the Scripture, and it is he alone who can interpret it. It was committed to paper by men inspired by God, the prophets and the apostles; and men inspired by God, the Holy Fathers, have interpreted it. Therefore, everyone who wished to have the true understanding of the Holy Scriptures must also read the Holy Fathers. For should you confine yourselves to reading the Scripture alone, you will try to understand and interpret it arbitrarily. And misconceptions will be unavoidable, because "the natural man receiveth not the things of the Spirit of God... neither can he know them, because they are spiritually discerned. Even so the things of God knoweth no man, but the Spirit of God" (I Cor. 2:14,11)... The Universal Church...has always had particular respect for the patristic writings, for they preserved the common Church tradition which had to have a commonly accepted, true and grace-giving interpretation of the Scriptures...

Praying Before Reading Scripture

The Fathers of the *Philokalia* emphasize the importance of praying before reading Scripture.

St. Isaac of Nineveh:

Do not approach the words of the mysteries contained in the Scriptures without prayer and without asking for God's help. Say, "Lord, grant that I may receive an awareness of the power that is within them." Consider prayer to be the key to the understanding of truth in Scripture.

The importance of praying before reading the Scripture is built into the liturgy itself. Fr. Alexander Schmemann wrote:

The celebrant reads the prayer before the gospel, in which he asks God to send down the "pure light of Thy divine knowledge. Open the eyes of our mind to the understanding of Thy gospel teachings." This prayer, which is now read silently, occupies the same place in the sacrament of the word that the epiklesis, the supplication for the Father to send down his Holy Spirit, occupies in the eucharistic prayer. Like the consecration of the gifts, understanding and acceptance of the word depend not on us, not only on our desire, but above all on the sacramental transformation of the "eyes of our mind," on the coming to us of the Holy Spirit. The blessing that the priest bestows on the deacon as he is about to read the gospel testifies to this: "May God...enable you to proclaim the glad tidings with great power, to the fulfillment of the gospel..."*

The Power of the Word

The Fathers of the *Philokalia* believed that great power resided in the Word of God. Augustine, for example, was converted through the reading of God's word in Rom. 13:13-14. He already knew of the conversion of Anthony of Egypt who was converted through the hearing of God's Word. In fact he wrote about it in his *Confessions*:

I had heard the story of Anthony and I remembered how he happened to go into a church while the Gospel was being read and taken it as a counsel addressed to himself when he heard the words, "Go, sell all that belongs to you and give to the poor...and come, follow me."

Augustine describes his own conversion through the power of God's word as follows:

So I rose and, throwing myself down under a certain fig tree, wept bitterly in contrition of heart. Suddenly I heard from a neighbor-

---

* "The Eucharist." Alexander Schmemann. SVS Press. Crestwood, NY. 1987. p. 76.

ing house the voice of a child, singing over and over again, "Take up and read, take up and read."

Checking my weeping I got up and went back to where I had been sitting, and had laid down the volume of the apostle, and read the first passage which met my eyes: "Not in rioting and drunkenness, not in impurity and wantonness, not in strife and envy; but put on the Lord Jesus Christ, and make no provision for the flesh, to fulfill its lusts."

I needed to read no further, for suddenly, as it were by a light infused into my heart, all darkness vanished away.

Tomas Spidlik describes how the Fathers of the *Philokalia* had devised ways of using the power of the word of God to resist evil:

The outstanding method against evil thought is called antirrhesis ("counter-speaking"). When tempted by the devil, Christ replied to his suggestions with texts from Scripture, and did not enter into discussion with the Evil One (Mt. 4:3-11). We read about certain ascetics that they knew "the entire Scriptures" by heart, that is, they were able to answer every question put to them with sacred texts, but, more than that, they knew a good quotation from Scripture against each demonic suggestion. The classical manual of this art is the Antirrheticus of Evagrius, divided into eight chapters according to the number of the eight vices. He cited scriptural texts pertinent to each thought, texts which help drive it away (taken from Genesis to the Book of Revelation, there are 487 altogether.)[*]

St. Ephrem says that it was the power of the word of God through the Holy Spirit that impregnated Mary:

The Theotokos was impregnated through her ear. She heard the Word of God and received it into her heart which became a womb.

"The desert fathers were convinced that the words of Scripture possessed the power to deliver them from evil," writes Douglas Burton-Christie, a scholar of early monasticism. "They believed that the Word of God has the power to effect what it says."

Abba Serapion

This truth is illustrated in the story about Abba Serapion and a prostitute. In the story, we hear that Serapion encountered a prostitute as he was passing through a village and told the woman, "Expect me this evening for I should like to come and spend the night with you."

---

[*] "The Spirituality of the Christian East." T. Spidlik. Cistercian Publ. Kalamazoo, MI. 1986. p. 243.

The prostitute, not wanting to bypass an opportunity, agreed to meet him and returned to her dwelling to prepare the bed. Upon arriving, Serapion asked her if the bed was ready, and being told that everything had been prepared, said to her that he must first fulfill his "rule of prayer." He then "took out the Psalter, and at each psalm he said a prayer for the prostitute, begging God that she might be converted and saved, and God heard him. The woman stood trembling and praying beside the old man. When he had completed the whole Psalter, the woman fell to the ground. Then the old man, beginning the Epistle, read a great deal from the apostle and completed his prayers. The woman was filled with compunction...." The power of the sacred texts to bring about conversion is clear from this story. Serapion made no attempt to say any words of his own to the woman. Rather, he recited the Psalter and the Epistles and let them do their own work. He "helped the word event to happen," which in this case meant enabling the words to pierce the woman's heart and initiate the process of transformation.[1]

Our Response to God's Word

Fr. George Florovsky writes of the response God expects of us as we read His Word:

We hear in Scripture also the voice of man, answering God in words of prayer or of thanksgiving or of praise. It is sufficient to mention the Psalms in this connection. And God desires, expects, and requires this response. God desires that man not only listens to his words but that man also responds to them. God wants to involve man in "conversation."[2]

This response on our part to the Word of God is greatly encouraged by the Fathers of the *Philokalia*. It is described by Bishop Kallistos Ware:

The real purpose of Bible study is...to feed our love for Christ, to kindle our hearts into prayer, and to provide us with guidance in our personal life. The study of words should give place to an immediate dialogue with the living Word himself. "Whenever you read the Gospel," says St. Tikhon of Zadonsk, "Christ himself is speaking to you. And while you read, you are praying and talking with him."

In this way Orthodox are encouraged to practice a slow and

---

[1] "The Word in the Desert." Douglas Burton-Christie. Oxford University Press. NY. 1993. p. 192.
[2] "Creation and Redemption." G. Florovsky. Nordland Publ. Co. 1986. p. 22.

attentive reading of the Bible, in which our study leads us directly into prayer.*

From "The Way of the Pilgrim"

In *The Way of a Pilgrim*, the spiritual classic that grew out of the great influence that the *Philokalia* exerted in Russia, we see again the importance and the power of God's Word.

The penniless pilgrim who seeks the secret of a deeper and more continuous life of prayer describes his worldly goods as "a knapsack with some dried bread in it on my back, and in my breastpocket a Bible. And that is all." The Bible was indispensable.

This same holy pilgrim meets up with a military officer whose life is almost completely destroyed by alcohol. He is given a Bible and told to read a chapter without delay as soon as he felt a longing for wine. He kept reading the Bible until his incurable habit completely disappeared. At the end he tells the pilgrim, "Since the time when I was cured of drunkenness, I have lived under a vow to read the Gospels every day of my life. I let nothing whatever hinder me."

An Effective Remedy for Sin

St. John Chrysostom recommends God's Word as an effective remedy for sin:

We must thoroughly quench the darts of the devil and beat them off by continual reading of the divine Scriptures. For it is not possible for anyone to be saved without continually taking advantage of spiritual reading. But when we are struck every day, if we do not use any medical care, what hope do we have of salvation?

Elsewhere St. Chrysostom says,

Reading the Scriptures is a great means of security against sinning. The ignorance of Scripture is a great cliff and a deep abyss; to know nothing of the divine laws is a great betrayal of salvation.

St. Isaac the Syrian describes the many ways in which God's Word comes to our assistance:

The holy occupation of the reading of the Scriptures...is a fortification of the mind, a cause of prayer, a helper, and a companion of vigils, a light of the mind, a guide on the way, and a seed of manifold inspirations during prayer. It is a check against distraction of the

---

* "The Orthodox Way." K. Ware. St. Vladimir's Seminary Press. Crestwood. NY. 1979. p. 48.

spirit and against occupying itself with idle things. It sows in the soul constant memory of God and of the ways of the Saints who have pleased Him. And it causes the mind to acquire wisdom and spiritual subtlety.

A Mirror

St. Ephrem delights to describe the Word of God as a mirror which reflects the image of divine reality but also reveals the truth about the one who reads it, uncovering whatever moral ugliness it comes upon:

You do well not to let drop from your hands the polished mirror of the holy Gospel of your Lord, for it provides the likeness of everyone who looks into it...it rebukes the defects of the ugly, so that they may remedy themselves, and removes the grime from their faces... For to everyone who peers into this mirror his sins are visible.... There the kingdom of heaven is depicted, visible to those who have a luminous eye.

Like a Sacrament

The Bible is treated like a sacrament in the Orthodox Church, like the real presence of Christ, "He who ignores the Scriptures," said St. Jerome (fifth century) "ignores the power of God and the wisdom of God, for the ignorance of Scriptures is the ignorance of Christ."

A Special Place of Honor

A special place of honor is reserved for the Gospel Book in Orthodox worship. It is enthroned in the center of the altar table where a votive light is kept burning. Every priest who approaches the Holy Table must, as his first duty, bow and kiss the Gospel. The elaborately bound Gospel Book is carried in procession during the Little Entrance of the Liturgy to signal the beginning of the Liturgy of the Word.

St. Tikhon of Zadonsk tells us that through His Word Christ is present in our midst today and speaks to us:

Blessed are those who saw Christ in the flesh. But still more blessed are we who see His image portrayed in the Gospels, and hear His voice speaking from them.

If an earthly king, our tsar, wrote you a letter, would you not read it with joy? Certainly, with great rejoicing and careful attention. The King of heaven has sent a letter to you, an earthly and mortal person. Yet, you almost despise such a gift, so priceless a treasure. Whenever you read the Gospel, Christ Himself is speaking to you. And while you read, you are praying and talking with Him.

No better words can conclude this chapter than those of Douglas Burton-Christie:

The high esteem in which the words of Scripture were held by the monks as well as the frequent recommendations to memorize and recite the sacred texts suggest the presence within desert monasticism of a culture nourished in significant ways on the Scriptures. Besides its place in the public synaxis, Scripture also played a key part in the life of the cells, where it was recited, ruminated, and meditated upon both in small groups of monks and by individuals in solitude.*

---

* "The Word in the Desert." Douglas Burton-Christie. Oxford University Press. NY. 1993.

CHAPTER TWENTY-TWO

Prayer According to the Fathers of the Philokalia

Someone may ask, "Why do these great and ineffable gifts only occur at this time of prayer?" Our reply is, "It is because at this time, more than at any other, a person is recollected and in a state of preparedness to gaze towards God, yearning and hoping for mercy from him." In brief, it is the time when a person is standing at the King's door, making his request, and it is appropriate that the request of someone who supplicates with real desire should be accorded to him then. For when is a person so attentive, and in such a state of readiness and preparedness, as he is at the time when he prays?

– St. Isaac of Nineveh

CHAPTER TWENTY-TWO

Prayer According to the Fathers of the Philokalia

A visitor to Mount Athos, the world center of Orthodox monasticism and spirituality, asked an abbot what message he could take to the world about the Holy Mountain.

The abbot replied, "Today everyone talks about the Holy Mountain in such a way that they make it an object of worship, an idol, which inspires curiosity, interest and admiration." Then he continued, "I sometimes think I should start an Athonite campaign for the destruction of this idol and the return to a proper understanding of the Holy Mountain."

The priceless spiritual treasures of the Fathers of the *Philokalia* need to be taken from Mount Athos and engraved on the tablets of our hearts (II Cor. 3:3). The Holy Mountain needs to be brought into our hearts, for this is where God is to be worshipped. It is in the inner chapel of the heart that we keep company with God and offer continual prayers to Him.

The purpose of this book is to accomplish exactly that: to bring Orthodox spirituality out of the monasteries and into our everyday living. As the *Philokalia* is a rich anthology of the writings of the Fathers, so we have endeavored to bring to you, albeit on a far limited basis, a similar anthology of their teachings on the various aspects of the spiritual life which they address.

The final topic is perhaps the most important of all. What do the Fathers of the *Philokalia* say about prayer?

What is Prayer?

First, let us see how some of the Fathers define prayer.

Evagrius of Pontus:

Prayer is an ascent of the mind to God. If you love God, you converse with him continually as you would with your father, banishing every passion from your mind.

Elsewhere he writes:

Prayer is the daughter of gentleness...
Prayer is the fruit of joy and gratitude...
Prayer is a continual intercourse of the Spirit with God...
Prayer is joy that gives rise to thanksgiving.

St. Gregory Palamas:
Prayer...uplifts and unites human beings with God.

St. Theophan:
Prayer is the test of everything...the source of everything...the driving force of everything...the director of everything.
Prayer is the raising of the mind and heart to God in praise and thanksgiving to Him and in supplication for the good things that we need, both spiritual and physical.

The blessed teacher Mar Jacob, a Syriac Father:
Prayer reveals the profundities of the
  Divine,
by it one enters to behold the
  mystery of hidden things.
It is the key able to open all doors.
From it one can clearly espy what is
  hidden,
by it the soul can approach to speak
  with God,
it raises up the mind so that it
  reaches the Majesty.
It is easy for prayer to learn the
  mysteries of the divinity...
no angel is as swift-winged as prayer,
nor do the seraphim fly up with it as
  it ascends;
it whispers its words in the ears of
  the Lord, without any
  intermediary,
it murmurs in the heart, and God
  hears it in his exalted place...

The seraph hides its face from the
*   divine Being with its wings,*
but prayer stands there unveiled
*   before the Majesty:*
nothing at all stands in the way
*   between it and the Lord...*
The cherubim are harnessed and
*   cannot see him whom they bear,*
but prayer goes up and speaks with
*   him lovingly.*

St. Theophan:

To pray is to stand before God with the mind in the heart, and to go on standing before Him unceasingly day and night until the end of life.

Commenting on these words of St. Theophan, Bishop Ware wrote:

Prayer is to stand before God. To pray is not necessarily to ask God for things; indeed, sometimes we may not use words at all. Prayer is far more than petitions, requests, verbal statements. It is a relationship, a personal encounter. To pray is to wait upon God, not only to speak to Him but also to listen in silence.

St. Isaac the Syrian:

Undistracted prayer is prayer which produces the continual thought of God in the soul.

St. John Climacus:

Prayer by nature is a dialog and a union of man with God. Its effect is to hold the world together. It achieves a reconciliation with God. Prayer is the mother and daughter of tears. It is an expiation of sin, a bridge across temptation, a bulwark against affliction. It wipes out conflict, is the work of angels, and is the nourishment of everything spiritual. Prayer is future gladness, action without end, wellspring of virtues, source of grace, hidden progress, food of the soul, enlightenment of mind, an axe against despair, hope demonstrated, sorrow done away with.... It is a mirror of progress, a demonstration of success, evidence of one's condition, the future revealed, a sign of glory. For the one who really prays it is the court, the judgment hall, the tribunal of the Lord—and this prior to the judgment that is to come.

St. John Climacus:

Prayer by reason of its nature is the intercourse (synousia) and union (enosis) of man with God.

St. Isaac the Syrian:

It is the same with all the revelations and visions which have come to the saints: they have all occurred at the time of prayer.

The Desert Fathers:

In the place where God is, there Anthony would be.

St. John Climacus:

A servant of the Lord is he who in body stands before men but in intellect is knocking at the gates of heaven.

St. John of Damascus:

God descends to the soul in prayer and the spirit rises to God.

Abba Theonas:

When we turn our spirit away from the contemplation of God, we become the slaves of carnal passions.

St. Syngletike:

It is necessary constantly to clean out the house and to see that nothing harmful to the soul penetrates into the chambers of the soul, by censing these places with the divine incense of prayer. For as poisonous creatures are sent away by certain other strong poisons, so also are evil thoughts banished by prayer and fasting.

Someone once asked a monk:

Father, who taught you to pray? He replied, "The demons!" They tempted me so badly that I could only defend myself from them by constantly resorting to prayer."

Aphahat reminds us that visiting the sick and helping the poor is also part of prayer:

Give rest to the weary, visit the sick, support the poor: for this also is prayer.

Prayer is the Root of All

Vasili Razonov wrote, "There is no life without prayer. Without prayer there is only madness and horror. The soul of Orthodoxy consists in the gift of prayer."

The Fathers of the *Philokalia* would endorse Razanov's statement wholeheartedly.

St. Nicodemos of the Holy Mountain believes that since prayer unites us to God, it is more than a means; it is an end:

There is no other virtue that is either higher or more necessary than sacred Prayer, because all of the other virtues—I mean fasting, vigils, sleeping on the ground, ascesis, chastity, almsgiving and all the rest—even though they are ways of imitating God, even though they cannot be taken away from us and constitute the immortal ornament of the soul—they do not unite man with God, but only render man fit to be united. Sacred prayer, and it alone, unites. It alone joins man with God and God with man, and makes the two one spirit.

Bishop Kallistos Ware wrote,

"Remember God more often than you breath," says St. Gregory of Nazianzus (d. 389). Prayer is more essential to us, more an integral part of ourselves, than the rhythm of our breathing or the beating of our heart. Without prayer there is no life. Prayer is our nature. As human persons we are created for prayer just as we are created to speak and to think. The human animal is best defined, not as a logical or tool-making animal or an animal that laughs, but rather as an animal that prays, a eucharistic animal, capable of offering the world back to God in thanksgiving and intercession."*

St. Seraphim of Sarov,

Prayer is always possible for everyone, rich and poor, noble and simple, strong and weak, healthy and suffering, righteous and sinful. Great is the power of prayer; most of all does it bring the Spirit of God and easiest of all is it to exercise.

St. Gregory of Nyssa:

It is necessary for us to persist in prayer which is like the leader in a circle of dancers which are the virtues. It joins the person who persists in prayer to God.

St. Theophan:

Prayer is the test of everything. If prayer is right, everything is right. Prayer is the root of all.

St. Benedict:

All goods are hidden in prayer—intimate, penetrating prayer, which obtains everything that transforms life.

---

* "Praying with the Orthodox Tradition." Compiled by S. Parenti. Triangle SPCK. 1989. London.

What Prayer Accomplishes

The Fathers of the *Philokalia* have much to say about what prayer can accomplish:

Evagrius of Pontus:

Prayer makes gentleness blossom in the heart. Prayer saves from despondency and discouragement.

Aphahat:

What then are we to say about the boundless power of Moses' prayer? For his prayer saved him from the hands of Pharaoh, and it showed him the Shekinah of his God. Through his prayer he brought the ten plagues upon Pharaoh, and it was his prayer again that divided the sea, and made bitter water sweet; it caused manna to descend, and it brought up the quails; it split the rock, and caused water to flow; it vanquished Amalek, and strengthened Joshua; it routed Og and Sihon in war; it brought the wicked ones down to Sheol, it averted the wrath of his God from his people; it pulverized the calf of sin; it brought the Tablets of stone down from the mountain and made Moses' face shine.

St. Gregory of Nyssa:

The effect of prayer is union with God, and, if someone is with God, he is separated from the enemy. Through prayer we guard our chastity, control our temper and rid ourselves of vanity. It makes us forget injuries, overcome envy, defeats injustice and makes amends for sin. Through prayer we obtain physical well-being, a happy home, and a strong, well-ordered society. It will refresh you when you are weary and comfort you when you are sorrowful. Prayer is the delight of the joyful as well as the solace of the afflicted.

An anonymous text from the Teaching of the Solitaries:

Prayer is a ladder leading up to God; for there is nothing more powerful than prayer. There is no sin which cannot be forgiven by means of prayer, and there is no sentence of punishment which it cannot undo. There is no revelation which does not have prayer as its cause, and there are no types or symbols which prayer cannot interpret.

St. Isaac of Nineveh:

Someone may ask, "Why do these great and ineffable gifts only occur at this time of prayer?" Our reply is, "It is because at this time, more than at any other, a person is recollected and in a state of preparedness to gaze towards God, yearning and hoping for mercy from him." In brief, it is the time when a person is standing at the King's door, making his request, and it is appropriate that the request of someone who supplicates with real desire should be accorded to him then. For when is a person so attentive, and in such a state of readiness and preparedness, as he is at the time when he prays?

St. Isaac continues:

It was also at the time of prayer that the angel appeared to Zechariah, announcing to him the conception of John; and in Peter's case, it was when he was praying on the roof, at the prayer of the sixth hour, that the revelation was seen by him, indicating the accession of the Peoples by means of the sheet let down from heaven with wild animals on it. And what is written about Cornelius' vision happened when he was praying.

Pentecost, too, occurred as the apostles were praying. See Acts 1:12-14.

Aphahat:

For it was through prayer that offerings were accepted, and it was prayer again that averted the Flood from Noah; prayer has healed barrenness, prayer has overthrown armies, prayer has revealed mysteries, prayer has divided the sea, prayer made a passage through the Jordan, it held back the sun, it made the moon stand still, it destroyed the unclean, it caused fire to descend. Prayer closed up the heaven, prayer raised up from the pit, rescued from the fire, and saved from the sea.

St. John Climacus:

Prayer is the queen of the virtues which summons us with a loud voice and says to us again: "Come to me all who labor and are heavy laden and I will give you perfect rest! Take my yoke upon you! You will find peace for your souls and healing for your wounds! For my yoke is easy and can restore the greatest fall" (Matt. 11:28-30).

It is the Holy Spirit Who Prays in Us

When we pray we need to realize that it is not we who are praying; it is the Holy Spirit Who is praying in us. St. Paul writes in Romans 8:26, "Likewise the Spirit helps us in our weakness; for we do not know how to pray as we ought, but the Spirit Himself intercedes for us with sighs too deep for words."

St. Isaac of Nineveh says,

When the Spirit takes up His dwelling place in a man, he never ceases to pray, for the Spirit will constantly pray in him. Then neither when he sleeps nor when he is awake will prayer be cut off from his soul; but when he eats and when he drinks, when he lies down or when he does any work, even when he is immersed in sleep, the perfumes of prayer will breathe in his heart spontaneously.

St. Theophan:

True prayer will not be achieved by human efforts; it is a gift of God.

Prayer Comes From the Depths

True prayer proceeds not only from the mouth but more especially from the heart, that is, from our whole being. It is a cry out of the deep; *de profundis*.

St. John Chrysostom:

By prayer, I understand not that which is found only in the mouth, but that which springs from the bottom of the heart. Indeed, just as trees with the deepest roots are not broken or uprooted by a violent storm...so too, prayers that come from the depth of the heart, rooted there, ascend to heaven with confidence. They are not turned aside under attack from any distracting thought at all. This is why the psalm says, "Out of the depths I have cried to you, O Lord" (Psalm 129:1).

Prayer Requires Effort

Paul Evdokimov says that "The existence of God is proved by adoration, not by proofs." Do we wish to "prove" God? Then let us adore, let us pray. Yet it is not easy to pray. The Fathers of the *Philokalia* remind us that praying involves struggle (*agona*):

The Desert Fathers:

The brethren asked Abba Agathon: "Amongst all our different activities, Father, which is the virtue that requires the greatest effort?" He answered: "Forgive me, but I think that there is no labor greater than praying to God. For every time a man wants to pray, his enemies the demons try to prevent him; for they know that nothing obstructs them so much as prayer to God. In everything else that man undertakes, if he perseveres, he will attain rest. But in order to pray, a man must struggle to his last breath."

Should one wait for the wandering thoughts to leave before one engages in prayer?

St. Isaac the Syrian replies,

You should not wait until you are cleansed of wandering thoughts before you desire to pray. If you only begin on prayer when you see that your mind has become perfect and raised above all recollection of the world, then you will never pray.

Evagrius advises on how we can pray without distractions:

Go, sell what you have and give to the poor; take up your cross and deny yourself. That is how you will be able to pray without distraction.

How to Pray

The Fathers of the *Philokalia* offer abundant advice on how to pray.

St. Macarius of Egypt:

Some people asked Abba Macarius, "How should we pray?" "There is no need to use a lot of words," he replied. "Just stretch out your hands and say, "Lord, as you will and as you know best, have mercy on me." And if the conflict grows fierce, say, "Lord, help me." He knows what we need and will show mercy to us.

Evagrius of Pontus:

Often in my prayers I have asked for what I thought was good, and persisted in my petition, stupidly trying to force the will of God, instead of leaving it to him to arrange things as he knows best. But afterwards, on obtaining what I asked for, I was very sorry that I did not pray rather for God's will to be done; because the thing turned out to be different from what I had expected. What is good, except God? Then let us leave all our concerns to him, and all will be well.

St. Theophan:

You must pray not only with words but with the mind, and not only with the mind but with the heart, so that the mind understands and sees clearly what is said in words, and the heart feels what the mind is thinking. All these together constitute real prayer.

John Cassian:

We have to take particular care to follow the Gospel precept that bids us go into our inner room and shut the door to pray to our Father.

This is how to do it.

We are praying in our inner room when we withdraw our heart completely from the clamor of our thoughts and preoccupations, and in a kind of secret dialogue, as between intimate friends, we lay bare our desires before the Lord.

Evagrius of Pontus:

Pray to obtain the gift of tears.

Pray that the Lord may soften the hardness of your soul.

Pray that the Lord may forgive the sins you confess to him.

Don't pray that what you want may come to pass. It does not necessarily coincide with the will of God.

Pray rather as you have been taught, saying: "Your will be done in me!"

Pray that the will of God may be done in everything. He, in fact, wants what is good and useful for your soul, while you are not always seeking that and only that.

Hippolytus in his *Apostolic Tradition* explains how often the early Christians prayed. Although written at the beginning of the third century, it purports to hand on customs that were much older:

If you are at home, pray at the third hour [nine o'clock in the morning] and bless God. But if you are elsewhere then, pray to God in your heart. For at that hour Christ was seen fixed to the wood. Hence even in the Old Testament the law ordered that the bread of proposition should be offered at the third hour as a type of the Body and Blood of Christ; and the immolation of the irrational lamb is a type of perfect Lamb. For Christ is the shepherd, and he is also the bread that came down from heaven.

Pray likewise at the sixth hour [noon]. For when Christ was fixed to the wood of the cross the day was broken and there was a great darkness. So let a powerful prayer be offered at that hour in imitation of the voice of him who prayed and caused darkness to overshadow all creation because of the unbelieving Jews.

Let a great prayer and a great blessing be offered also at the ninth hour [three o'clock in the afternoon] to imitate the manner in which the soul of the righteous praises God who does not lie, who remembers his holy ones and has sent his Word to glorify them. At that hour Christ, pierced in his side, poured forth water and blood and, illuminating the rest of the day, brought it to evening. And so, when he began to fall asleep, while causing the following day to begin, he imaged the resurrection.

Pray as well before your body rests on its bed. But toward midnight rise up, wash your hands and pray.... It is necessary to pray at that hour. For the ancients who have recounted the tradition to us told us that at that hour the entire creation rests for a moment in order to praise the Lord: the stars, the trees, the waters stop for a short space of time, and the whole army of angels who serve him praise God at that hour along with the souls of the righteous. That is why those who believe should hasten to pray then. And the Savior bears witness to this when he says: Behold, a cry is heard in the middle of the night of one saying: Behold, the bridegroom is coming; rise up to meet him. And he continues: Watch, therefore, for you do not know the hour when he is coming.

And at cockcrow rise up and pray once more. For at that hour, at cockcrow, the children of Israel denied Christ, whom we know by faith. In the hope of eternal light at the resurrection of the dead, our eyes are turned toward the day.

The Daily Rule of Prayer

George Gallup was commissioned by the Greek Orthodox Archdiocese a few years ago to make a study of our Church. He observed that one of ten trends in religion we are observing is an intense spiritual search and a desire for inward and individual spiritual growth.

The majority of respondents described our Church as *too concerned with organizational as opposed to theological values, as having lost the real spiritual part of religion.*

The report revealed that there was a need to *help young people develop a prayer plan for their lives.* Fewer than ten said they never prayed; 90 percent said they did pray. Yet there was a need to strengthen prayer life and to help people integrate prayer into their daily lives.

There is a "... need for helping individuals work out a prayer plan for everyday life. Most believe in the effectiveness of prayer, but few know how to bring prayer into their lives in a deep and meaningful way."

What help can the Church offer in this respect?

Orthodox Christians are encouraged to establish a Daily Rule of Prayer, whereby they set aside a regular period of time each day and devote it exclusively to prayer. In the words of Sergei Fudel, "You cannot wait to be in the mood of prayer; you have to use the spur of your Prayer Rule to force yourself to pray."

In the Orthodox tradition a basic outline of content is provided for the Rule of Prayer which begins with a simple invocation of the name of God, i.e., we make the sign of the cross and say, "In the Name of the Father and of the Son and of the Holy Spirit. Amen." This is followed by the prayer to the Holy Spirit, "O Heavenly King...". This is followed by the Trisagion Prayers. Of course, this is only the beginning of the Rule of Prayer. It may go on and include the reading of a psalm, a Scripture reading, the Prayers of the Hours, the Nicene Creed, some of the petitions from the liturgy, a period of silence, special petitions of praise and thanksgiving, intercessions for other people, etc. It can be as long or as short as one pleases. We suggest you set up your rule of prayer in consultation with your parish priest.

If you have not already started, begin to form a daily Rule of Prayer. Use the Trisagion prayers of the Church as the foundation upon which to build. Begin humbly and simply—but begin. You will be greatly blessed.

An excellent aid to use is the book *Renewed Day By Day: An Orthodox Prayer Workbook* by Fr. Alexander Goussetis.[*]

A Basic Sample of An Orthodox Rule of Prayer

In the name of the Father, the Son, and the Holy Spirit. Amen.
Glory to You, our God, glory to You.
God, have mercy on me, a sinner!

A Prayer to the Holy Spirit

Heavenly King, the Comforter, the Spirit of truth, present every-

---

[*] Light and Life Publ. Co., PO Box 26421, Mpls, MN 55426-0421.

where and filling all things, treasury of blessings and giver of life, come and abide in us. Cleanse us from every stain and save our souls, gracious Lord.

The Thrice-Holy Hymn

Holy God, Holy Mighty, Holy and Immortal, have mercy on us. (3 times) Glory to the Father, the Son, and the Holy Spirit, now, and forever, and to the ages of ages. Amen.

A Prayer to the Holy Trinity

All Holy Trinity, have mercy on us. Lord, cleanse us from our sins. Master, forgive us when we disobey You. Holy One, come to us and heal our weaknesses for the sake of Your Name.

Lord have mercy. (3 times)

Glory to the Father, the Son, and the Holy Spirit, now, forever, and to the ages of ages. Amen.

The Lord's Prayer

Our Father who art in heaven, hallowed by Thy Name; Thy kingdom come; Thy will be done on earth as it is in heaven. Give us this day our daily bread. Forgive us our trespasses as we forgive those who trespass against us. Lead us not into temptation, but deliver us from evil.

Theology and Prayer

Evagrius of Pontus says about prayer and theology: "If you are a theologian, you truly pray. If you truly pray, you are a theologian." According to the Fathers of the *Philokalia* doctrine is shaped by prayer and prayer by doctrine. The great Fathers of the Church theologized from their experience of God in prayer and in His Scriptural word. The doctrine of the Church is not only expressed through prayer; it comes from prayer. St. Gregory Palamas described a doctrine of God that was shaped entirely by prayer.

Pure Prayer

The Fathers of the *Philokalia* often speak of "pure prayer."

St. Macarius of Egypt defines "pure prayer" as follows:

And see to it that there be nothing of hindrance preventing your prayer from being pure, from your mind being totally occupied with the Lord as the concentration of the farmer is centered on his farming, the married man's concern with his wife, the merchant with his business...

From the Sayings of the Desert Fathers:

What is pure prayer? Prayer which is brief in words but abundant in actions. For if your actions do not exceed your petitions, then your prayers are mere words, and the seed of the hands is not in them.

The Daughters of Prayer

"Capture the mother (prayer) and you shall have the daughters," said St. Isaac the Syrian. The mother is prayer. The daughters of prayer are many and beautiful. They are:

1. Union with God. "Sacred prayer alone unites... God and man, and makes the two one spirit" (St. Nicodemos of the Holy Mountain).

2. The second daughter of prayer is love. The fruit of prayer is love. "Love comes from prayer," said St. Isaac the Syrian. St. Maximos the Confessor adds, "The person who truly loves God also always prays incessantly; and whoever prays incessantly, that person genuinely loves God."

3. The third lovely daughter of prayer is the Holy Spirit. "Great is the power of prayer; most of all does it bring the Spirit of God and easiest of all is it to exercise," said St. Seraphim of Sarov.

The Sacraments and Prayer

In his famous "Commentary on the Divine Liturgy," St. Nicolas Cabasilas emphasized that all sacraments are accomplished through prayer. He mentions the consecration of Chrism, the prayers of ordination, of absolution, and of the anointing of the sick. "It is the tradition of the Fathers," he writes, "who received this teaching from the Apostles and from their successors, that the sacraments are rendered effective through prayer; all the sacraments, as I have said, and particularly the Holy Eucharist."

St. Isaac the Syrian urges us never to approach the Scriptures without prayer:

Do not approach the mysterious words of Scripture without prayer and without asking help from God, saying: "Lord, grant me to perceive the power that is in them." Deem prayer as the key to the insight of truth in Scriptures.

Short Arrow Prayers

Bishop Ware mentions a special kind of short prayer that was emphasized by the Fathers of the *Philokalia*. "Already among the monks of fourth-century Egypt," he writes, "it was a custom to use 'arrow prayers,' short and fervent invocations frequently repeated, as an aid in preserving the continual 'remembrance of God.' This practice came to be known as 'monologic prayer,' prayer of a single *logos*, a single word or phrase."[*1]

St. Dimitri of Rostov teaches that "prayer should be short but oft repeated." Thus the mind will not be distracted in a search for words and is able to focus more effectively. The Jesus Prayer allows us to do this. It is often shortened just to the word "Jesus," which when prayed repeatedly causes a wave of calmness and joy to rise in us. "Let your prayer be completely simple, for both the Publican and the Prodigal Son were reconciled to God by a single phrase," says St. John Climacus.

St. Theophan:

This unceasing repetition of a short prayer kept the mind on the thought of God and dispersed all irrelevant thoughts.

Henri Nouwen wrote, "Such a simple, easily repeated prayer can slowly empty out our crowded interior life and create the quiet place where we can dwell with God. It can be like a ladder along which we can descend into the heart and ascend to God."[*2]

From the book *Themes from the Philokalia* we read about the importance of short sentence prayers:

The shorter prayers allow the mind to focus itself. The faithful repetition of the Jesus Prayer allows us to concentrate on the deeper reality that it conveys. After all, the purpose of all prayer is to place us in the presence of God. We must go beyond the words to the reality. Simple prayer, like the Jesus prayer, facilitates this process. It takes us a step beyond reason. We can let go. It makes it easier for us to contain the wandering of the mind. On Mount Athos, for example, the Jesus prayer is reduced to five words in Greek, "Lord Jesus Christ, have mercy on me."[*3]

[*1] "Praying with the Body." Kallistos of Diokleia. From a paper at the Fellowship Conference of 1991.
[*2] "The Way of the Heart." Henri Nouwen. Seabury Press. NY. 1981. p. 82.
[*3] "Themes from the Philokalia." No. 1. Watchfulness and Prayer. Light and Life Publ. Co. Mpls, MN. 1988.

The Stages of Prayer

Prayer takes two forms according to St. Theophan. The first is *"strenuous*, when man himself strives for it." The second is *"self-impelled*, when prayer exists and acts on its own." "First there is prayer which man himself makes; and (then) there is prayer which God Himself gives to him who prays" (St. Theophan).

The first part of prayer—the strenuous—is offered by man's conscious effort assisted by the grace of God. This leads to the second stage—the self-impelled prayer—where prayer rises spontaneously from the depths. Prayer becomes a gift. "Man is taken by the hand and forcibly led from one room to another" says St. Theophan. It is no longer man who prays but the Holy Spirit Who prays in him. "The soul is here taken captive by an invading force, and is kept willingly within" (St. Theophan). This type of prayer may come periodically, or it may be unceasing. Then there are no more acts of prayer but man's whole life becomes a state of prayer. St. Isaac the Syrian describes this last stage of unceasing prayer as follows:

When the Spirit takes its dwelling-place in a man he does not cease to pray, because the Spirit will constantly pray in him. Then neither when he sleeps nor when he is awake, will prayer be cut off from his soul; but when he eats and when he drinks, when he lies down or when he does any work, even when he is immersed in sleep, the perfumes of prayer will breathe in his heart spontaneously.

Degrees of Prayer

Theophan talks about the degrees of prayer. First, he says, there is *bodily prayer*, prayer with the lips, consisting of reading, standing, making prostrations, etc. The second degree is *prayer with attention* when the mind has learned to focus completely on the words being prayed or read. The third degree is *prayer of feeling* when the heart now begins to be warmed by the thoughts that existed formerly in the mind. The mind has now descended into the heart. Thought and feeling are now wedded. When the *prayer of feeling* becomes continuous, then, says St. Theophan, spiritual prayer has begun. This is the last stage of prayer where the Holy Spirit prays in us and for us.

Prayer for All of Creation

When the Fathers of the *Philokalia* pray, their prayers encompass all of God's creation.

St. Isaac the Syrian:

An elder was once asked, "What is a compassionate heart?" He replied:

"It is a heart on fire for the whole of creation, for humanity, for the birds, for the animals, for demons and for all that exists. At the recollection and at the sight of them such a person's eyes overflow with tears owing to the vehemence of the compassion which grips his heart; as a result of his deep mercy his heart shrinks and cannot bear to hear or look upon any injury or the slightest suffering of anything in creation. This is why he constantly offers up prayer full of tears, even for the irrational animals and for the enemies of truth, even for those who harm him, so that they may be protected and find mercy. He even prays for the reptiles as a result of the great compassion which is poured out beyond measure—after the likeness of God—in his heart."

When St. Basil prays, he remembers all of God's people. The following prayer is from his liturgy:

Fill their treasuries with every good thing; preserve their marriages in peace and harmony, raise the infants, guide the young, support the aged, encourage the fainthearted, reunite the separated, lead back those who are in error and join them to Thy Holy, Catholic and Apostolic Church; free those who are held captive by unclean spirits, sail with those who sail, travel with those who travel, defend the widows, protect the orphans, free the captives, heal the sick. Remember, O God, those who are in courts, in mines, in exile, in harsh labor, and those in any kind of affliction, necessity or distress. Remember, O Lord our God, ...those who love us and those who hate us...remember all Thy people, O Lord our God. ...Visit us with Thy loving-kindness, O Lord; manifest Thyself to us through Thy rich compassion. Grant us seasonable and healthful weather; send gentle showers upon the earth so that it may bear fruit; bless the crown of the year with Thy goodness... Receive us all into Thy Kingdom, showing us to be children of the light and children of the day. Grant us Thy peace and Thy love, O Lord our God, for Thou hast given all things to us.

Unceasing Prayer

The Fathers of the *Philokalia* emphasize the importance of unceasing prayer.

Peter of Damascus says:

The Apostle says, "Pray without ceasing." That is, he teaches men to have the remembrance of God in all times and places and circumstances. If you are making something, you must call to mind the Creator of all things; if you see the light, remember the Giver of it. ...If you put on your clothes, recall Whose gift they are and thank Him Who provides for your life. In short, let every action be a cause of your remembering and praising God, and lo! you will be praying without ceasing and therein your soul will always rejoice.

St. Nicholas Cabasilas encourages unceasing prayer:

At every hour invoke Him, He Who is the object of our meditations, in order that our spirit may be always absorbed in Him and our attention each day centered on Him. To call on Him there is no need for any lengthy preparation in prayer, nor for some special place, nor for reiterated groans. In effect He is nowhere absent; it is impossible that He should not be in us, for to all those who seek Him He is closer than our own heart.

The fact that perpetual prayer is a part of the Orthodox spiritual tradition is indisputable. The practice is not an exaggeration, yet many opinions have been expressed as to how unceasing prayer is to be understood.

Georgios Mantzarides writes,

"Origen, the first person to confront this problem in his work *On Prayer*, maintains that 'incessant prayer' can only be understood as a combination of prayer, in the customary sense, with the whole of the believer's Christian life. The saint's entire life is one great prayer, a part of which is also prayer as it is usually understood and which must be practiced at least three times a day. This attitude of Origen's exercised great influence on later theologians. Yet, in spite of this, many other mystical and ascetic Fathers wished to appear more faithful to the letter of the commandment. Besides those who introduced an increase in the frequency of praying, there were others who encouraged its continual practice. Basil the Great says, 'The time for prayer is one's whole life.' According to other monastic traditions, he who prays only at the appointed time does not pray at all. For the monk, there is no limit to prayer: 'It is good to praise God at all times.'"[*1]

If visiting the sick and supporting the poor is also part of prayer, as some believe, then it is not hard to believe that one can indeed pray unceasingly.

We can indeed pray unceasingly if, in addition to saying prayers we become prayer. Paul Evdokimov writes,

It is not enough to say prayers; one must become, be prayer, prayer incarnate. It is not enough to have moments of praise. All of life, each act, every gesture, even the smile of the human face, must become a hymn of adoration, an offering, a prayer. One should offer not what one has, but what one is.[*2]

Prayer as a Mirror

The Fathers of the *Philokalia* consider prayer, in addition to the Bible, to be a mirror of the soul. St. John Climacus said, "Your prayer will reveal to you your (spiritual) condition, for it is called the mirror of the monks by the theologians."

A story is told of a visitor who said to a monk one day, "I was in prayer last night and I saw an angel." The monk nodded but said nothing. He did this three times but the monk was not impressed.

Finally he said, "Did you hear what I told you?"

"Yes," said the monk, "but if you had told me that you had seen your sins while you were praying, I would have been impressed."

Prayer: The Queen of Virtues

St. John Climacus calls prayer "the queen of virtues." Prayer upholds the virtues and is itself upheld by them. "Prayer is indeed the wellspring of virtues" (St. John Climacus).

It is said that a monk went to his master in the morning, sad after a long night he had spent in meditation, during which time he was counting the virtues of one of his fellow monks. He said to his master, "Father, I have wasted the night in vain—sitting the whole night and counting the virtues of brother so-and-so. I found that he had thirty virtues; and I grew sad, since I found that I own nothing, not even one virtue of them.? But his master said, "Your sadness because your soul

---

[*1] "The Deification of Man." Georgios I. Mantarides. St. Vladimir's Seminary Press. 1984. p. 90.
[*2] "The Sacrament of Love." P. Evdokimov. St. Vladimir's Seminary Press. Crestwood. NY. 1985. p. 62.

is void of virtues, and your meditation on the virtues of another, is better than thirty virtues."

Prayer is indeed better than thirty virtues. Capture the mother—prayer—and all of her other daughters (virtues) will be yours!

St. John Climacus explains why prayer is the queen of virtues:

After a long spell of prayer, do not say that nothing has been gained, for you have already achieved something. For, after all, what higher good is there than to cling to the Lord and to persevere in unceasing union with Him?

We would be remiss if we did not conclude this chapter on prayer, in fact, the entire book, without a prayer:

Come, true light;
Come, eternal life;
Come, hidden mystery;
Come, treasure without name; ...
Come, incessant joy!
Come, light unfading;
Come, hope which will save all.
Come, resurrection of the dead;
Come, O powerful one, who fulfillest, transforms, and changes
    all things by thy will alone;
Come, garland never withered; ...
Come, breath of life consolation of my lowly heart.
Come, fill us with God's presence.
Come, make our bodies temples of God;
Come, fill us with power to overcome,
Come, restore the image of God in us.
Come, strengthen our faith.
Come, empower us to speak and work for You in the world.
Come, forgive our sins.
Come, breathe into us the life of God, immortal, everlasting.
Come, Holy Spirit, come!
As the fallow earth craves the rain, so we crave Your Presence.

– St. Symeon The New Theologian

ABOUT THE AUTHOR
Anthony M. Coniaris

Father Anthony M. Coniaris has served at St. Mary's Greek Orthodox Church in Minneapolis, Minnesota, since 1948. Ordained a Deacon in 1950 and a Priest in 1953, he is a native of Boston, Massachusetts, where he attended the Boston Latin School. He is a graduate of the Holy Cross Greek Orthodox Theological Seminary in Brookline, Massachusetts, as well as the Northwestern Theological Seminary in Minneapolis. He has attended postgraduate studies in the fields of religion and psychiatry at the University of Minnesota and at St. John's University in Collegeville, Minnesota.

Father Coniaris has been in charge of Eastern Orthodox student work at the University of Minnesota, where he served on the Council of Religious Advisors. He has served on the Standing Committee of Liturgical Translations of the Archdiocese. He was also an adjunct Professor of Homiletics at Holy Cross Seminary.

He is past President of the Minneapolis Ministerial Association, the Twin Cities Metropolitan Church Commission, the Minneapolis Professional Men's Club, the Minneapolis Kiwanis, and the Greater Minneapolis Council of Churches. He was a member of the Board of the Children's Heart Fund, and is listed in WHO'S WHO in RELIGION 1976-77. He received the WCCO Good Neighbor Award in 1973 and the Alumnus Citation from Holy Cross Seminary.

He retired in January 1993 after serving at St. Mary's for 44 years. He is currently the President of Light & Life Publishing Company. He is the author of over 85 books, pamphlets and brochures.

Other titles authored by Anthony M. Coniaris

Introducing the Orthodox Church

My Daily Orthodox Prayer Book

Making God Real in the Orthodox Christian Home

Let's Take A Walk Through Our Orthodox Church

Your Baby's Baptism in the Orthodox Church

Nicene Creed For Young People

Surviving the Loss of a Loved One

Confronting and Controlling Thoughts

Christ's Comfort for Those Who Sorrow

Getting Ready For Marriage in the Orthodox Church

For more titles by Anthony M. Coniaris, please visit our website at www.light-n-life.com